SPORT

2ND EDITION

Bob Harris • Ramela Mills
Shanon Parker-Bennett
Paul Beashel

www.heinemann.co.uk
✓ Free online support
✓ Useful weblinks
✓ 24 hour online ordering

01865 888058

Heinemann

Inspiring generations

Heinemann Educational Publishers
Halley Court, Jordan Hill, Oxford OX2 8EJ
Part of Harcourt Education

Heinemann is the registered trademark of
Harcourt Education Limited

Text © Bob Harris, Ramela Mills, Shanon Parker-Bennett, Paul Beashel, 2006

First published 2006

09 08 07 06
10 9 8 7 6 5 4 3

British Library Cataloguing in Publication Data is available from the British Library on request

10-digit ISBN 0 435 46219 9
13-digit ISBN 978 0 435 46219 2

Edited by Susan Ross
Designed by Wooden Ark Studio
Typeset by Saxon Graphics Ltd, Derby
Original illustrations © Harcourt Education Limited, 2006
Cover design by Wooden Ark Studio
Printed in the UK by Scotprint
Cover photo: © Corbis
Picture research by Zooid Pictures Ltd (Taryn Cass)

Acknowledgements

The authors and publishers are grateful to those who have given permission to reproduce material. Every effort has been made to contact copyright holders of material reproduced in this book. Any errors or omissions will be rectified in subsequent printings if notice is given to the publishers.

Photos

Alamy – pages iv, 118
Ron Angle/BEI/Rex Features – page 68
Pedro Armestre/AFP/Getty Images – page 37
Associated Press/Empics – page 289
Nathan Bilow/Allsport Concepts/Getty Images – page 223
Bryn Colton/Assignments Photographers/Corbis UK Ltd – page 346
S. Carmona/Corbis UK Ltd – page 32
Steve Chenn/Corbis UK Ltd – page 173
Robert Cianflone/Getty Images – page 163
Corbis – pages 30, 140, 152, 169, 210, 289 (top right), 294, 296, 340
Empics – pages 128, 136, 293
Stuart Franklin/Getty Images – page 200
Mark Gamba/Corbis UK Ltd – page 289 (top left)
Getty Images/PhotoDisc – pages 31, 40, 109, 241, 250, 264

Jeremy Hogan/Alamy – page 218
Kevin Lamarque/Reuters/Corbis UK Ltd – page 298
Andy Lyons/Getty Images – page 191
B. Pepone/Zefa/Corbis UK Ltd – page 1
Matthew Peters/Manchester United via Getty Images – page 235
PhotoDisc – page 244
Ken Redding/Corbis UK Ltd – page 149
William R Sallaz/The Image Bank/Getty Images – page 197
Science Photo Library – page 51
Tom Shaw/Getty Images – page 192
Andrew Stepan/Collections – page 112
Dan Tuffs/Rex Features – page 59
Peter De Voecht/Rex Features – page 120
Tim De Waele/Corbis UK Ltd – page 105
A Wire/Empics – page 317
Greg Wood/AFP/Getty Images – page 333

Text

The Football Association Ltd – page 114 (right)
Football Licensing Authority – page 101

International Olympic Committee – page 114 (left)

Contents

This unit is available for you to download from www.heinemann.co.uk/vocational. Click on *Sports Studies* in the subject list, and then *Free Resources* under the Resource Centre in the top right of the screen.

About this book

The sports industry continues to grow and develop at an amazing rate. Changes in technology and social factors such as the amounts of disposable income and free time people have are seeing a huge increase in the number of opportunities that are presented to us all.

A great many people make use of the goods and services that are offered in our 'free' or 'leisure' time for a number of reasons. These range from improving our health, meeting new people and learning new skills, to supporting our local sports team. To meet this increasing demand from consumers, a growing number of people are choosing the sports industry as a career. As more and more people access the sports industry, the demand for well-qualified people to work within it will grow.

This text is designed to accompany the new edition of the popular BTEC First courses in Sport which have been running for more than five years. In line with other qualifications, the First courses in Sport are changing from September 2006 and will offer learners a range of qualifications as per the National level qualifications. Thus, at First level, there will now be available:

- a BTEC First Certificate
- three different BTEC First Diplomas.

These qualifications will now be available with a range of industry 'flavours'. Thus, First Diplomas can be accessed in both Sport (Performance), Sport (Exercise and Fitness), and Outdoor Education. The Certificate level qualification is designed as a three-unit part-time course to be combined perhaps with other qualifications such as GCSEs. The three BTEC Diplomas are a six-unit course and follow the same basic format:

- two core units: Unit 1 – The Body in Action and Unit 2 – Health, Safety and Injury in Sport
- four other specialist optional units from a range to make up the total qualification. There are 15 specialist units from which centres can choose but it should be remembered that not all of these are available to a particular course.

For further advice and information, centres should visit the Edexcel web site on www.Edexcel.co.uk.

This book covers those units likely to be the most popular. A further web unit, Unit 13 – Work-based Project in Sport is available for users to download free of charge. The Contents page gives more details on how to access this unit.

Assessment

All units are now internally assessed by the centre which is responsible for designing assignment briefs that place students in a realistic vocational setting where the grading criteria for the unit can be covered and assessed. Each unit has a series of **learning outcomes**. These are headings which state what a student should be able to do after completing the unit. In addition, each unit has attached to it a series of Grading Criteria published by Edexcel at **Pass**, **Merit** and **Distinction** level. These criteria will be available for you to check your progress against. They guide the learner in respect of the evidence they must produce to gain a particular grade for the unit concerned.

The following is a list of words that you will come across in the Assessment activities in this book, and how you will be expected to answer them:

■ *Identify* – pick out what you regard as the key features of something, perhaps making clear the criteria you use in doing so

■ *Describe* – say what a thing looks, tastes, smells, sounds or feels like, or spell out the main aspect of an idea or topic or the sequence in which a series of things happened

■ *Explain* – tell how things work or how they came to be the way they are, including perhaps some need to 'describe' or to 'analyse'

■ *Discuss* – examine the topic through arguments for and against – write as if a debate

■ *Compare* – look for and explain points which are the same and those which are different

■ *Evaluate* – make an appraisal, show the value of, explore the similarities and differences that have been compared. You need to compare before you evaluate

■ *Analyse* – break an issue down into its component parts, discuss them and show how they relate to each other. Consider the reasons behind a choice.

Learners should note that in order to achieve an overall Pass for a unit, *all* Pass criteria must be achieved. To obtain a Merit grade, *all* Pass plus *all* Merit criteria must be achieved, and so on. The evidence presented can take many forms – practical assessments, video presentations, written projects, tests, verbal presentations, and so on. Centres should choose assessment methods that best meet the needs of the learner and the available resources as well as reflecting the nature and spirit of the unit concerned.

How to use this book

Each unit has been written by a practising deliverer of these qualifications with experience of the sports industry. Within each unit, there are a number of different features that are designed to assist the learner in understanding the content of the unit and to ensure that each learner has the best possible chances of success.

Key points
pick out and summarise
important concepts and ideas

Think about it features
designed to provoke critical
thinking and discussion

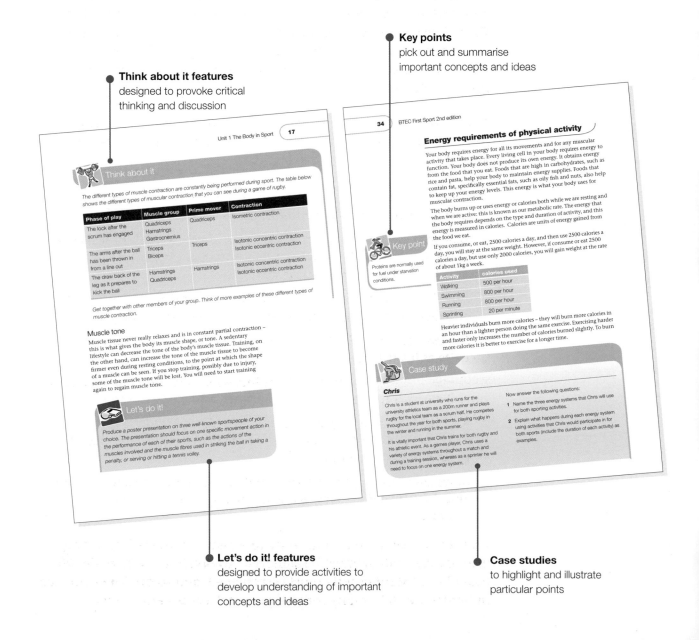

Let's do it! features
designed to provide activities to
develop understanding of important
concepts and ideas

Case studies
to highlight and illustrate
particular points

Assessment activities
designed to allow the learner to produce the
necessary evidence required to access all the
grades available in the unit

Check what you know!
questions relating to material
covered in the unit

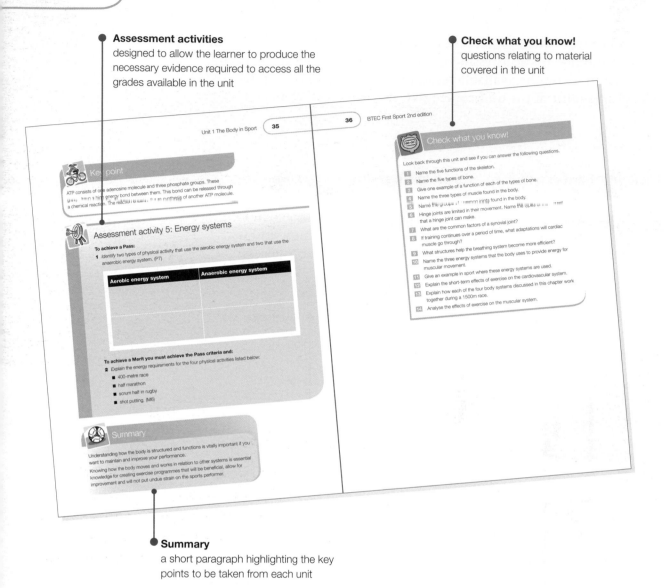

Key point

ATP consists of one adenosine molecule and three phosphate groups. These
groups form a high energy bond between them. This bond can be released through
a chemical reaction. The reaction remains in the synthesis of another ATP molecule.

Assessment activity 5: Energy systems

To achieve a Pass:
1 Identify two types of physical activity that use the aerobic energy system and two that use the
anaerobic energy system. (P7)

Aerobic energy system	Anaerobic energy system

To achieve a Merit you must achieve the Pass criteria and:
2 Explain the energy requirements for the four physical activities listed below:
- 400-metre race
- half marathon
- scrum half in rugby
- shot putting. (M6)

Summary

Understanding how the body is structured and functions is vitally important if you
want to maintain and improve your performance.
Knowing how the body moves and works in relation to other systems is essential
knowledge for creating exercise programmes that will be beneficial, allow for
improvement and will not put undue strain on the sports performer.

Check what you know!

Look back through this unit and see if you can answer the following questions.

1 Name the five functions of the skeleton.
2 Name the five types of bone.
3 Give one example of a function of each of the types of bone.
4 Name the three types of muscle found in the body.
5 Name the groups of common joints found in the body.
6 Hinge joints are limited in their movement. Name the types of movement
   that a hinge joint can make.
7 What are the common factors of a synovial joint?
8 If training continues over a period of time, what adaptations will cardiac
   muscle go through?
9 What structures help the breathing system become more efficient?
10 Name the three energy systems that the body uses to provide energy for
   muscular movement.
11 Give an example in sport where these energy systems are used.
12 Explain the short-term effects of exercise on the cardiovascular system.
13 Explain how each of the four body systems discussed in this chapter work
   together during a 1500m race.
14 Analyse the effects of exercise on the muscular system.

Summary
a short paragraph highlighting the key
points to be taken from each unit

Centres should encourage learners to keep up to date with current
developments in sport by accessing the media regularly, and
encourage discussion of issues and events as they happen. Learners
could keep a scrapbook of media clippings and stories, watch relevant
programmes on television and be encouraged to talk with current
sports professionals to bring to life the issues and topics being
covered.

The 2012 Olympic Games to be held in London will provide a wealth
of activities and case studies to support learning for years to come
and certainly for the life of this particular qualification. Being aware
of the potential the Games offer will help to stimulate learning and
make the features of this book highly relevant to the future careers of
learners. The more that learners can be encouraged to do this, the
greater their likely success will be!

1 The Body in Sport

Introduction

Knowledge of the body and how it works is essential in the field of sport. This unit will help you to understand more about human anatomy and how the body's systems change due to the effects of exercise. Anatomy is the study of the structure of the body. Physiology is the study of how the body structures work.

To perform skills in sport your body has to move in a variety of ways. Knowledge of the body's positions and movements is of vital importance for any sports performer, coach, teacher or student involved in sport. Without this knowledge, it is difficult to improve performance.

When you train and perform in sport, many changes occur in the body. The performer and the coach have to ensure that the performer's body develops through training, rests between training and performance, and is given the opportunity to recover if injury occurs. In this way, the performer will able to achieve his or her optimum performance levels.

▶ Continued from previous page

How you will be assessed

This unit will be assessed by an internal assignment that will be set and marked by the staff at your centre. It may be sampled as well by your centre's External Verifier as part of Edexcel's on-going quality procedures. The assignment is designed to allow you to show your understanding of the unit outcomes. These relate to what you should be able to do after completing this unit.

Your assessments could be in the form of:

- video recorded presentations
- case studies
- role plays
- written assignments.

After completing this unit you should be able to achieve the following learning outcomes.

1 Understand the skeleton and how it is affected by exercise.
2 Understand the muscular system of the body and how it is affected by exercise.
3 Understand the cardiovascular system and how it is affected by exercise.
4 Understand the respiratory system and how it is affected by exercise.
5 Know the fundamentals of the energy systems.

1.1 Understand the skeleton and how it is affected by exercise

Structure of the skeleton

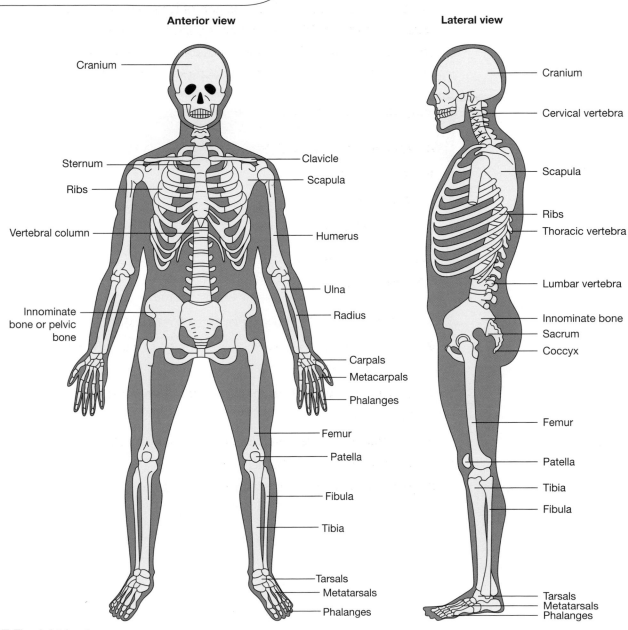

Anterior view

- Cranium
- Sternum
- Ribs
- Vertebral column
- Innominate bone or pelvic bone
- Clavicle
- Scapula
- Humerus
- Ulna
- Radius
- Carpals
- Metacarpals
- Phalanges
- Femur
- Patella
- Fibula
- Tibia
- Tarsals
- Metatarsals
- Phalanges

Lateral view

- Cranium
- Cervical vertebra
- Scapula
- Ribs
- Thoracic vertebra
- Lumbar vertebra
- Innominate bone
- Sacrum
- Coccyx
- Femur
- Patella
- Tibia
- Fibula
- Tarsals
- Metatarsals
- Phalanges

■ *The skeletal system*

The vertebral column

Your vertebral column, which is also called your spinal column or spine, is used for posture, movement, stability and protection. It is a strong and flexible structure and one of its primary roles is to protect the spinal cord. If the cord is damaged in any way it can cause considerable problems to the movements of the rest of the body, or can even lead to death.

Your spine is made up of 33 bones that fit together to form its shape. Some of these bones allow for movement at the joints where the bones fit together, and some allow for no movement at all. Between these joints are discs, which work as shock absorbers during impact.

The 33 bones that your vertebral column is made up of can be divided into five categories.

Category	Number of bones	Movement
Cervical	7	Yes
Thoracic	12	Very limited movement to create a stable structure for the organs found inside the rib-cage
Lumbar	5	2 lumbar vertebrae are movable, 3 are fused, therefore no movement
Sacrum	5	Fused, therefore no movement
Coccyx	4	Fused, therefore no movement

The cranium

Your cranium, or skull, sits on the vertebral column and is attached by a pivot joint (see page 7). It comprises many flat and irregular bones that give your head and face their shape.

Bone formation and development

The bones of an unborn baby start to develop from soft connective tissue. This is when the shape of the skeleton starts to form. After the baby is born, the bone of the skeleton becomes harder and more resilient to physical stresses. This process of bone formation is known as ossification.

Humans are born with more bones than they die with. At birth, a baby possesses over 300 bones yet the adult body is made up of approximately 206 bones. This is because some of the bones that make up the skeleton, especially those that are used for protection, fuse together to form a solid structure. A good example of this is the skull, which at birth is made up of six parts, and seven parts for the face. As the baby matures, the bones join together, to provide protection for the brain.

Key point

Ossification is the process of bone formation. This occurs at the site of the hyaline cartilage or the epiphyseal plate of bone.

The shape of the spine allows for the absorption of impact, for example, during sport. It is mainly the lumbar region of the spine which absorbs the impact and this area is where many back problems can be located.

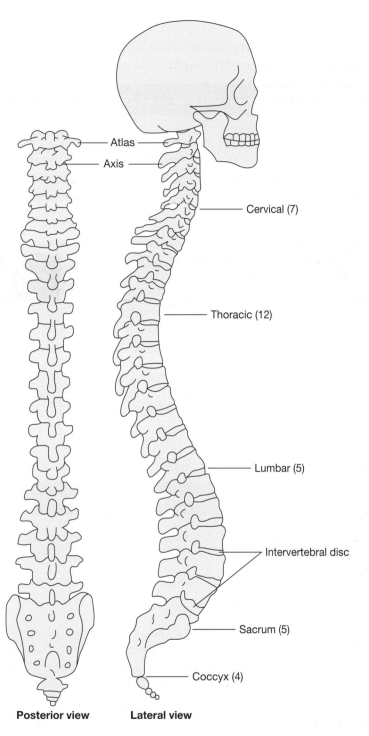

Atlas

Axis

Cervical (7)

Thoracic (12)

Lumbar (5)

Intervertebral disc

Sacrum (5)

Coccyx (4)

Posterior view　　**Lateral view**

■ *The vertebral column contains 5 sections, making up 33 vertebrae*

Types of bone

The bones that make up the skeleton can be placed into groups according to their shape and function.

Types of bone	Example found in body	Example of function
Short bones	Carpals Metatarsals	Small movement
Long bones	Femur Humerus	Large movements Cell production
Irregular bones	Vertebrae	Protection Support
Flat or plate bones	Pelvic girdle Cranium	Attachment of muscle Protection
Sesamoid bones	Patella	Prevention of hyper-extension of the femur

Let's do it!

Complete the following table.

Description of the bone	Type of bone	Main function of the bone
Humerus		
	Sesamoid	
		Muscle attachment and protection
Phalanges		
		Protects and support internal organs

Key point

Exercise increases the strength of bones. They adapt to the stress imposed by exercise by laying down more calcium.

Joints

Joints are found where two or more bones meet. Not all joints provide movement. Bones that work together to provide movement are joined by soft tissues called ligaments.

Joints can be divided into three main groups.

Types of joint	Movement	Example of joint
Fixed joints	No movement	Cranium Sacrum
Slightly movable joints	Limited movement	Vertebral column (thoracic vertebrae)
Synovial joints/freely movable	Free movement	Ball and socket Hinge Sliding Saddle Pivot

Key point

Ligaments attach bone to bone.

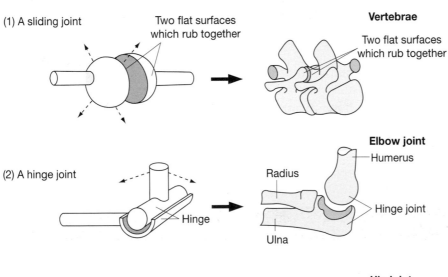

(1) A sliding joint — Two flat surfaces which rub together

Vertebrae — Two flat surfaces which rub together

(2) A hinge joint — Hinge

Elbow joint — Humerus, Radius, Hinge joint, Ulna

Key point

There is one more joint, found only in the thumb – the saddle joint. This type of joint allows a wide range of movement.

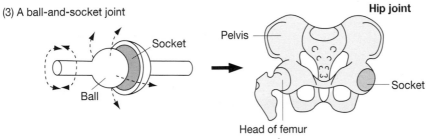

(3) A ball-and-socket joint — Socket, Ball

Hip joint — Pelvis, Socket, Head of femur

Let's do it!

Produce a clearly-labelled poster of a synovial joint and identify the function of each feature.

(4) A pivot joint — Peg of axis

Atlas and axis in cervical spine — Atlas vertebra, Axis vertebra

■ *Different types of synovial joint and where they can be found in the body*

Features of synovial joints

All synovial joints, whatever their type and the degree of movement they afford, contain the following common features.

- **Joint cavity** – the space within the joint.
- **Articular cartilage** – this covers the end of the bones. It provides a smooth sliding surface for the bones assisting in reducing friction and improving the shock-absorbing qualities of the joint.
- **Synovial membrane** – this lines the whole of the interior of the joint, with the exception of the bone ends, and secretes synovial fluid.
- **Synovial fluid** – the fluid that nourishes the cartilage and cells, and lubricates the joint to reduce friction as the joint operates.
- **Joint capsule** – this forms the outer membrane surrounding the joint. It holds the bones together and encloses the joint cavity. It is strengthened on the outside by ligaments that help to stabilise the joint.

Joints need the help of muscle to produce movement. The muscle pulls on the bone to allow for the movement to happen. The muscle is attached to the bone by another soft tissue known as a tendon. Tendons are linked strongly to bone by fibres that are extensions of collagen (protein) fibres.

Key point

Tendons attach muscle to bone.

Let's do it!

Look at the list of skills in the following table. For each one:

- identify the joint(s) used to perform the skill
- state where you would find the joint in the body
- identify the bones that make up the joint(s)
- give an example of another joint of the same type, and where it can be found in the body.

Skill	Joint	Location	Bones	Example of another joint
Squatting (lower body) from the ankle				
Throwing a javelin (upper body) from the wrist				
Trail leg of hurdling (lower body) whole leg				

Function of the skeleton

Your skeleton has many different functions to enable you to live and survive. These include:

- protection
- movement
- shape
- support
- blood cell production
- bone growth.

Protection

The organs that are supported by the tissues and the skeleton also need to be protected throughout life. The organisation of your skeleton's bones allow for this. Many of the internal organs are protected by adipose (fatty) tissue and also by the hard structure of bone. The flat-type bones that your body possesses function in this way. For example, the pelvic girdle provides protection for the female reproductive organs and the cranium provides protection for the brain.

Movement

Your body is able to move because of the co-operation between its muscles and bones. The muscles are attached to the bones of the skeleton, creating a lever and joints system that allows the body to move.

Shape

Your skeleton provides the framework to give your body its shape. Without it, you would look like a blob of jelly.

Support

Your skeleton also supports the visceral organs within your body. These important organs are held within the body structure by a network of tissues. As with all of the body's systems, these tissues do not work in isolation. They are attached to the matrix of the bones' structure and this enables them to support the body's organs.

Blood cell production

Bone also produces blood cells. This occurs in the marrow of the bone that is found in the epiphysis region and the shaft (diaphysis) of all long bones.

Key point

Bone is your body's largest storage tank for the mineral calcium. Calcium is important for bone formation and maintenance. Calcium is also used for muscular contraction.

Key point

It is important to remember that many of the other systems of the body are also required for the production of movement.

Key points

- Your bones are constantly changing in structure, and to do this they require specific amounts of certain nutrients. It is essential to follow a diet that is specific to your needs to ensure your bones develop and maintain the correct level of bone density and strength.

- It is also important to participate in regular physical activity. By doing this, your bones will develop a greater density. This means your bones will become stronger and more able to bear more weight.

Bone growth

Osteoclasts are cells that are responsible for breaking down old bone and cleaning the bone environment. Osteoblasts are bone-forming cells. They help to develop new bone throughout life. Once they have carried out their job they become osteocytes. Osteocytes are the cells within bone that maintain bone formation. The periosteum is a tough layer of fibres wrapped around the surface of the bone, except at the ends. This layer is vital for bone growth and blood supply.

Movement

Your body can move in a variety of ways and these movements link your skeleton and muscular system together. The table below shows the terms that are used to describe the movements that different parts of the body perform.

Think about it

Choose two of the terms in the table. Think of one joint movement for each of them.

Movement term	Description of movement
Abduction	The limb moves away from the mid-line of the body
Adduction	The limb moves closer to the mid-line of the body
Rotation	The limb moves towards the mid-line and changes the position of the body, e.g. medial rotation results in the anterior surface of the body moving medially
Extension	The joint angle of two or more bones increases, or the limb straightens
Flexion	The joint angle of two or more bones decreases, which results in a bending position

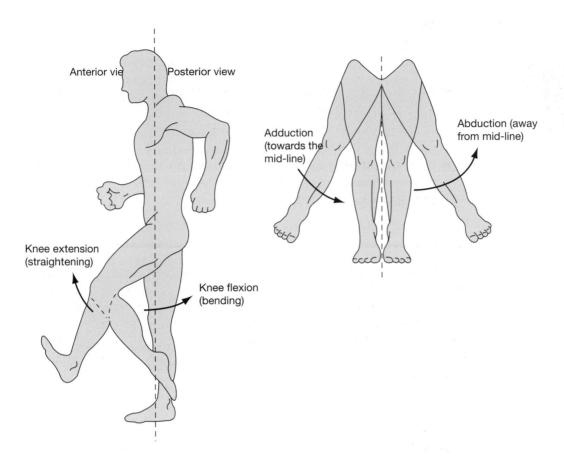

Anterior view   Posterior view

Adduction (towards the mid-line)

Abduction (away from mid-line)

Knee extension (straightening)

Knee flexion (bending)

■ *Terms relating to muscle action*

Let's do it!

Complete the following table.

Structure or movement	Functions	Examples in sport
Long bone	Mineral storage	Provides calcium needed for muscular contraction
Fixed joint		
Hip and socket joint		
Adduction		
Extension		

Effects of exercise

The skeletal system changes due to exercise; however the changes depend on the type of exercise that individuals may participate in. The skeletal system sees changes both short term and long term. In the short term, for example, changes can occur in the increased production of synovial fluid, which can be found around all synovial joints. In the long term, changes can result in the increased thickness of the hyaline cartilage that can be found on the articulating (jointed) surface of the long bones.

Synovial joints and hyaline cartilage

When you participate in exercise your body moves more rapidly, which means that the joints need to work more than at rest. This extra demand on the joints causes a release of synovial fluid around the joint site that helps movement occur more easily. Hyaline cartilage increases in its thickness around the joint site (where two bones meet) as exercise continues; this can help with preventing the surface of the bones from wearing away too soon. However, if injury occurs at a joint, for example the knee or elbow, movement can be hindered in the short term and lead to further problems in the long term if treatment is not given. (See Unit 2.)

Bone density

Regular participation in weight-bearing exercise helps to increase bone density, resulting in the bones becoming stronger.

Assessment activity 1: Skeletal system

To achieve a Pass:

1 *Describe* the structure of the skeleton. (P1)

2 *Describe* the function of the skeleton and how the skeleton grows. (P1)

3 *Identify* the effects of exercise on bones and joints. (P2)

To achieve a Merit you must achieve the Pass criteria and:

4 *Identify* the movement occurring at the synovial joints during the following physical activities.

Activity	Movement	Synovial joint
Knee when kicking a football (leg drawn back as ball is kicked)		
Bowling arm of a cricketer		
Wrist of a darts player (hand throwing the dart)		

5 *Explain* the effects of exercise on bones and joints. (M2)

1.2 Understand the muscular system of the body and how it is affected by exercise

Major muscles

Your body has over 600 muscles to enable it to move.

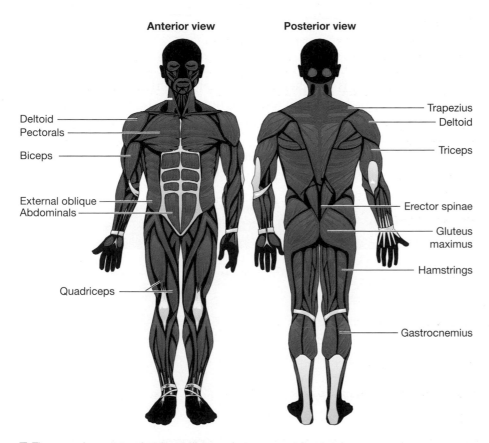

Anterior view   **Posterior view**

Deltoid
Pectorals
Biceps
External oblique
Abdominals
Quadriceps

Trapezius
Deltoid
Triceps
Erector spinae
Gluteus maximus
Hamstrings
Gastrocnemius

■ *The muscular system, showing major muscle groups*

Types of muscle

Three different types of muscle tissue make up the muscular system.

1 **heart (cardiac) muscle**, which is only found in the heart
2 **involuntary muscle**, also known as smooth muscle
3 **voluntary muscle**, also known as skeletal muscle.

The structure and function of each of these muscle tissues are very different, and they are controlled by different methods.

Cardiac/heart muscle

Heart muscle has a built-in 'pacemaker', known as the sino-atrial node, that controls the rate of the heartbeat. The rate of the heartbeat is an involuntary action but can be influenced by factors such as stress, medication, illness and exercise. These influencing factors change the reaction of the nervous system and the hormones that are released, which results in a change in heart rate.

Involuntary (smooth) muscle

Examples of this type of muscle can be found in the visceral organs, propelling food through the digestive system, and the blood vessels that aid the blood flow away from the heart to all parts of the body. These muscles are controlled by the autonomic nervous system.

Voluntary (skeletal) muscle

This type of muscle is attached to the skeleton of the human body and its major functions are to provide movement and stability. It is also called striated muscle, because of its stripy appearance under a microscope. These muscles are controlled by the central nervous system, therefore it requires conscious thought for movement to occur. These are the muscles that you will concentrate on through this section.

Muscle type	Muscle structure	Primary function of muscle	Control mechanism of muscle	Location of muscle
Heart muscle	A combination of striated and smooth muscle tissue	Allows the pumping action of the heart, during rest and exercise	The heart's automatic nervous system assisted by the autonomic nervous system (ANS)	In the heart
Involuntary muscle	Smooth	Maintains the different functions of many vital organs of the body	Controlled without conscious thought Autonomic nervous system (ANS)	Blood vessels and visceral organs
Skeletal muscle	Striated or striped	To provide movement of the body	CNS with conscious thought	Attached to the bones

The structure of voluntary (skeletal) muscle

As a result of a great deal of research, we now know that skeletal muscles are made up of many thousands of fibres rather than just one. Each skeletal muscle in the body consists of many individual fibres. These in turn are made up of even smaller fibres called myofibrils. It is within these smallest fibres that the contraction of muscle takes place. Actin and myosin are the proteins in myofibrils that are responsible for muscular contraction.

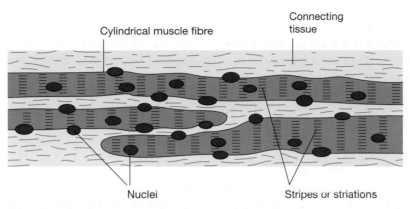

■ *The microscopic structure of skeletal muscle*

Key point

Skeletal muscle performs any visible movement that your body makes. Movements that are not visible are the result of other muscular tissues performing a job that you do not have to think about. You can sometimes feel these movements, in your abdomen or chest for example.

Muscle movement

Skeletal muscle has a vast supply of nerve and blood vessels. It is one of many links between the systems of the body, which work together to help movement to occur. Skeletal muscle is also termed voluntary muscle because movement is created via conscious thought processes.

A tendon is a tough but flexible tissue that connects muscle to bone. It is skeletal muscle that is responsible for movement during sporting activity, and it does this by working together with your bones.

Muscles can **only** pull, therefore, during muscular contraction, muscles pull on bone to cause movement. However, it is the tendon that transmits the force of the muscular contraction to the bone. Tendons move with ease as the muscle contracts.

There are many factors that help produce muscle movement. Nutrition is one that is often overlooked. Muscles pull to produce movement. In other words, the cells of the muscle tissue contract and then relax to their original size. The cells of the body use chemical energy to work. This energy is created from the foods that we eat. Carbohydrate foods are the main fuel provider for muscle contraction. Minerals such as calcium are also essential.

Antagonistic pairs

Muscles work in pairs to provide movement for physical activity.

- **Prime mover (agonistic)** – this muscle determines the movement of an action via contraction. For example, during the biceps curl, the prime mover during the flexion phase is the biceps.

- **Antagonistic** – this muscle works together with the prime mover but creates an opposition action. Using the example of the biceps curl again, during the flexion phase the triceps enables the arm to bend at the elbow joint for the bar to move toward the shoulder girdle.

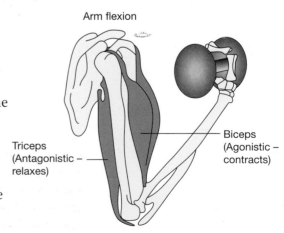

Arm flexion

Triceps (Antagonistic – relaxes)

Biceps (Agonistic – contracts)

■ *The upward phase of a biceps curl*

Muscle contraction

Muscles contract to produce movement. There are three main types of muscle contraction: two where obvious movement occurs and one where there is no obvious movement visible.

- **Isometric contraction** is where the muscle stays the same length during contraction, or when the activity is being carried out. A good example of isometric contraction is during the crucifix position on the rings in gymnastics. Tension occurs in the muscle but the distance between the ends stay the same.

- **Concentric contraction** is where the muscle shortens when performing an action. There is obvious movement when the ends of the muscle move closer together. A good example of isotonic concentric contraction is the leg kicking or striking a ball.

- **Eccentric contraction** occurs when the muscles lengthen under tension. The ends of the muscle move further away during an action. A good example of isotonic eccentric contraction is when the biceps lengthens during the downward phase of a biceps curl.

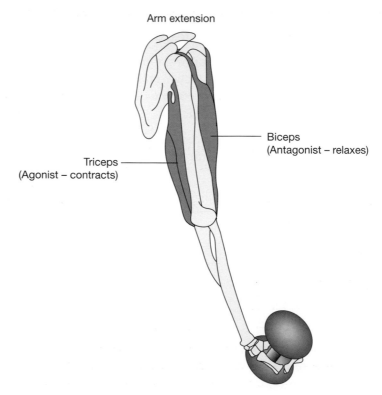

Arm extension

Biceps
(Antagonist – relaxes)

Triceps
(Agonist – contracts)

■ *The biceps lengthen during the downward phase of a biceps curl*

Think about it

The different types of muscle contraction are constantly being performed during sport. The table below shows the different types of muscular contraction that you can see during a game of rugby.

Phase of play	Muscle group	Prime mover	Contraction
The lock after the scrum has engaged	Quadriceps Hamstrings Gastrocnemius	Quadriceps	Isometric contraction
The arms after the ball has been thrown in from a line out	Triceps Biceps	Triceps	Isotonic concentric contraction Isotonic eccentric contraction
The draw back of the leg as it prepares to kick the ball	Hamstrings Quadriceps	Hamstrings	Isotonic concentric contraction Isotonic eccentric contraction

Get together with other members of your group. Think of more examples of these different types of muscle contraction.

Muscle tone

Muscle tissue never really relaxes and is in constant partial contraction – this is what gives the body its muscle shape, or tone. A sedentary lifestyle can decrease the tone of the body's muscle tissue. Training, on the other hand, can increase the tone of the muscle tissue to become firmer even during resting conditions, to the point at which the shape of a muscle can be seen. If you stop training, possibly due to injury, some of the muscle tone will be lost. You will need to start training again to regain muscle tone.

Let's do it!

Produce a poster presentation on three well-known sportspeople of your choice. The presentation should focus on one specific movement action in the performance of each of their sports, such as the actions of the muscles involved and the muscle fibres used in striking the ball in taking a penalty, or serving or hitting a tennis volley.

Let's do
it!

Take five minutes to consider all the movements your muscles have contributed to in the last hour. List the different activities you have identified. How many are there? Discuss your findings with other members of your class.

Effects of exercise

As with all systems of the body, changes occur in both the short term and the long term due to the participation in exercise.

Short-term changes

Short-term changes are also classed as the response to exercise; these are the immediate changes that can be seen or experienced when you start to exercise.

Short-term effects are:

- An increase of blood flow to the exercising muscles, due to the increased demand of oxygen by these muscles

- An increase in the demand of fuel by the working muscles to complete the activity

- An increase in the waste products that are produced by the working muscles resulting in the demand for these waste products (e.g. carbon dioxide and lactic acid) to be removed by the body muscles

- An increase in body temperature due to muscles working harder to provide movement.

Long-term changes

Long-term changes are classed as the adaptations to the body as a result of long and regular participation in exercise.

Long-term effects are:

- Muscles become bigger and stronger depending on the type of exercise that you undertake. It can take up to six weeks for changes to the body to be seen. However, it often only takes two weeks for these changes to be lost if exercise does not continue.

- Participation in strength-type exercises increases the size and strength of muscle tissue. This type of muscle tissue allows for fast movements to be carried out during sprint or power type activities. This type of muscular development can be termed hypertrophy.

Assessment activity 2: Muscular system

To achieve a Pass:

1. *Describe*:

- the different types of muscle found in the body

- the major muscles in the body (see the diagram on page 13)

- how the major muscles move. (P3)

2. *Identify* the effects of exercise on skeletal muscles. (P4)

To achieve a Merit, you must achieve the Pass criteria and:

3. *Identify* the muscles and the contraction that is taking place during each of the following activities. (M3)

	Muscular contraction of muscle groups	
Physical activity	**Muscle group**	**Muscular contraction**
Kicking leg in rugby as the leg contacts the ball during a conversion		
Lifting a barbell		
Taking off from the diving blocks in swimming (legs)		
Pulling back arm in archery		

To achieve a Distinction you must achieve the Pass and Merit criteria and:

4. *Analyse* the four sporting movements in the table above, detailing:

- the musculoskeletal actions that are occurring

- the contractions that are necessary for the movement to take place. (D1)

5. *Analyse* the effects of exercise on the musculoskeletal system. (D2)

1.3 Understand the cardiovascular system and how it is affected by exercise

Structure of the cardiovascular system

This system is the body's delivery and transport system, where blood moves from the heart and delivers oxygen and nutrients to every part of the body. On the return trip the blood picks up waste products so that they can be removed from the body.

The cardiovascular system is made up of three components:

1   the heart
2   the blood vessels
3   the blood.

The heart

The heart is a muscular pump, usually the size of your clenched fist, which can increase in either size or thickness as a result of training. It is made up of special cardiac muscle, which contracts regularly without tiring. Cardiac muscle becomes bigger and stronger if regular exercise is carried out. This means the heart becomes more efficient in pumping blood around the body.

Structure of the heart

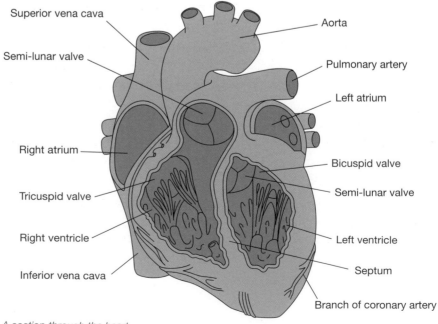

■ *A section through the heart*

Key points

- The atria are the top chambers of the heart. They are commonly known as the collecting chambers.
- The ventricles are the bottom chambers. They are commonly known as the pumping chambers.
- The right side of the heart collects and pumps de-oxygenated blood (blood with less oxygen or blood rich in carbon dioxide).
- The left side of the heart collects and pumps oxygenated blood (blood carrying more oxygen).

Key points

- **Cardiac output** can be defined as the amount of blood pumped out of the left ventricle per minute.
- **Stroke volume** is the volume of blood pumped out of the left ventricle per beat.

Let's do it!

For this activity you will need an open space in which you can run or walk, or a sports hall or fitness facility with a treadmill.

Before you start:

- *Calculate your maximum heart rate using the formula: **220 – age in years**.*
- *Take your pulse and calculate your heart rate at rest in beats per minute.*

Then:

- *Walk for 2–3 minutes. Remain standing and immediately take your pulse using a 10-second count, then multiply by six to give beats per minute. Record your reading.*
- *Increase your pace to a jog for 2–3 minutes or as long as you can sustain your chosen pace. Remain standing and immediately take your pulse using a 10-second count, then multiply by six. Record your reading.*
- *Increase your pace to a run for 2–3 minutes or as long as you can sustain your chosen pace. Remain standing and immediately take your pulse using a 10-second count, then multiply by six to give beats per minute. Record your reading.*
- *Now perform 30 burpees (squat thrusts) or as many as you can. Remain standing and immediately take your pulse using a 10-second count, then multiply by six to give beats per minute. Record your reading.*
- *Take 5–10 minutes to do a thorough warm down and then consider the body changes that you have experienced during all the above activities. Record your thoughts for later discussion with your tutor.*

Key points

- The heart has its own nervous control. If the central nervous system is damaged, the heart can still function.
- The left ventricle is the largest chamber of the heart. One of the changes brought about by endurance training is that the cavity of this chamber increases in size.

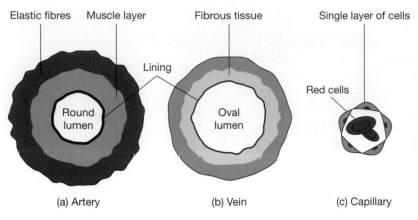

Elastic fibres   Muscle layer   Fibrous tissue   Single layer of cells

Lining

Round lumen   Oval lumen   Red cells

(a) Artery   (b) Vein   (c) Capillary

■ *Major blood vessels*

The structure and function of blood vessels

The blood vessels are the routes that the blood travels along to carry nutrients and gases to all of the many body parts.

There are three types of blood vessel in the body.

1 **Arteries** – these are thick and elastic in texture. They carry blood away from the heart. The muscle action of these vessels pushes the blood through the arteries to the relevant stops.
2 **Veins** – these are two layers thick. They carry blood back to the heart from both the upper and lower sections of the body. They contain structures called pocket valves to ensure that blood returns back to the heart.
3 **Capillaries** – these are narrow and thin in structure. Capillaries connect the arteries and veins to enable the delivery of nutrients and the removal of waste products to occur. The process of delivery and removal of chemicals in the network of capillaries is called diffusion.

There are two smaller vessels that help with the diffusion of gases between the arteries, veins and capillaries.

■ Arterioles are the smallest vessels found in the body; they direct blood from the arteries to the capillary network.

■ Venules are the second smallest group of vessels; they direct blood from the capillary network to the veins so that blood can return back to the heart.

Function of the cardiovascular system

The cardiovascular system is primarily responsible for the blood flow through the heart, the body and lungs.

Blood is pumped from the left ventricle through the aorta to the body, delivering oxygen to each cell. Once blood has delivered oxygen to the cells, it picks up carbon dioxide on its return to the heart.

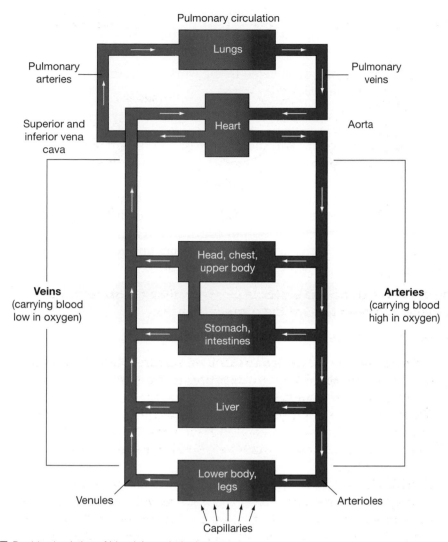

Pulmonary circulation

Lungs

Pulmonary arteries

Pulmonary veins

Heart

Superior and inferior vena cava

Aorta

Veins
(carrying blood low in oxygen)

Head, chest, upper body

Arteries
(carrying blood high in oxygen)

Stomach, intestines

Liver

Venules

Lower body, legs

Arterioles

Capillaries

■ *Double circulation of blood through the heart*

Blood contains the following elements:

- **plasma** – a watery liquid which contains salts, calcium, nutrients, hormones, carbon dioxide and other waste from body cells

- **red blood cells** – these contain haemoglobin, which carries oxygen from the lungs to our body cells

- **white blood cells** –these are more plentiful than the red cells. Their role is to fight infection and disease

- **platelets** – their role is to produce clots when blood vessels are damaged.

Carbon dioxide-rich blood enters the right atrium of the heart via the vena cava, where it passes through to the right ventricle to be pumped to the lungs. The blood 'unloads' the carbon dioxide, which is exhaled by breathing out, and oxygen-rich blood starts it journey back to the heart to be distributed once again around the body and head.

The process of exchange between oxygen and carbon dioxide is called gaseous exchange; this is covered in more detail on page 28.

Effects of exercise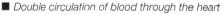

Short-term changes

There are changes in the body as you start to exercise. These are called the response to exercise as they are short-term changes.

- Your heart rate increases as you start to exercise and will continue to increase as exercise intensity continues to rise.

- Stroke volume (the volume of blood being pumped out per beat) also increases when exercise starts, due to the increase of oxygen demand by the working muscles.

- The volume of blood delivered to the working muscles increases with every beat of the heart.

- Blood delivery rate increases as heart rate continues to increase.

Stroke volume does not continue to increase in the same manner as cardiac output and heart rate. Therefore, as exercise intensity increases, the increase in oxygen demand is supplied by the increasing beats of the heart (the heart rate). In the short term, both heart rate and stroke volume increase, resulting in an increase in cardiac output. As exercise increases in intensity, cardiac output continues to increase due to the continued increase in the heart rate rather than an increase in stroke volume.

Factor of the cardiovascular system	Definition	At rest	During exercise
Heart Rate (HR)	The number of heart beats per 1 minute	60–80 beats per minute	Max. = 220 – age in years (beats per minute)
Stroke Volume (SV)	The volume of blood pumped from the left ventricle per heart beat	70 ml per beat	140 ml per peat
Cardiac Output (Q)*	The volume of blood pumped from the left ventricle per 1 minute	5 litres per minute	20–25 litres per minute
*Cardiac Output = Heart Rate x Stroke Volume			

As you start to exercise, your heart rate increases and your body temperature also increases. These are the immediate responses to exercise. Once the body gets used to changes in the environment or when exercise stops, the body will eventually return to its original resting state.

Long-term changes

As fitness levels increase, the recovery time (returning to resting levels) decreases.

Think about it

For this activity you need to find somewhere to cycle for a 10-minute period. Warm up and then undertake this activity.

- *While cycling, try to note the acute responses your body appears to make to this bout of exercise.*

- *Consider the chronic adaptations you would expect to occur if you were to cycle two or three times per week for a six-week period.*

Adaptations to the body due to exercise are the long-term changes that occur. For example, resting heart rate lowers, making the heart more efficient – the heart needs to beat less rapidly to pump the same amount of blood around the body. This would be the same for breathing frequency. As this lowers, due to regular participation in exercise, you need to breathe fewer times to take in the same amount of oxygen.

The heart increases in size as does any other muscle tissue due to long-term training. Therefore, the strength of the contraction pumping the blood from the left ventricle to the body also increases, resulting in an increase in blood being pumped out per beat.

Case study

Megan

Megan plays tennis on a regular basis for her local tennis club. She trains twice a week and plays once a week during the summer league season. However, Megan injured her elbow after a tennis match at the start of the season and she was forced to stop training and playing for a period of six weeks. However, Megan wanted to maintain some fitness and continued to run around her neighbourhood for approximately 30 minutes, twice a week.

Megan was referred to physiotherapy. She was placed on a circuit training programme for twelve weeks to help build her upper body strength back to pre-injury levels. As a result of the training programme, Megan's overall performance improved.

Megan continued with the muscular endurance training for six weeks after the initial programme. She found

that her strength and her ability to continue with repetitive exercises increased.

Now answer the following questions.

1   List three responses that Megan will experience as she starts training or starts playing in her tennis match.

2   What type of changes is Megan's cardiovascular system making as she continues to exercise over a sustained period of time?

3   Explain the long-term changes that will occur to both Megan's resting heart rate and heart rate during exercise.

4   Give two other changes that Megan's cardiovascular system might experience due to regular participation of endurance exercise.

Assessment activity 3: The cardiovascular system

To achieve a Pass:

1   *Describe* the structure of the cardiovascular system. (P5)

2   *Describe* the function of the cardiovascular system and how it is affected by exercise. (P5)

To achieve a Merit you must achieve the Pass criteria and:

3   *Explain* the effects of exercise on the cardiovascular system. (M4)

To achieve a Distinction you must achieve the Pass and Merit criteria and:

4   *Analyse* the long-term effects of exercise on the cardiovascular system. (D3)

1.4 Understand the respiratory system and how it is affected by exercise

The respiratory system helps the body take in oxygen and remove carbon dioxide and heat. The average adult breathes in and out between 12 and 16 breaths per minute.

Structure of the respiratory system

The respiratory system is the breathing machine of the body. It includes the mouth, nose, larynx (voice box), trachea (wind pipe), lungs, diaphragm, intercostal muscles, and the thoracic cage (rib cage).

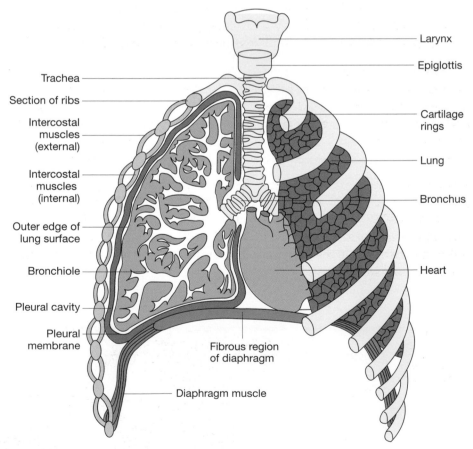

■ *The structure of the respiratory system*

Let's do it!

Sit on a chair with a back rest and relax. Do not cross your legs or arms. Count how many breaths you breathe in and out in one minute. Count in and out as one breath. Compare your results with the rest of the group. Breathing rate is different for different groups of individuals. Some of these differences are due to gender, age, health and fitness.

Function of the respiratory system

The mechanics of breathing

When we breathe in, oxygen comes in through the nose and mouth. It travels down the trachea until it arrives at the bronchi. The bronchi can be described as thick trunks split into two parts that direct the air into the right lung and the left lung. These trunks are divided further into smaller branches, known as bronchioles. The bronchioles have little air sacs (alveoli) at the tips. These air sacs allow oxygen and other nutrients to change place with waste products that need to be removed from the body.

Expiration and inspiration

Oxygen and nutrients are used by the body. Blood takes them to the different parts of the body that need them. Blood picks up carbon dioxide and other waste products on the return journey to the heart. It is essential that these chemicals are removed from the body. They are carried by the blood to the lungs and removed when we breathe out (expiration).

A high concentration of oxygen found in the alveoli during inspiration (breathing in) moves to the smaller vessels of the pulmonary vein. This is so that the blood can take the oxygen to the heart for distribution. The high concentration of carbon dioxide in the smaller vessels of the pulmonary artery moves to the alveoli, so that it can be removed during expiration (breathing out).

Key points

- The method by which oxygen and carbon dioxide change places is called **gaseous exchange**.

- These gases can only change places through the process of diffusion. This is where a high concentration of gas moves to a low concentration of gas.

- The exchange of these gases occurs in the capillary network.

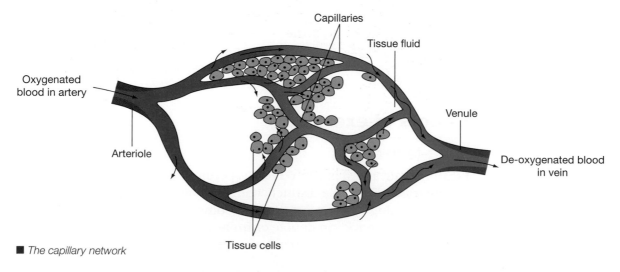

■ *The capillary network*

The passage of oxygen through the body and the removal of waste products is the primary function of the respiratory system. The diaphragm and the intercostal muscles help with the process of breathing. The diaphragm is found below the lungs. It contracts and flattens when you breathe in (inspiration). During breathing, the intercostal muscles lift and expand the thoracic cage to allow for the lungs to fill up with oxygen. When you breathe out (expiration), the diaphragm and the intercostal muscles relax and the lungs deflate.

These intercostal muscles are classed as involuntary muscles because they relax and contract without conscious thought. You can override this involuntary control, however, through conscious thought, for example by forcibly pushing out a breath further than a normal breath.

Term	Description	Amounts at rest
Breathing frequency	The number of breaths per minute	12–16 breaths for an average adult
Tidal volume	The volume of air breathed in or out per breath	0.5 litres per breath
Minute ventilation	The volume of air breathed per minute	6 litres per minute
Vital capacity	Maximum amount of air that can be forcibly inhaled and exhaled in one breath	500 ml
Total lung capacity	All the air in the lungs after a maximum inhalation	6000 ml
Residual lung volume	The amount of air left in the lungs after a forced breath out	1200 ml

Gaseous exchange

All forms of respiration (breathing) need some form of gaseous exchange. Gaseous exchange is the exchange of oxygen and carbon dioxide across a breathing surface. Oxygen must enter your blood and carbon dioxide must leave the blood through the lungs.

The lungs have an enormous surface area so that oxygen can get into the blood, and carbon dioxide can be removed from the blood, quickly. The lungs contain billions of very tiny sacs called alveoli. As well as having an enormous surface area, the walls of the alveoli are extremely thin, so the distance that the air in the lungs must travel to get to the blood in the capillaries is very small. Therefore, gaseous exchange can be seen as being an efficient process.

Effects of exercise

Short-term effects

Breathing rate at rest is 12–16 breaths per minute, but as exercise starts this increases. There is a distinct change in the way that you breathe when exercising – that is, breathing becomes more rapid and heavier. Breathing frequency can double or triple as exercise intensity increases. This is due to the rise in demand of oxygen by the working muscles and a build-up of carbon dioxide. Therefore, it is vitally important that breathing frequency increases to help provide the body with the oxygen that it needs, and to remove carbon dioxide and lactic acid, to avoid exercise stopping completely.

Long-term effects

Breathing becomes more efficient due to the participation in regular aerobic-type exercise. The muscles that aid the respiratory system become stronger and help with the efficiency of this system during rest and exercise. These adaptations lead to an increase in vital capacity.

Assessment activity 4: The respiratory system

To achieve a Pass:

1 *Describe* the structure of the respiratory system. (P6)

2 *Describe* the function of the respiratory system and how it is affected by exercise. (P6)

To achieve a Merit you must achieve the Pass criteria and:

3 *Explain* the effects of exercise on the respiratory system. (M5)

To achieve a Distinction you must achieve the Pass and Merit criteria and:

4 *Analyse* the effects of exercise on the cardio-respiratory system. (D3)

1.5 Know the fundamentals of the energy systems

Energy systems

The body uses energy systems to produce adenosine triphosphate (ATP). These systems work by re-synthesising the molecule of ATP.

■ *This athlete is using a short burst of energy*

The body uses different types of energy, depending on the intensity and duration of the activity. There are three energy systems that the body can call upon to provide the energy that is needed.

1 The alactic acid or ATP system (anaerobic).
2 The lactic acid system (anaerobic).
3 The aerobic system.

Alactic acid system

The alactic acid system provides the body with energy for sports that require short bursts of energy without the presence of oxygen. These include sports such as the 100-metre sprint, javelin, long- and high-jump and shot putt. The advantage of the alactic acid system is that it is our immediate energy source, and provides us with faster energy than the other two systems. However, the disadvantage of this system is that it only lasts for very short periods of time.

The muscular contractions that are required for sports that use the alactic acid system rely on a chemical compound called adenosine triphosphate (ATP) that can be found directly in the muscle tissue. This is the main reason why energy can be gained immediately. But there is a limited amount of this compound that can be stored in the muscle; therefore, the energy that is provided is very limited, lasting about 10 seconds under extreme exercise conditions.

Think about it

Can you think of any other sports or events where the activity is completed within the 10 seconds that this system provides energy for?

Lactic acid system

This is another anaerobic system, that is, energy provided either without or with little presence of oxygen. This system kicks in when exercise continues longer than 10 seconds but where there is still insufficient time for oxygen to be used and the ATP stores have been used. The lactic acid system relies on glucose to provide the energy for exercise that lasts for about 90 seconds. Due to the insufficient amounts of oxygen being available, a build-up of lactic acid occurs as exercise intensity continues. This build-up of lactic acid causes muscles to stop working if the intensity of exercise does not decrease.

The types of activities that predominately use the lactic acid system are: 400-metre running, 100-metre swimming, basketball, and speed skating.

■ *World-class swimmers in 100-metre swimming events use anaerobic energy*

Aerobic system

The aerobic system is a long-term energy system. It requires oxygen to ensure that sufficient energy is available for the re-synthesis of ATP. The aerobic system provides energy for continued low to moderate intensity exercise. There is a much greater amount of energy available during this system compared with the other two, and this helps in the re-synthesis of ATP. The aerobic system goes through various chemical reactions that produce carbon dioxide and water as by-products. The aerobic system makes available vast amounts of energy during exercise.

The advantages of this system are that:

- it has a great capacity to store energy
- energy provision is available from the three main fuels – carbohydrates, fats and proteins
- energy for low- to moderate-intensity activities can be sustained
- because oxygen is present, there is no build-up of lactic acid
- waste products (water and carbon dioxide) are removed via the breathing process.

The disadvantages of this system are that:

- the chemical reactions are greater and therefore slower to change levels
- it is an aerobic system and therefore requires the presence of oxygen.

Examples of the aerobic system in sport

The sports that predominantly use this type of energy system are low- to moderate-intensity events that last longer than five minutes. An example is the 1500-metres running event.

■ *Athletes in low- to moderate-intensity events use aerobic energy*

How the body uses the energy systems

All three systems operate to enable your body to carry out the normal functions necessary for living, and for completing day-to-day tasks. If you exercise, the demands on your body increase. The energy that is required to complete the exercise or the task will determine which of the energy systems dominates the provision of energy. The factors that determine which energy system leads an activity are:

- the type of activity or sport
- the speed of the task
- the intensity of the task
- the duration of the task
- the standard or level of the sport
- individual factors, such as personal fitness level and the type of training that you carry out.

Under resting conditions your body obtains the majority of the energy it requires from the aerobic pathway. This enables the cell functions that keep you alive to be carried out. During rest there is enough time for the aerobic system to break down fats which then provide the energy required at a steady rate and for a prolonged period of time.

During exercise your muscles require more oxygen. If the intensity of the exercise continues to increase, the demand for oxygen continues to increase. Eventually, the point will be reached at which the demand exceeds your body's ability to provide sufficient levels of oxygen to complete the task. The body then calls on the anaerobic system to provide the necessary energy for exercise. This point is termed the 'anaerobic threshold'.

As the anaerobic pathway continues to provide the energy for exercise, there is an increase in the production of lactic acid within the muscle tissue. Lactic acid build-up can change performance. If the intensity of performance is reduced then the lactic acid can be dispersed; if the intensity of performance continues at the same level then lactic acid can prevent further contraction of the muscle.

Let's do it!

Identify when each of the energy systems is being used during a game of hockey for a player on the right wing.

Let's do it!

Using the knowledge you have gained about the skeletal and muscular systems, visit your local health club or leisure centre to observe and analyse the range of fitness equipment available. Draw a chart of your research to include information on:

- *the range of fitness equipment available*
- *the muscle groups targeted by this equipment*
- *the muscle actions brought about by the execution of the range of exercises utilising this equipment.*

Think about it

Analyse a sport of your choice and identify when each of the energy systems is being used in the activity.

Energy requirements of physical activity

Your body requires energy for all its movements and for any muscular activity that takes place. Every living cell in your body requires energy to function. Your body does not produce its own energy. It obtains energy from the food that you eat. Foods that are high in carbohydrates, such as rice and pasta, help your body to maintain energy supplies. Foods that contain fat, specifically essential fats, such as oily fish and nuts, also help to keep up your energy levels. This energy is what your body uses for muscular contraction.

The body burns up or uses energy or calories both while we are resting and when we are active: this is known as our metabolic rate. The energy that the body requires depends on the type and duration of activity, and this energy is measured in calories. Calories are units of energy gained from the food we eat.

If you consume, or eat, 2500 calories a day, and then use 2500 calories a day, you will stay at the same weight. However, if consume or eat 2500 calories a day, but use only 2000 calories, you will gain weight at the rate of about 1kg a week.

Key point

Proteins are normally used for fuel under starvation conditions.

Activity	Calories used
Walking	500 per hour
Swimming	800 per hour
Running	800 per hour
Sprinting	20 per minute

Heavier individuals burn more calories – they will burn more calories in an hour than a lighter person doing the same exercise. Exercising harder and faster only increases the number of calories burned slightly. To burn more calories it is better to exercise for a longer time.

Case study

Chris

Chris is a student at university who runs for the university athletics team as a 200m runner and plays rugby for the local team as a scrum half. He competes throughout the year for both sports, playing rugby in the winter and running in the summer.

It is vitally important that Chris trains for both rugby and his athletic event. As a games player, Chris uses a variety of energy systems throughout a match and during a training session, whereas as a sprinter he will need to focus on one energy system.

Now answer the following questions:

1 Name the three energy systems that Chris will use for both sporting activities.

2 Explain what happens during each energy system using activities that Chris would participate in for both sports (include the duration of each activity) as examples.

Key point

ATP consists of one adenosine molecule and three phosphate groups. These groups have a high energy bond between them. This bond can be released through a chemical reaction. The reaction enables the re-synthesis of another ATP molecule.

Assessment activity 5: Energy systems

To achieve a Pass:

1 *Identify* two types of physical activity that use the aerobic energy system and two that use the anaerobic energy system. (P7)

Aerobic energy system	Anaerobic energy system

To achieve a Merit you must achieve the Pass criteria and:

2 *Explain* the energy requirements for the four physical activities listed below:

- 400-metre race
- half marathon
- scrum half in rugby
- shot putting. (M6)

Summary

Understanding how the body is structured and functions is vitally important if you want to maintain and improve your performance.

Knowing how the body moves and works in relation to other systems is essential knowledge for creating exercise programmes that will be beneficial, allow for improvement and will not put undue strain on the sports performer.

Check what you know!

Look back through this unit and see if you can answer the following questions.

1 Name the five functions of the skeleton.

2 Name the five types of bone.

3 Give one example of a function of each of the types of bone.

4 Name the three types of muscle found in the body.

5 Name the groups of common joints found in the body.

6 Hinge joints are limited in their movement. Name the types of movement that a hinge joint can make.

7 What are the common factors of a synovial joint?

8 If training continues over a period of time, what adaptations will cardiac muscle go through?

9 What structures help the breathing system become more efficient?

10 Name the three energy systems that the body uses to provide energy for muscular movement.

11 Give an example in sport where these energy systems are used.

12 Explain the short-term effects of exercise on the cardiovascular system.

13 Explain how each of the four body systems discussed in this unit work together during a 1500-metre race.

14 Analyse the effects of exercise on the muscular system.

2 Health, Safety and Injury in Sport

Introduction

In any sporting environment health and safety is of the utmost importance. It must be maintained in order to prevent injuries occurring to participants, visitors or staff. Sports are fun and enjoyable, but participating in any sporting activity carries an element of risk including sports injuries and exercise-induced illnesses.

Sports centres, leisure centres, outdoor facilities and gymnasiums also carry risks of different kinds. They may have large pieces of machinery, there may be lots of different people of different ages using the facilities or there may be a swimming pool. All of these have potential hazards that could cause harm to visitors, staff and customers if correct procedures for ensuring health and safety are not followed.

Anyone working in the sports industry, from management to general staff, should be aware of the issues that surround health and safety in the work place. They should be fully trained in certain aspects, for example the use of chemicals in a swimming pool, or trained as a first aider to deal with minor injuries or accidents that may occur. It is important for all who are involved in sport, be it participants, coaches or facility managers to be able to identify potential risk factors, look for ways to prevent or minimise the risk and take appropriate steps to avoid unsafe practice.

▶ Continued from previous page

How you will be assessed

This unit will be assessed by an internal assignment that will be set and marked by the staff at your centre. It may be sampled as well by your Centre's External Verifier as part of Edexcel's on-going quality procedures. The assignment is designed to allow you to show your understanding of the unit outcomes. These relate to what you should be able to do after completing this unit.

Your assessments could be in the form of:

- video recorded presentations
- case studies
- role plays and practicals
- written assignments.

After completing this unit you should be able to achieve the following learning outcomes.

1 Know the different types of injuries and illnesses associated with sports participation.
2 Be able to deal with injuries and illnesses associated with sports participation.
3 Understand risks and hazards associated with sports participation.
4 Be able to prepare a risk assessment relevant to sport.

2.1 Know the different types of injuries and illnesses associated with sports participation

There are many different types of injuries associated with participation in sports. Some may be minor, such as cuts and bruises, but other more serious injuries can occur. In order to prevent these from occurring or re-occurring it is important to have an understanding of how they can be caused in the first instance.

Causes of injury

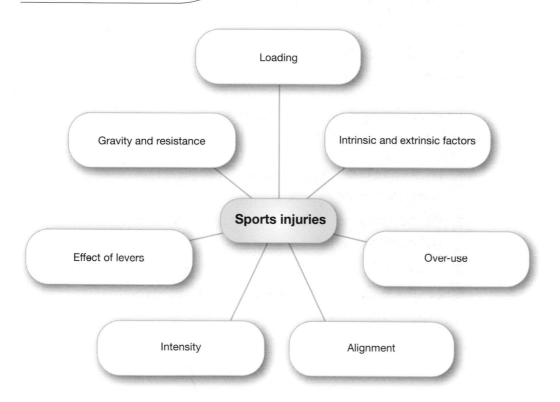

■ *Different causes of injuries associated with sports participation*

The principle of overload means that the body will adapt to the stresses placed upon it. If you stress your body by lifting a weight you are not used to lifting, your body will react so that it is better able to handle that stress the next time it occurs.

Loading

Loading refers to the stresses that we place on the body when we are training. For example, in a gym you might increase the amount of weight or load to increase or improve your muscular strength. For any individual wanting to increase their muscular strength or cardiovascular endurance, the principle of overload must be applied.

The principle of overload states that the body will adapt to any stresses placed upon it. When training, a greater stress or load than what the body is used to must be applied in order for any changes to take place.

Imagine a weightlifter who is used to lifting 65 kilograms every time he trains. His muscles will become accustomed to this weight. In order for him to become stronger, or for any training adaptations to take place, he will have to use a greater stress or load, which in this case will refer to the need to use more weight. However, it must be noted that this process of overload must be gradual.

■ *The process of overload needs to be gradual*

Think about a runner who wants to improve her cardiovascular endurance. She will have to work against a load greater than what she is used to. In other words, if she can comfortably run for six miles, and the heart, lungs and muscles of her body are used to this, then they need to be made to work harder by progressively running a greater distance than what they are used to for any adaptation to occur.

How do injuries occur because of loading?

Go back to the example of the weightlifter who is comfortably lifting 65 kilograms. If he suddenly decided to go to the gym and lift 110 kilograms (a stress that is greater than what he is used to) he would probably sustain an injury because he wouldn't have given his body and muscles time to adapt to the new stress or load. His use of a greater weight or stress needs to be progressive or gradual. Lifting such a heavy weight could result in muscle or tendon strains, ligament sprains, or even minute muscle tearing.

Key point

Overloading can be safely achieved by applying the FITT Principle.

- **F**requency – this refers to how often you train or take part in any physical activity.

- **I**ntensity – this refers to how hard you exercise, or the amount of effort you should put in to your training programme.

- **T**ype – this refers to the type of exercise or activity which you are doing, for example, rowing, walking, weights or swimming.

- **T**ime – this refers to the duration of your exercise session or how long you exercise for. It is recommended that you spend a minimum of 20–60 minutes training, but again this could depend upon fitness levels, goals and time available.

For weight loss training, 20–40 minutes of exercise is recommended. For cardio-respiratory fitness training, 40–50 minutes of specific exercise is recommended.

Intrinsic and extrinsic risk factors

Intrinsic risk factors can be the cause of sports injuries and refers to a person's physical characteristics. For example, an individual's body type or size could make them more prone to injuries.

An extrinsic risk factor is caused by an external force – something outside of the body. For example, inappropriate footwear or equipment could lead to an injury being sustained. Other risk factors are identified in the table on page 42.

The causes of sports injuries must be identified and measures taken to avoid the re-occurrence of the injury.

Intrinsic factors	Extrinsic factors
Age Performance How often a person gets injured How quickly they recover	**Environmental conditions** *Playing sport in different weather conditions* Hot weather Cold weather Humid/snow/rain Excessive sunshine
Body Type/Somatotype/Size Endomorph Mesomorph Ectomorph	**Surfaces** *Running or participating in sporting activities on different surfaces* Hard – concrete/wooden floors Soft – grass
Muscle imbalance/Muscle weakness	**Shoes** *Injuries can be caused by incorrect footwear* Inappropriate for activity Worn out Ill fitting
Lack of flexibility	**Equipment** Equipment which is inappropriate for the activity Broken/faulty or worn equipment
	Training principles *Incorrect training methods can cause sports injuries* Training too often Training excessively hard A **sudden** change in type of exercise or activity Inadequate recovery or rest periods An incorrect or poor technique

 Let's do it!

Working in small groups and using the table above, discuss the reasons why you think each of the intrinsic and extrinsic factors given could potentially cause a sporting injury. Give an example for each.

For example, a gymnast with a lack of flexibility wouldn't be able to perform quality movements required by gymnasts. A lack of flexibility would restrict or reduce their movement considerably, resulting in the gymnast pushing themselves or trying harder which could result in strains, sprains or tears.

Over-use

Over-use is one of the most common causes of sports injuries. Over-use injuries tend to be sports specific and come on as a gradually increasing pain, directly associated with repetitive movements or activities. The physical demands of some sports require the athlete constantly to use specific but repetitive techniques. For example, in racquet sports where excessive movements at the wrist such as gripping and twisting can cause an over stretch or strain of tendons.

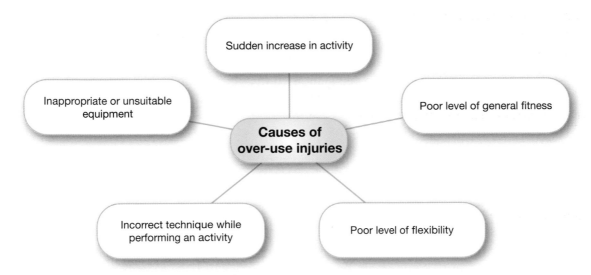

■ *Possible causes of over-use injuries*

Alignment

Incorrect posture or body alignment can result in injuries. Correct posture and body alignment is crucial not just for sportspeople but for everyone else too. An athlete with poor posture or alignment may be susceptible to frequent injuries, or may not perform to the best of his or her ability due to the restrictions that incorrect alignment or poor posture may present.

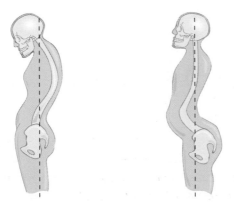

■ *Examples of poor posture*

It is necessary for a sportsperson's body to be in proper alignment in order for it to function effectively and work at its peak performance.

Runners can sometimes have poor alignment. If you observe two or three runners and note the differences in running style, you will find that some athletes run with their feet or toes turned out, or with the outside of their feet rolled over. Incorrect alignment in running can result in injuries to the foot, the ankle and the leg.

Intensity

Training at the wrong intensity, specifically an intensity that is too high for you or one that your body is not used to, can be a cause of injury. Training at the wrong intensity can also result in poor body alignment or a poor posture being adopted to compensate for the extra work you are doing, such as slumping forward, or arching the back.

Effects of levers

Movement is made possible because of the relationship of a system of levers (see Unit 1, pages 15–16). In the human body our bones act as levers, with the joints acting as the fixed points or fulcrums that allows the turning motion or action to occur. Muscle contractions provide the force (or effort) that allows these movements to take place.

If the load is too great for the effort or muscle then it more likely that an injury could occur, because the muscle will have to work twice as hard to lift the load. A soft-tissue injury such as tearing is an example of an injury that could occur in this situation.

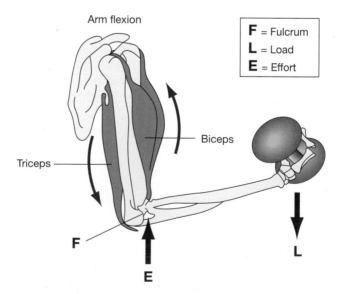

■ *The elbow joint acts like a lever*

Gravity

Gravity can be described as a downward force and an object's weight is directed downwards. In sports such as hurdling, long jump and triple jump, the athletes will experience a gravitational pull, which results in their bodies being propelled forwards. Injuries can therefore result from the impact of landing, as there will be considerable force applied to the knees and heels.

Consider the example of a hurdler. After a certain number of strides between hurdles, the athlete will jump over the hurdle and land with first one foot hitting the ground then the other. This action is repeated a number of times until the athlete crosses the finishing line. Because of this action and the downward force of gravity, the soft tissues of the body, (the muscles, bone, ligaments and tendons) will suffer from repetitive overloading, which increases the risk of impact injuries to these structures.

Resistance

Athletes who exercise at high performance levels may use resistance to help develop muscular strength, which refers to the maximum force that can be generated by a muscle.

Resistance refers to the use of weights; injuries can be caused if the weight or resistance is too great or inappropriate loading has taken place. If an athlete performs a biceps curl, as he is lifting the weight he is working against gravity. As he lowers the weight, gravity is assisting because of the downward force. If the weight is too heavy then the athlete might lower it too quickly, which could result in minute muscle tearing.

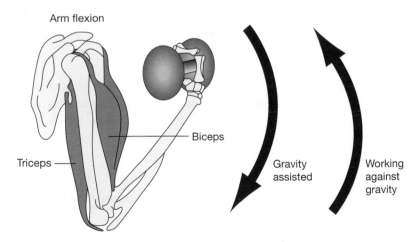

■ *Example of a biceps curl*

Types of injuries

There are many different types of injury that can occur as a result of sports participation. Some are more common than others and usually occur if care has not been taken to minimise the risk of injury. The following spidergram identifies some of the most common types of injury.

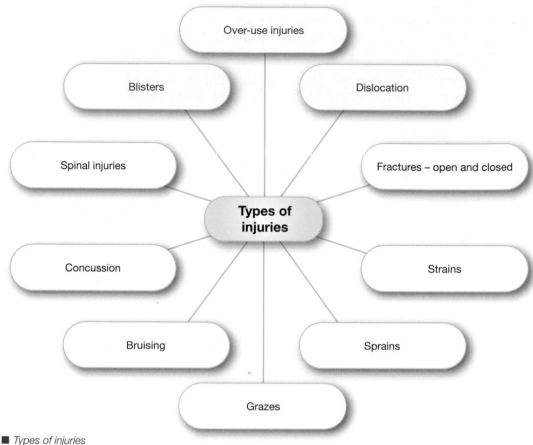

■ *Types of injuries*

Over-use injuries

These injuries usually occur as a result of an excessive repetition of a specific movement or series of movements that put too much stress on the bones and muscles. Over-use injuries can occur in both adults and children who play sport, but are, not surprisingly, more problematic in children as their bones are still growing and the injury could have an effect on bone growth.

Over-use injuries are most common in the following sports and include injuries such a shin splints and tendonitis:

■ running (shin splints)

■ racket sports (tennis elbow)

■ throwing sports – javelin, shot put

■ football

■ gymnastics (spondylolysis, which is caused by arching of the back)

■ athletics – running, jumping

■ swimming.

Tendonitis or tendinitis
Tendonitis is a common over-use injury and is characterised by inflammation of a muscle tendon that causes pain and tenderness. Tendonitis can sometimes restrict movement of the muscles attached to the inflamed tendon. The most common areas or tendons in which tendonitis occurs are those found in the knee, foot, elbow and shoulder.

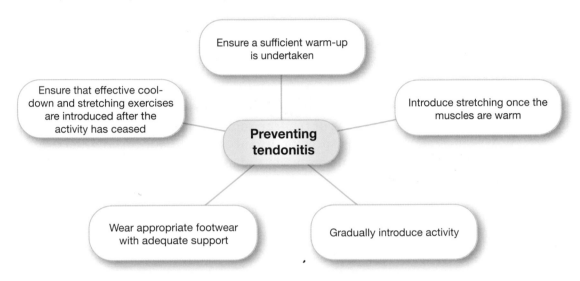

Ensure a sufficient warm-up is undertaken

Ensure that effective cool-down and stretching exercises are introduced after the activity has ceased

Preventing tendonitis

Introduce stretching once the muscles are warm

Wear appropriate footwear with adequate support

Gradually introduce activity

■ *How to prevent tendonitis*

Tennis elbow			
Causes and risk factors	**Signs and symptoms**	**Minimising risk of injury**	**Treatment**
Tennis elbow is caused by partial tears of the tendon and the attached covering of the bone. This can occur because of: ■ sudden stress on the forearm ■ incorrect grip of the racket ■ the wrist snapping at contact point with the ball ■ incorrect technique when hitting the ball ■ incorrect equipment.	Pain or tenderness in the elbow, which gets worse if the arm rotates or attempts to grip an object	■ Do not play racket sports for long periods of time without adequate rest periods ■ Perform strengthening exercises for the forearm ■ Undertake a thorough warm-up and cool-down ■ Use strapping	First aid: ■ Advise the athlete to rest. Tennis elbow can also respond well to heat treatments. ■ Alternatively, refer the athlete to a doctor for a corticosteroid injection, which will reduce inflammation and relieve pain

Shin splints

Shin splints is an over-use injury and is characterised by pain and discomfort at the front or inside (medial side) of the lower parts of the leg. Repeated running on hard surfaces, an inappropriate running style such as running on tiptoes, or over-training can cause shin splints. This is also a common injury in sports such as hurdling, where jumping and landing are involved, and other athletic events which involve running. Even dancers are prone to this injury. This condition usually involves having one leg that is dominant. For example, if an athlete is right-handed then it is almost certain that it would be the right leg that would be affected by shin splints.

The underlying causes of shin splints may be different for each athlete and could include weak muscles or tight posterior muscles (muscles on the back of the leg), running on hard surfaces, an increase in running speed or distance without adequately-timed progression, and inappropriate and unsupportive footwear.

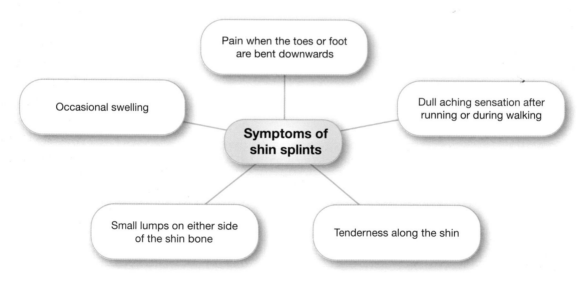

Pain when the toes or foot are bent downwards

Occasional swelling

Symptoms of shin splints

Dull aching sensation after running or during walking

Small lumps on either side of the shin bone

Tenderness along the shin

■ *Symptoms of shin splints*

Dislocation

Dislocations usually occur at joints. They can be caused by a direct force, or by placing joints in an abnormal position. A common site of dislocation is the shoulder joint, where the upper arm bone comes away from its socket.

The following are the most common symptoms of a dislocation. However, each individual may experience different symptoms. Symptoms of dislocation may include:

■ pain in the injured area

■ loss of movement to the injured area

■ swelling

- deformity of the dislocated area
- warmth to the area
- bruising or discolouration
- redness.

Dislocations			
Causes and risk factors	**Signs and symptoms**	**Minimising risk of injury**	**Treatment**
Dislocations are commonly caused by falling onto an outstretched arm or by a blow, for example to the shoulder. They are most common in: ■ contact sports ■ football and basketball ■ wrestling ■ falling from a horse ■ throwing activities in athletics, for example the javelin ■ weight or power lifting.	■ Severe pain ■ No movement ■ Visible bone deformity ■ Swelling ■ Bruising ■ Numbness	■ Adequate warm-up ■ Adequate strength training for the sport in question ■ Protective equipment ■ Wear strapping	First aid: ■ Call for a trained person if one is present, or phone 999 ■ Ensure the athlete is kept warm to prevent shock occurring ■ Immobilise neck and dislocated shoulder with padded splints or a sling ■ Do not attempt to reposition the dislocated bone; only a trained person should do this

Key point

It is important to ask an injured person if they are in pain. The pain could be defined as discomfort, stress or agony resulting from the physical activity. Pain signals that something is wrong. You are not a doctor and cannot give qualified medical help. What you can do is make the injured person feel comfortable, reassure them, and send for medical help. Under no circumstance should you give any painkillers to an injured person in pain.

Simple and compound fractures

A fracture can be defined as a crack or break in the bone or cartilage. A simple fracture is a clean break in a bone and is sometimes referred to as a closed fracture. There may be visible bruising and swelling to the area.

A compound fracture is where part of the bone breaks through the skin, which causes bleeding. This is sometimes referred to as an open fracture.

This type of fracture carries the risk of complications as there may be damage to the tissue surrounding the bone, which in turn brings the possibility of infection occurring through the open wound.

Fractures are usually the result of a strong force applied to the bone; this could be due to a bad tackle in football or from falling- or tripping-related accidents.

Open

Closed

■ *Open and closed fractures*

Fractures			
Causes and risk factors	**Signs and symptoms**	**Minimising risk of injury**	**Treatment**
Fractures are caused by indirect or direct forces	■ Simple fracture: pain, redness, swelling, bruising and discolouration ■ Compound fracture: bone breaking through skin, bleeding, pain, swelling, redness and bruising	Wear protective clothing if required	■ Simple fracture: support the injured part and take casualty to hospital for medical attention ■ Compound fracture: ask someone to call for medical help or telephone 999. To prevent blood loss and reduce the risk of infection, cover the site of the fracture with a sterile dressing and apply pressure to stop the bleeding (do not apply pressure over the fractured bone)

Sprain

Bones in the body are held together and supported by strong bands of connective tissue called ligaments.

A sprain involves overstretching or slightly tearing this ligament. Sprains can occur in many sports but are particularly common in gymnastics. Ankles, knees and wrists are the areas of the body most susceptible to sprains. A sprained ankle can occur when the foot turns inwards away from its normal alignment, resulting in the ligaments being overstretched or torn.

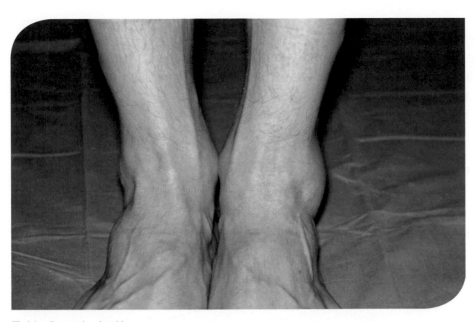

■ *A badly sprained ankle*

Ankle sprains

Causes and risk factors	Signs and symptoms	Minimising risk of injury	Treatment
An ankle sprain is caused by stress that is placed on either side of the ankle joint, which then forces the ankle from its normal alignment. The ligaments that hold the joint in place are then torn or overstretched. For example, a runner may unintentionally land on the side of the foot, resulting in the ankle being forced from its normal position. This type of injury in common in the following sports: ■ running ■ basketball ■ football ■ skiing ■ running or playing sport on a rough surface ■ any sport where the athlete may 'go over' on his or her ankle.	The main symptoms are: ■ pain at the ankle joint at the time of the injury ■ a feeling of popping or tearing of the ankle joint in the outer region. Some other symptoms are: ■ swelling and tenderness in the area ■ slight loss of function with slight injuries to the ankle joint ■ more severe loss of function with more severe injury ■ bruising, which usually appears a few hours after the injury has occurred.	■ Perform thorough warm-up prior to training ■ Wear protective shoes ■ Tape or strap the ankle	First aid: ■ Use the RICE method (rest, ice, compression and elevation). After the initial treatment of the area, apply ice to the injury for 20 minutes, three or four times per day.

Wrist sprains			
Causes and risk factors	**Signs and symptoms**	**Minimising risk of injury**	**Treatment**
Wrist sprains can be caused by: ■ a sudden twist ■ overstretching ■ stress on ligaments. They are very common in: ■ gymnastics ■ boxing ■ pole vaulting ■ falling on an outstretched arm when the wrist is hyperflexed (this may occur as force is applied during techniques such as vaulting, or floor exercises in gymnastics).	■ Pain during the activity ■ Pain on performing passive extension of the wrist ■ Swelling in the wrist	■ Use strapping or a support ■ Reduce intensity of training ■ Strengthen the muscles of the wrist and forearm	First aid: ■ Use the RICE method (rest, ice, compression and elevation).

Strain

A strain involves: muscles, the connective tissue which attaches muscles to bone, and tendons. A strain usually occurs as a result of an injury when a tendon or muscle has been torn or stretched suddenly, or with some degree of force.

Adductor muscle strain (inner thigh)			
Causes and risk factors	**Signs and symptoms**	**Minimising risk of injury**	**Treatment**
Adductor muscle strain is caused by quick changes in direction during running, taking the adductor muscle beyond the point of alignment or range of motion. Footballers are prone to this type of strain.	■ Sharp pain in the groin area, which may increase as the activity continues ■ Weakness during flexion of the hip and adduction movements	■ Perform thorough warm-up prior to training	First aid: ■ Carry out ice treatments immediately ■ Stretching and gentle massage will reduce discomfort.

Triceps strain			
Causes and risk factors	**Signs and symptoms**	**Minimising risk of injury**	**Treatment**
Triceps strain is most commonly an over-use injury, where prolonged action has been experienced by the muscles and tendons of the strained area. The action could be constant extension when throwing a ball, for example. A single force to the area can also cause damage to the soft tissue of the area of the arm and elbow. Triceps strain is most common in the following sports: ■ baseball ■ football ■ throwing sports ■ weight lifting.	■ Pain experienced during motion of the elbow or during a forceful extension of the forearm at the elbow joint ■ Muscle spasm ■ Swelling around the injured area	■ Perform thorough warm-up prior to training	First aid: ■ Use the RICE method ■ Advise the athlete to rest, so that the damaged soft tissue has time to repair itself ■ Give ice treatments immediately, to reduce and prevent further swelling, as these treatments won't be effective 24–48 hours later ■ Once swelling has stopped, heat treatments can be applied.

Soft-tissue injuries

These are injuries that occur to the soft tissues of the body, and include cuts, grazes, blisters, sprains and strains. Soft-tissue injuries can occur in any sport.

Cuts

Clean a cut with cold water to help stop the bleeding, then dry the cut and cover it with a sterile dressing.

Grazes or abrasions

These usually occur during a slip or fall on a rough surface when playing sport. The superficial layer of skin is usually rubbed off. Treat grazes in the same way as cuts.

Blisters

A blister can be described as a bubble which forms on the skin, and which is caused by friction or heat. If the blister is broken then it needs to be protected and covered by a dry, non-adhesive dressing to prevent infection. The dressing will also allow the blister to reduce and heal of its own accord, without further irritation from clothing or shoes.

Bruises

A bruise usually occurs as a result of direct contact or a hard blow. The capillaries under the skin become damaged and bleed into the tissue. As

Think about it

Discuss some of the injuries you have learned about with others in your group. Have you personal experience of any of them? If so, how were you treated? Was the treatment given correct for your injury?

a result the skin becomes discoloured, swelling occurs and the area becomes painful to touch.

To treat a bruise, elevate the injured area and apply an ice pack for 10 to 15 minutes. Check the area after a few minutes for any increased swelling or discolouration. Also feel to check the temperature of the skin.

If there is increased swelling or discolouration, apply the ice for a further 10 minutes. If swelling still does not cease, you will need to get medical help.

Serious injuries

Concussion

Concussion can be defined as a disturbance of the brain function and is usually brought about by a blow to the head, which in turn can result in a temporary loss of normal brain function. Concussion can occur in football when two players' heads collide when going to head the ball. It is not unheard of for people who have sustained a concussion to have problems with their memory, in particular remembering what happened before or after the injury occurred.

Someone who has a concussion may appear confused or lose their balance; muscle coordination and speech can be affected too. If concussion is suspected it is important for the injured to obtain medical attention straight away. This might mean calling an ambulance and getting them to hospital.

Concussion			
Causes and risk factors	**Signs and symptoms**	**Minimising risk of injury**	**Treatment**
Concussion can be caused by a blow to the head, which results in a short period of unconsciousness and then a full recovery. It is most common in: - contact sports - motor cycling.	- Memory loss - Change in breathing rate - Temporary loss of consciousness - Loss of balance - Disturbed vision - Dilated pupils	Wear protective headgear for sports where there is a high risk of sustaining a head injury	First aid: 1 Prepare an ice pack and place on head if there is any bleeding. Leave on for 15 minutes. After five minutes check the injured area to see whether the bleeding has stopped. Ensure that there is a towel or cloth between the ice and the skin. Never place the ice directly onto the skin as this could result in ice burns. 2 Ensure that the head is higher than the heart (elevation) to reduce swelling. 3 If symptoms persist, refer the athlete to his or her doctor or hospital. 4 At home, ensure the athlete is in the care of a responsible person, who should look out for the signs and symptoms indicated on this table.

Head injuries

Causes and risk factors	Signs and symptoms	Minimising risk of injury	Treatment
Head injuries are common in sports such as football, for example when two players attempt to head a ball at the same time, resulting in their heads colliding. They are also common in contact sports such as boxing, wrestling and ice hockey, or any sport where a fall could occur. Someone who has sustained a head injury may be conscious or unconscious. All injuries to the head are dangerous and require immediate treatment, especially if the athlete is unconscious	The signs and symptoms of a head injury depend on its extent but could include some or all of the following: ■ blurred vision ■ drowsiness ■ nausea ■ different-sized pupils ■ headache ■ temporary loss of memory ■ bleeding from the scalp ■ irritability ■ confusion.	Wear protective headgear if the sport allows it	Unconscious athlete: 1 Ask someone to dial 999 and tell them you have an unconscious athlete with a head injury. 2 Place the injured person in the recovery position (see page 64) and keep a regular check on his or her breathing pattern, pulse and level of response. 3 If the athlete regains consciousness, keep monitoring and under no circumstance allow him or her to rejoin the sporting activity. Any athlete who has been unconscious must go to hospital. 4 Following medical examination, an athlete recovering from unconsciousness may be kept in for observation. This is because the first 24 hours after a head injury are critical and the symptoms can reappear. If the athlete is allowed home, then a responsible person must watch the athlete, and check each hour for a response. If any of the following symptoms appear, they must be reported immediately to the doctor or hospital: ■ stiff neck ■ inability to move arms or legs ■ vomiting/nausea ■ blurred vision ■ severe headache ■ confusion ■ different-sized pupils ■ high temperature.

Key point

Lots of active people suffer from recurring injuries. These are usually triggered if an injury has not been treated previously, or if the athlete had an insufficient rest period and resumed activity without being fully recovered. You will need to refer the athlete to a physiotherapist or a doctor for further investigation.

Spinal injuries

An example of a spinal injury that could occur in sports is a stress fracture. This is when a small fracture develops after repeated stress is placed on the spine.

Spinal injuries			
Causes and risk factors	**Signs and symptoms**	**Minimising risk of injury**	**Treatment**
A spinal stress fracture is caused by twisting or direct stress to the bone. It is common in the following: ■ contact sports, such as football and boxing ■ gymnastics.	■ Pain in the back or neck ■ Swelling and bruising ■ Redness and warmth ■ Tenderness to touch ■ Numbness	■ Increase calcium intake ■ Perform strengthening exercises for surrounding muscles to help protect underlying bone	There is no first aid treatment, as the fracture is something that gradually develops. If a spinal stress fracture is suspected, refer the athlete to his or her doctor

Key points

■ Spinal injuries can be extremely dangerous. If the injured person has fallen from a horse or a motorbike, or is at the bottom of a rugby scrum and hasn't moved, then a severe spinal injury is possible. In these situations, do not move the athlete and call for appropriate help.

■ If the athlete is unconscious but has a pulse, then he or she needs to be moved into the spinal injury recovery position in order to protect the airway. This is an adaptation of the normal recovery position. It is important that the head and trunk are kept aligned at all times.

■ If an athlete is wearing any type of head gear or a motorcross racer is wearing a helmet, this should only be moved if there is an airway obstruction. The head must be stabilised while the helmet is being removed.

Key point

Here are some useful terms and explanations of methods involved in injuries.

Acute injuries – a single force is directed upon a structure that produces an injury

Chronic injuries – repeated force or loading, over a period of time, resulting in an injury

Compression – a force directed along the length of a structure, a bone or soft tissue

Cryotherapy – a therapy which uses cold application methods to reduce swelling and pain

Ice massage – massage technique that uses iced water in a foam cup. The ice protrudes from the cup and massage is performed over the area in circular movements. Usually carried out three or four times per day for approximately 15 minutes, for the initial 24–72 hours after the injury has taken place

Laceration – a wound that opens the skin and goes through to the subcutaneous layer of the skin, muscles, associated nerves and blood vessels

Spasm – temporary muscle contractions

Sprain – injury to soft tissues, e.g. ligaments

Strain – the amount of deformation that a structure goes through compared with its original shape and size

Synovitis – inflammation of the synovial membrane that surrounds a synovial joint

Tendonitis – inflammation of a muscle tendon

Let's do it!

With a partner, practise putting each other into the spinal recovery position.

Assessment activity 1: Causes and types of injuries

Individually devise a series of fact sheets, which discuss injuries associated with sports participation. You can look at a number of sports or focus on just one sport. Identify the type of injury, the causes of the injuries, signs and symptoms, and identify treatment aims.

To achieve a Pass:

1 *Describe* four different injuries associated with sports participation and their underlying causes. (P3)

To achieve a Merit you must achieve the Pass criteria and:

2 *Explain* why certain injuries are associated with sports participation, give examples, and identify signs and symptoms. (M3)

To achieve a Distinction you must achieve the Pass and Merit criteria and:

3 Give a *detailed account* of why participants are at risk of injury while taking part in sport. Give examples to support your answer. (D1)

Types and signs of illnesses

Asthma

Asthma is a common illness which can be exercise-induced. It is a condition which affects the respiratory system and is characterised by a narrowing of the airways. Because the airways are narrowed, this leads to difficulty passing air, which in turn will result in wheezing, shortness of breath and a feeling of tightness in the chest. Asthma can turn suddenly and unpredictably into a life-threatening condition if left untreated.

There are many different triggers that individuals have which could bring on an asthma attack. If someone already has asthma then they will be aware that it can be brought on if they take part in physical activity. Other triggers include:

- grass pollen
- animal hairs
- exercise
- peanuts
- a cold that goes on to the chest
- dust
- feathers.

Each individual will know their triggers and hopefully take steps to avoid an asthma attack occurring.

Medication used for asthma

Asthma is diagnosed by a doctor, who will prescribe preventative inhalers to help to prevent an asthma attack. These inhalers are usually taken every day.

Inhalers which help to combat wheezing and reduce muscle spasm of the airways are called relievers and are usually **blue**. If a sports participant is having an asthma attack they will require this inhaler and not the preventative.

The drugs found in inhalers include:

- preventative inhalers – becotide, flixotide
- reliever inhalers – ventolin, salbutamol.

■ *Blue inhalers help to combat wheezing*

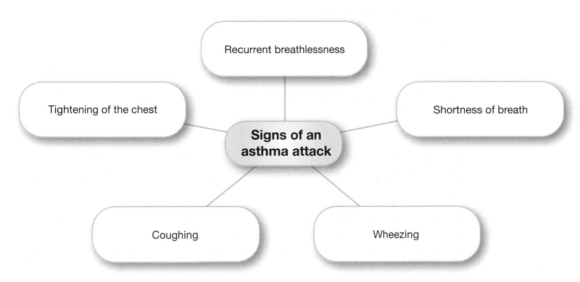

■ *Signs of an asthma attack*

Heart attack

A heart attack is characterised by pain in the chest. It is sometimes referred to as a coronary because the coronary artery, which supplies blood to the heart muscles, is affected, usually by a blood clot or coronary thrombosis. This clot or blockage will reduce the blood and oxygen supply to the part of the heart muscle affected, which becomes damaged and may even die.

In some cases only a small amount of heart muscle is damaged and the rest of the heart, which is unaffected, continues to beat. In other cases the damage to the heart muscle could cause the heart to stop.

Signs of a heart attack include:

- crushing sensation or tightness in the chest
- pain in the neck, jaw or arms
- breathlessness
- sweating
- pallor
- rapid, weak and irregular pulse
- if severe, the pain may cause nausea and shock
- fall in blood pressure.

Key point

If you suspect a heart attack call for an ambulance straight away.

Viral infections

These include influenza, the common cold and other minor illnesses, which are common during the winter months. Symptoms or signs of a viral infection may include:

- high temperature or fever
- sore throat
- aching muscles and joints
- mild headache
- shivering.

A viral infection usually begins as a common cold, but as the virus multiplies, other symptoms such as a chest infection could occur.

Think about it

- *Have you ever had a viral infection?*
- *What symptoms did you experience?*
- *How did it make you feel?*
- *How long did it last?*

Hypoglycaemia

Diabetes is a disorder where the affected person has problems with their sugar or glucose levels. In the body we have an organ called the pancreas, which produces a substance called insulin. Insulin functions to lower the level of glucose or sugar in the blood. In a person who is a diabetic this process is not effective.

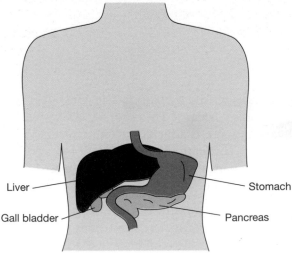

Liver

Gall bladder

Stomach

Pancreas

■ *The pancreas produces insulin*

Hypoglycaemia refers to low blood sugar levels or too little sugar in the blood. This is a condition which is associated with, and often caused by, diabetics not eating enough sugar after injecting themselves with insulin.

The affected individual will become sweaty, shaky, disorientated, confused and may even become aggressive. They may also rapidly lose consciousness. This can be an extremely dangerous condition if aid is not given immediately.

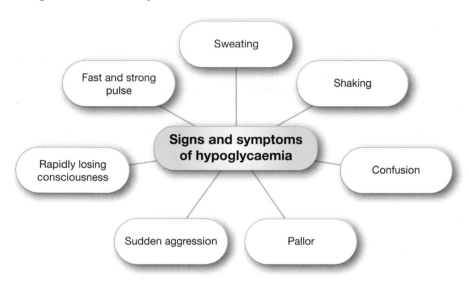

■ *Signs and symptoms of hypoglycaemia*

Other injuries/illnesses that can occur as a result of sports participation

Dehydration
Dehydration can be described as a loss of water and salts from the body.

Dehydration			
Causes and risk factors	**Signs and symptoms**	**Minimising risk of injury**	**Treatment**
Dehydration can be caused by: ■ excessive sweating while training or participating in a sporting activity ■ training during hot weather ■ inadequate fluid intake ■ the use of drugs.	■ Dry mouth/tongue ■ No urine (or very little) ■ Drowsiness/confusion ■ Deep sunken eyes ■ Dry skin ■ Tiredness or even collapse	Athletes should maintain a regular fluid intake when training or during physical activity, and small but frequent amounts of fluid in hot weather	First aid: ■ Give the athlete small amounts of water to drink and refer him or her to a medical person. ■ If the dehydration is severe, the athlete may need to go to hospital in order to receive intravenous fluids to replace lost fluids and essential salts.

Key point

Hypothermia

Hypothermia can be defined as a dramatic fall in body temperature to below 35 degrees Celsius.

Death usually occurs when the body temperature falls below 25 degrees Celsius.

Hypothermia			
Causes and risk factors	**Signs and symptoms**	**Minimising risk of injury**	**Treatment**
Hypothermia can be caused when an athlete trains in extreme, cold conditions for a prolonged period of time	■ Shivering ■ Muscle rigidity ■ Cramps ■ Low blood pressure ■ Low pulse and breathing rates ■ Confusion ■ Disorientation ■ Cold, pale, dry skin	■ Be equipped for all kinds of weather ■ Wear extra, thin layers of clothing ■ Wear a waterproof and windproof outer layer of clothing ■ Wear a hat and gloves ■ Eat extra energy foods and warm drinks	First aid: ■ Cover athlete with foil blanket ■ Replace any wet clothing with warm dry clothing ■ If the athlete is otherwise fit and healthy, bathe him or her in a warm bath to increase body temperature ■ In the case of severe hypothermia, send for medical help straight away and keep the athlete warm and dry.

Assessment activity 2: Types of injuries associated with sports participation

To achieve a Pass:

1 *Describe* four types of injuries associated with sports participation and their underlying causes in each of the following sports:

■ ice hockey

■ football

■ gymnastics

■ rugby. (P3)

To achieve a Merit you must achieve the Pass criteria and:

2 *Explain* why certain illnesses and injuries are associated with sports participation. (M3)

To achieve a Distinction you must achieve the Pass and Merit criteria and:

3 Give a detailed account of why participants are at risk of injury whilst taking part in sport. (D1)

Assessment activity 3: Types and causes of illnesses associated with sports participation

Joshua is a very active eight-year-old boy and has suffered from asthma since he was 18 months old. He currently plays basketball twice a week and participates in a very active martial arts class three times a week. He is prescribed two types of inhalers – flixotide, his preventative inhaler, and ventolin or salbutamol, his reliever.

To achieve a Pass:

1 If Joshua began to feel ill during physical activity/sports participation what signs and symptoms might indicate that he is having a asthma attack? (P4)

To achieve a Merit you must achieve the Pass criteria and:

2 *Explain* why asthma and other illnesses can be associated with sports participation. Give examples. (M3)

2.2 Be able to deal with injuries and illnesses associated with sports participation

Procedures and treatment

Protection of a casualty and other people from further risk

When an injury or accident occurs it is extremely important to assess the situation quickly, carefully and safely. When it is safe to do so, the casualty or the injured athlete must be quickly examined to check for any life-threatening conditions that may need urgent attention. You should be prepared to resuscitate if necessary.

If you are first on the scene, it is your responsibility to provide first aid. When medical help arrives you will need to give a report of the casualty and what treatment you have given. If the casualty is responsive, try to get as much information as you can to give to the paramedics or doctors. A checklist of relevant information should include the following:

■ Casualty's name and age

■ Details of any injuries

■ Time the injury occurred

■ Details of other individuals involved

■ First aid treatment given

■ Date

■ Time.

You may not always be able to gather this information from the casualty. If there are people around, they may have seen what happened or know the casualty. Do not be afraid to ask. Also look around for clues that indicate how the accident or incident happened.

The six checks

Before making any type of assessment it is important to go quickly through a series of checks to establish the casualty's need for treatment or to identify any life-threatening conditions.

1 **Assess situation and environment.**
   Are you, the casualty or other people at risk from further danger?
2 **Make an assessment of the casualty's response/level of consciousness/unconsciousness.**
   Gently shake the casualty's shoulders and say, 'Hello, I'm (your name), can you hear me?' If there is no response the casualty may be unconscious.

3 **Shout for help if you are on your own with the casualty.**

4 **Open the airway.**

Place one hand on the casualty's forehead and two fingers of the other hand under the casualty's chin. Gently tilt the head backwards to open the airway. Remove any obstructions that might be affecting breathing.

5 **Assess breathing.**

Is the casualty breathing?

Yes – Place in the recovery position.

No – Ensure that an ambulance has been called for and give two rescue breaths.

Look at and feel the chest, to ascertain whether it is rising.

6 **Make an assessment of circulation.**

Feel for a pulse in the neck or at the wrist. Check for any signs of bleeding.

Key point

Blood loss needs to be controlled. If it is not, the blood won't be efficiently transported to the vital organs of the body and the casualty could go into shock.

Key point

Remember the four Ps!

Preserve your own life first by ensuring that you are not in any danger of being harmed. Never put yourself at risk. Also, preserve the life of the injured.

Protect the injured from further danger by ensuring that the area is safe.

Prioritise urgent matters and assess injuries and illnesses to determine treatment priorities. You must treat any condition that is deemed to be life-threatening first. For example, imagine a situation in which two football players both go to head the ball and collide. Both players fall to the ground. You need to assess the situation quickly. If one player has stopped breathing and the other has concussion, prioritise and treat the player who has stopped breathing.

Promote recovery – help the injured to recover by applying the necessary first aid to relieve pain or discomfort, or to control bleeding and so on.

Key point

Perform the six checks and establish if the casualty is:

- conscious, breathing, with a pulse
- unconscious, not breathing, with a pulse
- unconscious, not breathing, without a pulse
- unconscious, breathing, with a pulse.

Then give the immediate necessary treatment without delay.

What to do if the casualty is conscious, breathing and has a pulse

- Call 999.
- Make the casualty comfortable.
- Place the casualty into the recovery position.
- Treat any other injury.
- Keep monitoring breathing until medical help arrives.

What to do if the casualty is unconscious, not breathing and has a pulse

- Call 999.
- Lay the casualty on his or her back and tilt the head back to open the airway.
- Remove any obstructions and start mouth-to-mouth ventilation.
- Once breathing has started unaided, place the casualty in the recovery position.

What to do if the casualty is unconscious, not breathing and does not have a pulse

- Call 999.
- Tilt the head back and ensure the airway is open and free from obstructions.
- Start mouth-to-mouth ventilation.
- Apply 15 chest compressions (cardio-pulmonary resuscitation).
- Give another two breaths.
- Apply another 15 chest compressions.
- Repeat this process until the casualty starts breathing and there is a pulse. If the casualty does not respond, continue with this until medical help arrives.

What to do if the casualty is unconscious, breathing and has a pulse

- Call 999.
- Place the casualty in the recovery position with the head tilted back to ensure the airway is open.
- Keep on monitoring breathing and pulse until medical help arrives.

Key point

To perform mouth-to-mouth ventilation:

1 Pinch the casualty's nose and seal your mouth around the casualty's mouth.

2 Breathe into the mouth and watch to see if the chest rises.

3 Perform this technique twice.

4 If there is still a pulse and the chest has risen, continue with ten breaths per minute until breathing is unaided.

Key point

To perform chest compressions (cardio-pulmonary resuscitation):

1 Find where the lower ribs meet the breastbone.

2 Place your middle finger on this spot and your index finger above it.

3 Place the heel of your other hand on the breastbone. Move it until it reaches your index finger.

4 Link fingers and apply a downward pressure leaning over the casualty with arms straight.

Let's do it!

Ask your tutor for a first aid box. List everything it contains, and describe what each piece of kit is for.

Types of qualified assistance

When dealing with injuries or illnesses during sports participation, dependent upon the scale of the sporting event there could be lots of qualified assistance there to help deal with medical situations or injuries. For example, at an event such as a boxing match there are usually doctors or paramedics on hand to treat injuries that could be sustained, since boxing is a dangerous sport where rapid blows to the body and head are executed with speed and a great degree of power.

Doctor

Doctors may provide assistance to local sports clubs or for larger sporting events. For example, a local rugby team, premiership football matches, the London Marathon and events such as the Olympics will all have doctors on hand whose presence and assistance will contribute towards the smooth running of the sporting event. Doctors are on hand during an event to deal with any medical problem that may arise; they can make a diagnosis and provide immediate treatment or make a referral to hospital.

Paramedic

Paramedics are health care professionals and are usually the first medical people at the scene of any accident such as a car crash. They give immediate care and treatment to casualties. Usually, they have no indication of what type of injury they may meet on any day.

Key point

At large-scale football matches there may be a team of health care professionals including doctors, paramedics, physiotherapist, sports massage therapist and first aiders.

Physiotherapist

Specialised physiotherapists help and treat people of all ages with sports injuries or with injuries caused by accidents. Football and rugby teams usually have physiotherapists who attend all their matches and who help to deal with injuries as they arise.

A physiotherapist is also crucial in the rehabilitation stages after injury. He or she will provide advice, assess and diagnose injuries, prescribe exercises and perform massages and other manipulative techniques to aid the injured person back to full recovery. Physiotherapy treatments can include manual therapy, massage, therapeutic exercise and the application of electrotherapy modalities.

Sports therapy practitioner

Sports therapy practitioners are trained, and specialise, in the rehabilitation of sports injuries, using treatments such as sports massage, electrotherapy and exercise. They may also provide advice in areas such as nutrition and sports training. Sports therapy practitioners will be able to recognise signs of injury and provide an injury-management plan. They will have also undertaken first aid training, and therefore are found at sporting events, football and rugby matches, athletic events and can also be found working in private practice.

 Key point

If there are a few people in the vicinity of a serious accident then one person should start the necessary basic life support and others should go for help and call for medical assistance.

■ *Sports therapy practitioners may provide sports massage*

Organisation's first aider and emergency services

Every organisation, whether a leisure centre, gymnasium or supermarket, should, under the Health and Safety at Work Act 1974 and the Health and Safety (First Aid) Regulations Act 1981, have qualified and appointed first aiders who are trained to give basic life support until the emergency services arrive. The relevant legislation also states that there should also be a fully stocked first aid box.

Methods of providing reassurance and comfort

Illnesses and injuries can be frightening. The casualty or injured may panic, especially with problems such as asthma attacks in which the breathing can be affected. Sometimes the casualty will think they are going to die. This thought in itself makes the casualty panic even more, which will cause them to hyperventilate and lead to even greater difficulty in breathing.

No matter what the age of the casualty, reassurance and comfort are important.

Ways in which to reassure and comfort

- Talk to the casualty in a quiet and calm manner.
- Hold their hand.
- Tell them not to worry and that help is on the way.
- Ask them questions to take their mind off what is happening.
- Encourage slow, controlled breathing.

Accident reporting procedures

You may need to report details of accidents or illnesses to medical professionals or others involved in the treatment of the casualty. You will need to be able to communicate effectively and give clear and accurate information.

For example, if the casualty has suffered from an injury or asthma attack you will need to obtain the following information.

History

In this instance you need to find out what happened. If the casualty is conscious and alert, ask them; if not, then there may be people around who witnessed the incident. Look around you to see if there is anything that could tell you how the incident occurred.

NB: This may not always be achievable, for example, if someone is having difficulty breathing.

Symptoms

Make a note of the symptoms that the casualty is experiencing. Are they in pain? Where does it hurt? If two footballers have collided heads and are complaining of double vision, hold a few fingers up and ask them to tell you how many you are holding up.

Key point

No one knows when someone will suddenly become ill or when an accident will happen; therefore, organisations should ensure that first aid provision is always available. Everyone in an organisation should have information on who the appointed first aiders are and how to contact them.

Let's do it!

If you attend a sports club or a leisure centre, make a point of finding out who the organisation's first aiders are and how to contact them.

If you are in school or college, ask your teacher who the appointed first aiders are and where they can be found.

Signs

Look for signs of injury or illness.

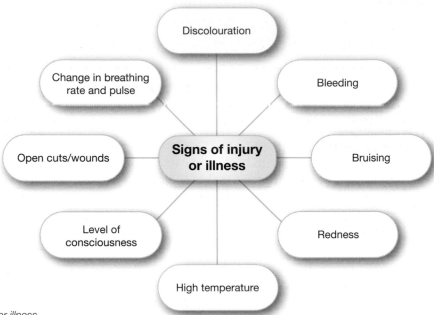

■ *Signs of injury or illness*

First aid treatment given and any response to treatment

Note down any treatment given in order to report it to the medical emergency services or other health care professionals. It is also important to write down how the casualty responded to the treatment given.

All organisations will have an accident book in which any injury or first aid treatment given on the premises must be officially recorded. Below is an example of a page from an accident book.

ACCIDENT REPORT FORM

Name

Address

Occupation of injured/casualty

Date of accident

Details of accident	First aid treatment given	Name of First Aider	Signature

■ *A page from an accident book*

Let's do it!

Choose two different types of injuries. Prepare an injury report form like the one below, which could be given to a medical professional with information filled in about an injured athlete.

Injury report form

Date and time of injury: 05/05/2006 2.00 pm
Venue: Barracks Lane Sports Ground
First aider: Milly Smith
Time of observation: 2.01 pm

Pulse: 85 bpm
Breaths per min: 23
Breathing: quiet

	General information	Details of the injured party	Additional comments
1	Name and age of injured	Nathan Murray – 14 yrs	
2	How did the injury occur/cause of the injury	Two football players went to head the ball at the same time. Collision of heads	Nathan fell to the ground clutching his head
3	The insured's symptoms, for example: a) Numbness b) Blurred vision c) Severe pain d) Mild pain, etc.	He is conscious but is complaining about severe blurred vision, dizziness and a throbbing headache	Nathan feels scared
4	Visual signs, for example: a) Swelling b) Bleeding c) Dislocation d) Discolouration e) Redness f) Bruising g) Breathing difficulties h) Unconsciousness i) Concussion j) Other	A lot of swelling at the front and side of the head	
5	Speech a) Responds well to questions b) Confused c) Other	Confused	
6	First aid treatment given	Ice pack for head Kept calm and warm	
7	Ambulance/Medical help sent for	Ambulance called	2.04 pm
8	Referred to hospital	Yes	Parents contacted – minor
9	Resume play	No	
10	Advice given	Reassurance, kept talking/kept awake, felt sleepy	
11	Home treatment plan	N/A	Referred to hospital

Types of casualty

Able-bodied people and people with disabilities, old and young, and children all participate in sporting activities, so you may deal with a wide variety of different people who may be unfortunate to sustain an accident, illness or injury.

Types of casualty include:

- men
- women
- young children
- teenagers
- participants with special needs including:
  - wheelchair use
  - visual impairment
  - neurological disorders.

Types of injury/illnesses

Becoming injured in sport is a common occurrence, especially if steps haven't been taken to avoid injury. Where illness is concerned the participant normally knows that they have an illness and would usually take precautions to stop them from becoming ill while taking part in their sporting activity. For example, if a known asthmatic was going to take part in a football match then he or she would normally use a preventative inhaler before taking part. However, in doing this there is nothing to say that the condition may not worsen, particularly if the asthmatic were wheezing or showing signs of a mild asthma attack before playing.

Active participants who regularly take part in a sporting activity and who have suffered from an illness such as a viral infection may be eager to get back to their sport as soon as possible. Many participants don't like to get behind with training, or if they play for a team may feel like they are letting their team-mates down. This thought process usually results in the sufferer going back to the sport too early, before their body has had time to recover from the illness, and in effect may worsen the condition and ultimately affect their performance, or, if contagious, infect others.

As we have discussed previously, many different types of injuries or illnesses can occur while taking part in any sporting activity. Some of these can be dealt with on site, in the changing rooms or pitch side, and those that are more serious may require medical attention in hospital.

Key point

If a sports person has an illness or viral infection it is important that they allow the body to have sufficient rest to aid in their recovery.

Case study

Roger

Roger is a 48-year-old runner training for the London Marathon. He is training every day and gradually building up his distance. His wife has influenza (flu) and has been bedridden for a week. Roger has started to show signs of fatigue, high temperature and chills. Tomorrow he is due to run 15 miles during training.

1 What is your advice to Roger?
2 Do you think anything could happen to Roger if he goes running? Give reasons for your answer.

Certain types of minor injuries are common in certain sports. For example, facial injuries such as cuts, bruises and swelling are more common in contact sports such as rugby than in non-contact sports such as badminton. Most minor sports injuries can be recognised by a first aider and the necessary treatment provided. An example of a minor injury that can be dealt with on site is cramp.

Cramp
Cramp occurs in muscles and is characterized by a sudden tightening or painful contraction of a muscle, which can last from a few minutes up to an hour. It is thought that there are many factors which can contribute to cramp. These include inadequate warm up and stretch, inadequate rest and recovery after training, insufficient cool down and stretch programme, dehydration or loss of fluid, or an electrolyte imbalance due to excessive sweating.

Treatment: The affected muscle should be held in a stretch position until the cramp subsides. For relief, athletes should hold the affected muscle in a stretched position until twitching subsides. They should also be encouraged to breathe deeply in order to take in more oxygen.

Minor illnesses that can be dealt with on site
Heat exhaustion is an example of a minor illness that can be dealt with on site. However, if the signs and symptoms are not recognised then this could turn into a major illness requiring medical attention. Weakness, chills, disorientation, thirst and headache are just some of the common symptoms of heat exhaustion.

Treatment: A cool drink should be given and the casualty taken out of the sun to a shaded area. If the casualty has lots of clothes on then some of these should be removed. Sports drinks with electrolytes can be given.

Major injuries requiring medical attention
A head injury or concussion is an example of a major injury which would require medical attention if the casualty has lost consciousness or

Key point

Electrolytes are required for maintaining fluid levels and healthy muscle contractions. Electrolytes include sodium, potassium and chloride. Sweating results in the loss of electrolytes; these can be replaced by food and drink in a healthy diet.

Let's do it!

Think about and research other minor injuries and their treatments that can be dealt with on site, and complete the injuries and illnesses table.

Let's do it!

Think about and research other major injuries and their treatments that require medical attention, and complete the injuries and illnesses table

has disturbed vision. If an athlete has sustained a head injury, this could get progressively worse so he or she must be closely observed. See page 54 for signs and symptoms of concussion.

Asthma is another major illness which is described on page 58. If a child or adult is participating in sport and suddenly becomes increasingly breathless and his or her inhaler has no effect, then he or she may require urgent medical treatment. See page 59 for the signs and symptoms of an asthma attack.

Let's do it!

Copy the table below, and working in pairs or small groups do the following.

1 Research minor and major injuries that can occur in the sports highlighted in the table. Don't be afraid to use your own personal experiences if you have been injured.

2 Research minor and major illnesses associated with sports participation.

3 Complete the table, following the example of boxing that has been given.

Sporting activity	Minor injuries that can be dealt with on site	Minor illnesses that can be dealt with on site	Major injuries requiring medical attention	Major illnesses requiring medical attention
Boxing	Cuts Bruising Swollen lip	Virus – high temperature	Knock-out which renders participant unconscious Large open wound – carries the risk of infection Blow to the chest Repeated blows to the head which render participant dizzy and confused	Heart attack Blood clot
Football				
Running a marathon				
Swimming in a pool				
Rugby				

Alternative methods of treating injuries

Increasingly, sportsmen and women are turning to forms of alternative medicine to help the healing process and to recover more quickly from an injury.

Method	Description
Acupuncture	A method of healing using needles, developed in China thousands of years ago. The needles are used to influence the balance of the body's natural health by stimulating points in the channels of energy (Qi) that flow through the body
Homeopathy	This method uses medicines that are given in an extremely dilute form, and which work by influencing the energy level of the body. Homeopathy tends to see illness as an expression of disharmony within the whole person
Chiropractic	This method specialises in and focuses on muscular and skeletal problems through manipulation of the spine
Medical herbalism	This method treats disorders with medicines that have been derived from plant materials
Sports massage therapy	Sports massage is an effective and beneficial form of physical therapy, which aims to enhance a sportsperson's performance, help to prevent injuries and aid in the recovery of an athlete after an event

Assessment activity 4: Role play

Your teacher will observe you.

Scenario 1

Requirements:

- Five or six students in a group
- One student to act as the first aider
- Two students to simulate playing football
- The other students should act as spectators.

Two football players have collided heads while going for the ball; one falls unconscious to the ground, and the other is suffering from concussion.

Scenario 2

Requirements:

- Five or six students in a group
- Two students to act as the first aiders
- Three students to simulate playing rugby one of whom is the casualty
- The other students should act as spectators.

Thirty minutes into a rugby match you notice a player struggling out on the pitch. He seems to be clasping his chest and gasping for air. Two players running for the ball, unaware that he is having any problems, knock him to the ground; he bangs his head and is bleeding from a small head wound.

To achieve a Pass or Merit:

1 Deal with the casualty in the appropriate manner. Don't forget to use people around you to help or call for help if necessary. (P5 or M4)

2.3 Understand risks and hazards associated with sports participation

Key point

Here are some important definitions to help you through this unit.

- **Health** – being free from illness, injury or disease and having a general sense of well-being
- **Safety** – being free from anything that could cause harm
- **Injury** – anything that occurs or happens to an individual that causes bodily harm
- **Hazard** – anything that can cause physical bodily harm, for example a slippery floor, fire or certain items of sports equipment, for example javelins or darts
- **Risk** – the probability or chance of injury occurring because of a hazard. The risk could be great or small

A risk assessment is an analysis or check of any working environment, be it sports hall, swimming pool or football pitch, to make sure that there are not any hazards which could be potentially harmful or cause an injury to participants, spectators or coaches.

You can break down the main risk factors and hazards which can be associated with sports participation. Factors that can lead to or cause sporting injuries to occur include:

- the participant or sporting individual
- the coach
- the environment
- other users and participants
- equipment and personal protective equipment
- lifestyle (e.g. alcohol)
- parental influence.

People

The participant or sporting individual

The participant or sporting individual, through their own actions, can be an injury risk factor, particularly if he or she is misbehaving, has a negative attitude towards the sport or is not following the rules. The following spidergram identifies the risk factors related to the sporting individual or sports participant.

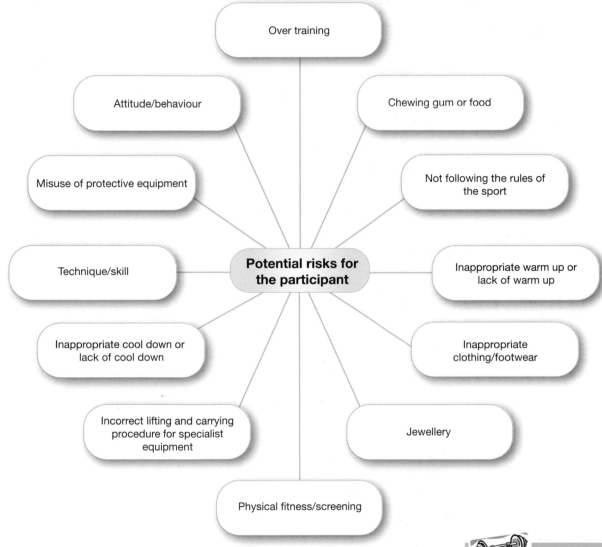

■ *Potential risk for participant or sporting individual*

Attitude/behaviour

If you have the wrong attitude to the sport or to the coach, you are more likely not to listen and to think that you know what is best. This could lead to you being injured through wrong practice, misuse of equipment, or performing a skill or technique incorrectly.

Over training

Continuous training without adequate rest or recovery periods can place a lot of stress upon the soft tissues of the body (muscles, ligaments, tendons and joints). All these areas are prone to injury. Over training can result in athletes injuring themselves, and will also have a profound effect on the athlete's mental state.

Think about it

Get together with two or three others in your group and discuss your own experiences of being coached. Was your coaching experience positive or negative? Identify how your coach helped you, or didn't help you, to improve.

Think about it

Imagine if high profile football players such as Thierry Henry or David Beckham began a continuous training programme of five hours a day, seven days a week leading up to the World Cup, without appropriate rest or recovery.

1   How do you think this would affect their performance?
2   How do you think it would affect them mentally?
3   How do you think this scenario may cause them to sustain a sports injury?

Think about it

Have you ever injured yourself because you performed a technique or skill incorrectly? Discuss your experiences with your group.

Poor technique/level of skills training

Skill development or skills training is a very important component of any training regime and is necessary for safety in sport. If you do not develop the specific skills needed for your sport, you are more likely to become injured.

Visualise the technical arm movements and release of a field athlete such as a javelin thrower. During training sessions they would practise and develop their skills in the correct throwing or releasing techniques through repetition, practice and feedback from a coach or from analysing a video recording. If the athlete doesn't take on board what their coach is advising or doesn't practise and improve their technique, then they will be at risk of sustaining an injury to the shoulder complex, back and neck through poor technique. Therefore, skill development and training can be a means of preventing injury.

Lack of warm up

A warm up is designed gradually to increase the flow of blood around the body. This in turn increases the core temperature of the muscles and allows for freer movement at the joints. It prepares the body for the exercise or activity and it also prepares the athlete mentally for the work ahead.

The warm up must be specific to the individual and should also be sports specific, encompassing techniques and skills to be used in the training session. The warm up should include pulse raising, mobility and stretching exercises or activities. If you don't perform an adequate warm

Let's do it!

In a group, discuss the different warm up and cool down exercises that you have experienced. Try to think about what each exercise is designed to do. Together, create a suitable warm up and cool down routine for an aerobics session, or other sport of your choice.

up of about 10–15 minutes, your muscles, ligaments and tendons are more prone to injury.

Lack of cool down

The aim of a cool down is to gradually decrease the heart rate back down to near its non-exercising state, to improve recovery time by removing the waste products from the muscle tissue, and to help reduce the pain associated with muscle soreness and stiffness. All training sessions should finish with a cool down. If you don't cool down after exercising, you are more likely to be stiff and your muscles may be sore. This could affect the range of movement of your joints, your flexibility and your performance.

Physical fitness/screening

Any sports participant must be in good health. If you are not physically fit, you may become tired and injuries may result. You may not be able to execute skills correctly because you lack the stamina to do so.

All participants in sport should undergo health screening. This may involve filling in a PARQ (Physical Activity Readiness Questionnaire), which asks questions about your health, lifestyle and medical history. This will ensure that it is safe for you to take part in physical activity. If the screening questionnaire highlights any problems then you will require a letter from your GP stating that you are 'fit' to participate.

Inappropriate clothing or footwear

All sports participants must wear the appropriate clothing for their particular sporting activity. Clothes that are too baggy can get trapped or caught in equipment. Clothes that are too tight can restrict movement. This may make it difficult for you to perform in a technically correct way, which could result in some form of injury.

Footwear is for support and protection. Fashion footwear must not be worn for sports, and it is crucial that footwear is suitable for the sporting activity that you are participating in.

Inappropriate footwear could result in unnecessary stresses being placed upon the feet, ankles, legs, or even the back.

Jewellery

Jewellery should not be worn during any sporting activity; it could cause an injury to you or to others. Earrings can be ripped out during contact sports; chains and necklaces could get caught up in equipment and could cause choking accidents. During exercise the blood flow is increased around the body so that the fingers may swell slightly. If you are wearing a ring it will become increasingly tight and could even restrict the blood flow to the finger. Participants wearing jewellery can cause cuts and lacerations to others.

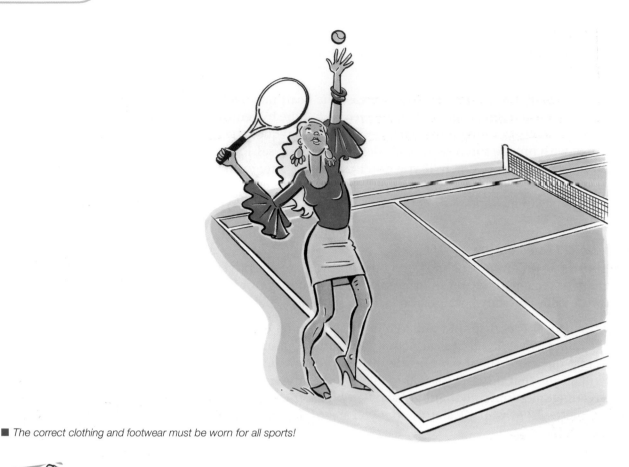

■ *The correct clothing and footwear must be worn for all sports!*

Misuse of protective equipment

A sports participant who does not use protective equipment has a greater risk of becoming injured during play. Helmets, shin pads, mouth guards and gloves are just some of the protective equipment that is used in sport.

Incorrect lifting and carrying procedure for specialist equipment

Sports participants should always be taught how to lift and carry any heavy specialist equipment. Incorrect lifting and carrying can result in injuries to the back.

Not following the rules of the sport

All sports have specific rules that need to be followed. These rules are usually set by the governing body or association for each sport, for sport participants' enjoyment and safety. Injuries and accidents can occur when sports rules are ignored.

Appropriate physique required for a specific sport

Having the right body to suit a particular sport can make a difference to the performance of an athlete – the difference between success and failure. Have you ever see a marathon runner with the physique of a sumo wrestler, or an ice dancer with the physique of a rugby player?

Think about it

1 *What type of physique do marathon runners have?*
2 *What types of physique do weightlifters have?*
3 *Are their physiques suitable for their chosen sport? Justify your answer.*

Food and chewing gum

It is important that anyone undertaking any physical activity doesn't eat or chew gum while playing sport. Running around with food or gum in the mouth could cause choking, especially if two players collide or falling occurs. The gum or food could block the airway, making breathing difficult, and unconsciousness and death could follow if immediate help is not given.

Think about it

Think of other instances in sport where rules have not been followed. The examples can be from professional televised sport or from your own personal experiences.

Let's do it!

Risk factor	Who might be harmed?	How might the risk affect sporting performance?	How could the risk be minimised?
Over training	The athlete	Puts stress on muscles, joints, tendons and ligaments, resulting in a restricted range of movement, muscle soreness and stiffness, or minute tearing of the muscles. All of the above have a negative effect on performance	Devising an effective but safe training programme. Providing adequate rest periods. Sports massages to help prevent injuries or reduce the risk of injuries occurring
Lack of warm up	The athlete	Training heavily on muscles that are cold and have not been sufficiently warmed can lead to injuries, such as tears	Allow sufficient time to warm up and stretch before any type of activity begins
Misuse of protective equipment	The athlete; other participants	Not wearing protective equipment increases the risk of injury	Follow the rules for the specific sport. Wear protective equipment when necessary. The coach should check that equipment is worn/used properly

The table above shows three of the risk factors that can cause sporting injuries. Draw a similar table and complete it for the remaining risk factors described on pages 77–81. State who might be harmed and how this might affect sporting performance, and suggest ways in which the risk could be minimised or prevented.

The coach

A sport's coach could contribute to injuries being caused by inappropriate coaching methods or even his or her desire to win at all costs. Risk factors related to coaching behaviour include:

- coaching styles
- pushing too hard
- no knowledge of sporting activity
- incorrect technique
- desire to win
- over training
- no first aid provision.

Coaching styles

The style of coaching that the coach adopts could result in injuries occurring to the participant. For example, if you find it difficult to talk to or approach your coach, you are less likely to ask for advice or pose questions. This may lead to you learning to perform skills in a technically incorrect way, and this could result in a soft tissue injury.

Pushing too hard

If the coach pushes the participant very hard, with little time for recovery, this will make the participant more susceptible to injuries.

No knowledge of sporting activity

It is important that a coach has knowledge and experience of the sport that he or she is coaching. He or she must have tactical awareness skills, be able to analyse strategically, and be able to implement and apply the rules of the sport. The coach must also be able to plan a programme of training to match each individual's needs and abilities. If the coach has no knowledge of the sport, then he or she is more likely to teach incorrect techniques.

Incorrect technique

If the coach does not teach technically correct skills or techniques then the participant will execute those skills and techniques incorrectly. This will leave him or her more prone to injury. For example, if a karate coach is teaching a side kick that requires specific movement at the hips, and is teaching it with no movement, then this could lead to groin injuries.

Desire to win

Coaches who just have a desire to win are probably not thinking about the stresses placed upon the athlete's body. Continuously pushing in training sessions is not the right way to get the best out of an athlete.

Over training

Continuous pushing from the coach may lead to over training. Too much training places severe stresses on the muscles and joints, which could result in muscle soreness, stiffness, minute tearing and over-use injuries. If you over train you will also become fatigued, make silly mistakes, and may sustain an injury as a result of this.

No first aid provision

Adequate first aid provision is vital. Minor injuries may become worse if immediate treatment is not to hand. A good example of this is an impact injury where swelling occurs. If no ice or ice packs are available to help reduce the swelling then it will become worse and effectively lengthen the recovery time following injury.

 Let's do it!

Risk factor	Who might be harmed?	How might the risk affect sporting performance?	How could the risk be minimised?
No first aid provision	The athlete; other participants	Minor injuries may take longer to heal	Provide adequate first aid, e.g. a fully stocked first aid kit. A qualified, appointed first aider must be present at all times
No knowledge of the sporting activity	The athlete; other participants	Skills may be taught incorrectly. Rules may not conform to those laid down by the sports associations	Coach must be fully qualified to teach the sport. Coach should regularly update knowledge and take further training courses
Coaching styles	The athlete; other participants	An athlete knows his or her own body and whether or not a specific skill or drill is suitable – if the coach will not listen or the athlete is too afraid to speak, injury may result	Coach should be selective in coaching styles, depending on whom he or she is training. Coach should be aware of how the different coaching styles will affect the athletes and their sporting performance. Coach should be willing to listen to the athletes he or she is training

The table above shows three of the risk factors that can cause sporting injuries. Draw a similar table and complete for the remaining risk factors described on pages 82–3. State who will be harmed, how it will affect sporting performance and suggest ways in which the risk could be minimised or prevented.

Case study

Coach

The coach of a local athletics team usually teaches 16–18 year olds. He has been asked to cover ten sessions coaching 8–10 year olds in high jump. He is not a high jump specialist and his knowledge is limited. His coaching style is dictatorial, and winning is his main aim.

Answer the following questions.

1 What potential hazards and risks can you see in this scenario?

2 How might injuries occur?

3 What are the health and safety implications?

Equipment and personal protective equipment

Equipment that is not checked regularly or properly maintained can become a big risk factor. Most sporting associations and governing bodies specify what protective equipment must be worn during each particular sport. It is important to remember that, as well as those listed below, vandalised equipment or not wearing protective equipment at all are risks factors.

- Faulty or damaged equipment
- Inappropriate specialist equipment

Faulty or damaged equipment

Equipment must be regularly checked, maintained, repaired or replaced in order to prevent injuries occurring to individuals who use it. If you notice faulty equipment you need to take appropriate steps and report it immediately to a coach or facility manager so that they can take it out of use, thus preventing others from becoming injured.

Imagine what would happen if you knew a trampoline was faulty but you forgot to report it? Can you visualise what could happen or what the potential risks could be to others?

Lack of protective clothing or inappropriate specialist equipment

Specialist equipment necessary for specific sports must be made available and be in good condition. If it is not, certain areas of the body will either not be fully protected, or not be protected at all. High-risk sports, such as contact sports, require more preventative measures.

Let's do it!

1 Make a list of the protective equipment required by the following sports:
- football
- cricket
- ice hockey
- hockey
- boxing
- rugby.

2 What type of injury do you think the protective equipment could prevent from happening?

3 Are there any sports that you know of that should have protective equipment but don't?

The environment

The environment can pose a risk to sports participants. For example, running on a hard surface can increase the likelihood of shin splints. Certain weather conditions will affect playing surfaces and can lead to injuries being sustained. The following spidergram identifies some of the environmental risk factors.

■ Environmental risk factors

Facilities

If facilities are hired for training purposes it is the responsibility of the coach and of the owner to liaise with each other to ensure that the facilities are safe to use. Indoor facilities must be clean and well maintained. Current health and safety regulations covering the facility must be regularly checked and updated.

Weather conditions/temperature

Weather conditions can cause injuries to occur. For example, rain, snow or frost could make playing surfaces slippery, leading to falls that could result in breaks and sprains.

Playing in severely cold weather for any length of time could result in hypothermia, especially if the participant is not dressed appropriately for cold weather.

Extremely hot weather could lead to dehydration, so it is important that participants drink lots of fluid and wear the correct clothing, and that training time is minimised. A cap is essential to protect the head from the sun and to prevent sunstroke occurring. The sun can also cause an accident or injury to happen by temporarily blinding participants.

Flooding or muddy pitches caused by heavy rain can cause slipping and falling accidents. In these instances, training or the match should be cancelled or moved to another safe venue.

Playing surfaces

Playing surfaces must be correct for the sport in question. A good example is aerobics, or any type of dancing activity, which should be undertaken on a sprung floor. This type of floor is designed to reduce the impact on the joints, thereby reducing any impact-associated injuries. Hard surfaces can cause injuries to the soft tissues of the body, especially when you are not used to playing or training on them. If a playing surface is constantly being changed, for example from grass to concrete or wood, it is likely that this will have an effect on the legs and could induce injury.

Think about it

In your group, discuss all the different playing surfaces you know about.

1 *What experience do you have of them?*
2 *Have any of you been injured through playing on the wrong surface?*

Hazards and obstacles

All playing or training surfaces must be free from obstacles or hazards that could cause injury. It is the coach's responsibility to check the areas before each session. He or she should also encourage the participants not to drop litter or leave things lying around that could cause harm to others. Wet floors in changing rooms are another common hazard.

Inadequate lighting/ventilation

Adequate lighting and ventilation need to be provided for any training or playing that takes place indoors. Everyone must be able to see what they are doing and be able to move around safely.

Let's do it!

Risk factor	Who might be harmed?	How might the risk affect sporting performance?	How could the risk be minimised?
Unsafe facilities	The athlete; other participants; visitors	May be the cause of injury, e.g. old or broken tiles on a changing room floor might cause minor or serious injury to the feet	Ensure facilities are in good working order. Deal with hazards immediately to prevent injuries occurring
Hazards/obstacles	The athlete; other participants; the coach	May be the cause of injury, e.g. broken glass on a football pitch puts players at risk of cutting themselves if they fall or slip	Conduct a risk assessment of the sporting environment before any activity, to ensure it is safe to play in and free from any hazards that could cause bodily harm
Inadequate lighting and ventilation	The athlete; other participants; the coach	May cause injury, e.g. if athletes can't see what they are doing this could lead to an accident happening	Be aware of the time when it starts to get dark and ensure that training is scheduled in daylight. If using a floodlit pitch, ensure that all floodlights are in good working order. If using indoor facilities ensure that all lighting is working and report if necessary to facilities' owner

The table above shows three of the risk factors that can cause sporting injuries. Draw a similar table and complete for the remaining risk factors described on pages 84–6. State who will be harmed and how it will affect sporting performance, and suggest ways in which the risk could be minimised or prevented.

Floodlights are usually provided at specialist facilities for playing outdoors. If they are not then it is important that you are aware of the time when it starts to get dark, to ensure everyone's safety.

Other users and participants

When playing sports in any environment there are often other participants and users of the sporting facilities. Their actions and behaviour could lead to other participants being injured.

Risk factors related to other participants and users include:

- attitude and behaviour
- misuse of equipment
- vandalism and graffiti
- peer pressure.

Attitude and behaviour

The attitude and behaviour of other participants is very important. A small group misbehaving with equipment, for example throwing javelins when they have been told not to, can result in serious injuries occurring to others within the training environment.

Misuse of equipment

Many situations require participants to be supervised when setting up or taking down equipment, as well as when using specialist equipment. If the coach does not supervise the participants, then they could misuse the equipment.

Vandalism and graffiti

If equipment has been vandalised, this must be reported to prevent accidents occurring. If there is a fault with a trampoline, for example, or it has been vandalised, the next group of people to use it could sustain an injury.

Peer pressure

Peer pressure is another factor that could cause, or lead to, an injury in sport. If you try to train like one of your most experienced counterparts from a higher ability group, you might injure yourself. If you feel under pressure to be as good as your peers, you might over train, which can lead to over-use injuries.

Lifestyle

An athlete's lifestyle could have a bearing on his or her performance. Alcohol and drugs affect an athlete's ability to think logically or react quickly. Some of the injury risk factors associated with lifestyle include:

- inadequate diet/sleep
- alcohol and drugs
- irregular training.

Inadequate diet/sleep

The types of food you eat will have a major bearing on your health, fitness, training and performance. If you are not eating a healthy balanced diet, or not eating much but training heavily, this will lead to light-headedness, dizziness or even fainting. This is true for sleep too – too little sleep could lead to slow reactions and increase the risk of injury.

■ *Drinking alcohol before or during a sporting activity is not permitted and can lead to serious accidents or injury*

Alcohol and drugs

Training or playing when alcohol or drugs are in your system can be dangerous to yourself and other participants. Some sportspeople in the past have used alcohol as a way to calm nerves before a competition or event. But alcohol slows down reaction time and affects balance and coordination. It also affects the way in which you think about, and judge, situations and will negatively affect your athletic performance.

Irregular training

Regular guided training, together with adequate recovery and rest time, is a requirement of any sport. If you train only when you feel like it, and have no specific routine, then your body will not be trained to cope with the demands of your sport and injuries can occur as a result.

Let's do it!

Risk factor	Who might be harmed?	How might the risk affect sporting performance?	How could the risk be minimised?
Inadequate diet	The athlete	The athlete will fatigue quickly and performance will be hindered due to tiredness and low energy levels	Educate the athlete on the right and wrong foods to eat. Ensure the athlete perseveres with the new nutritional plan

The table above shows one of the risk factors that can cause sporting injuries. Draw a similar table and complete for the remaining risk factors described on pages 88–90. State who will be harmed and how it will affect sporting performance, and suggest ways in which the risk could be minimised or prevented.

Parental influence

Some parents are very demanding, and want their child to be the best. This can create an adverse reaction in the child. The child athlete may train harder to please his or her parents, or the parents may push the child to train harder. Both these scenarios could lead to over-use injuries.

In summary

Ways to minimise the risk of injury occurring include:

- obeying the rules
- wearing the correct clothing and footwear
- warming up
- cooling down
- using appropriate training methods
- training under a qualified, knowledgeable and experienced coach
- wearing personal protective equipment
- ensuring activities are suited to age and ability levels
- following a suitable training and fitness programme
- ensuring adequate supervision
- avoiding over training
- following correct lifting and carrying procedures
- removing obstacles and hazards
- health screening
- following a good diet
- practising skills and techniques.

Assessment activity 5: Risk and hazards associated with sports participation

The following is a list of different sporting situations.

- A crowded ice rink.
- A crowded swimming pool with one lifeguard on duty.
- A fitness instructor giving an induction to a busy over-50s session at the gym.
- A football match at a ground with stadium capacity of 10,000. Tickets are being sold on the gates and more people are being let inside than the stadium is designed to hold.

To achieve a Pass:

1 *Describe* all of the injury risk factors and hazards associated with each of the four sports. (P1)

To achieve a Merit you must achieve the Pass criteria and:

2 *Explain* why you think each could be the cause of an injury. (M1)

To achieve a Distinction you must achieve the Pass and Merit criteria and:

3 Give a *detailed account* of why participants are at risk while taking part in sport and discuss the impact of injury risk factors on successful sports performance. (D1)

Rules, regulation and legislation

You, health and safety and the law

When you are working in sport, it is important to be aware of the relevant laws that deal with health and safety. These laws are sensible and are there to protect you and others who participate in sport. Whether a facility or training ground is large or small, it is covered by the laws laid down by the government in Acts of Parliament. The coach and facilities provider have to ensure that everyone is aware of, and abides by, relevant regulations and legislations. In this way, the health, safety and welfare of athletes, staff and other participants within the working environment will be maintained.

It is also the responsibility of the facilities owner and coach to obtain updated information on any changes in regulations. Breaking the law, by ignoring or not updating this information, could result in severe punishment. This in turn is likely to be costly to the sporting environment in a number of ways, which could include any of the following:

- closure of the sports ground/stadium or playing environment
- a bad reputation
- a hefty fine
- imprisonment
- an order to pay compensation if a preventable injury occurs.

In addition, some facilities may have voluntary codes of practice. These are rules which the organisation wants you to follow for goodwill, and are not usually laid down by law. A common example of this is a sign in a swimming pool saying 'No running, no eating or drinking, no diving, and no splashing'. These are all voluntary codes of practice and are there to ensure the safety of yourself and other users.

Health and Safety at Work Act 1974

Under the Health and Safety at Work Act 1974, all employers have a duty of care to ensure that a safe working environment is provided which is free from anything that could cause harm or cause a risk to health or life. In this instance, the employer would be the coach and the facility provider. The act states both employers and employees have responsibilities.

Employer responsibilities

- To provide for the health, safety and welfare of *all* of their employees or those who work for them.
- To provide a written health and safety policy.
- To ensure the safety of customers or participants who visit the premises or facilities.

Key point

A health and safety policy is required in an organisation that employs five or more people. A health and safety policy is a written document which describes important health and safety procedures or safe working practices. All employees should have access to a copy of their company's health and safety policy.

Let's do it!

Arrange to visit a local leisure or sports centre and see if you can identify any risk factors within the environment. Look in all areas of your chosen facilities, such as:

- *swimming pool/changing rooms*
- *sports hall*
- *gym*
- *reception area.*

Decide whom these risk factors might affect, for example members of staff, visitors and/or customers. Then discuss the best ways in which to minimise the risk of injury or prevent them from occurring.

Think about it

- *Think of any sporting situation where you might be required to lift something heavy.*
- *How can you minimise or prevent injuries occurring when you lift something heavy?*

Think about it

Think of four sports for which you are required, by its rules or regulations, to wear protective equipment.

Employee responsibilities

Employees have to abide by the facility rules and regulations and ensure that by their own actions they do not put themselves or any customer, visitor or other member of staff, at risk of injury or harm. For example, when dealing with chemicals in a swimming pool, the right amount of chemical needs to be added. If the employee does not take reasonable care, then a lot of visitors to the pool could be affected by their actions.

Manual Handling Operations Regulations 1992

Working in the sports industry may involve lifting and carrying heavy equipment. The Manual Handling Operations Regulations 1992 state that all employees who are involved in lifting and carrying must have sufficient training in these procedures, in order to promote safe practice and to prevent injuries occurring.

Personal Protective Equipment at Work Regulations 1992

This regulation requires all employers to provide protective clothing if necessary. For example, those involved with handling swimming pool chemicals may need to wear gloves, boots or goggles. Sports participants may also be bound by law to wear protective equipment, for example in motorbike racing.

Control of Substances Hazardous to Health Regulations 2002 (COSHH)

Under this regulation, employers must ensure that anyone who uses chemicals or substances that could cause harm to others is aware of safe practices relating to handling, use and storage. In a leisure or fitness centre a wide range of harmful or toxic substances are used to maintain swimming pools or jacuzzis, and also for cleaning and disinfecting, so it is important that the following are adhered to.

- Chemicals are stored correctly, or locked away out of reach of the general public and children.

- All staff are trained and continue to have regular training in the correct usage and storage.

- Employers should provide protective clothing where necessary, for example gloves, aprons, goggles.

- All staff should be trained in emergency procedures or first aid in order to cope with situations where chemicals get into the eyes, are ingested, or cause irritation to the skin.

Let's do it!

Visit a leisure centre to find out:
1 about the chemicals, which are used in a swimming pool
2 whether staff have to wear any protective clothing
3 whether staff have had training on how to use the chemicals.
Identify:
4 risk factors to the public (via the swimming pool) or to the staff (using chemicals)
5 the methods used to minimise any injuries or accidents occurring.

Health and Safety (First Aid) Regulations 1981

Accidents happen when we least expect them to, so it is important to be prepared!

The key intentions of these regulations are that there must be qualified first aiders within leisure facilities, companies or any organisation. These people need to be able to take control of first aid situations and look after the first aid equipment. A fully-stocked first aid kit must also be available.

The qualified first aider who provides treatment must also record details of the accident (when, why, how, what happened) and also must record details of what treatment was given.

Children Act 1989

There are many services in sport and leisure aimed at children, for example football and rugby coaching, half-term and out-of-school activities, so this act is of major importance as it looks at safe working practices for children. The facility or centre providing the sports or leisure services must be also registered.

Let's do it!

1 If the Health and Safety (First Aid) Regulations were not followed at a big athletics meet, what would the injury risk factors be?
2 Identify the best ways to minimise the risk.

This act protects children and states that anyone working with children must:

- obtain clearance from the police and criminal records bureau before he or she can actually work with children
- be suitability qualified to work with children
- be trained to recognise the signs of abuse
- be trained in methods of dealing with abuse, and in reporting procedures and referral.

Safety at Sports Grounds Act 1975

What would the World Cup, the Ashes or the Olympics be like without spectators? Spectators buy tickets and may travel quite far to attend such events to support individuals or teams. So it is important that while they are in a large venue such as a stadium that their safety is not compromised.

This act is designed to protect the safety of spectators at sports events. It is the responsibility of the organisers of the event to ensure that spectators, participants and staff are all within a safe environment. If the capacity of the stadium is 10,000, then a safety certificate is required.

To ensure the health and safety of all spectators, the following need to be considered.

- Ensure that the stadium does not exceed the maximum number of spectators.
- Ensure there are enough exits/entrances.
- Ensure that spectators/fans of different clubs are seated in different areas of the stadium.

Let's do it!

1 A newly qualified coach, who was trained with adults, is employed to work with children. Identify the injury risk factors in this situation.

2 Identify ways to minimise or prevent injuries occurring.

Let's do it!

There have been some instances where safety has been compromised at sporting events, and serious injures and, tragically, deaths have occurred.

In small groups do the following.

1 Research breaches of health and safety in the following sporting events, for example where accidents have happened.

- *Football matches.*
- *Motorcross racing.*

2 Discuss what happened and how health and safety was compromised.
   a Was anybody injured?
   b What happened as a result of the event?

Case study

Hillsborough

The Hillsborough football disaster in April 1989 claimed 96 lives, with a further 170 people being injured. These people had gone to watch the FA cup semi final between Nottingham Forest and Liverpool, at the Hillsborough stadium in Sheffield. A gate was opened to allow a big crowd of fans into an already crowded centre section of the stadium. This resulted in fans being crushed in the entrance tunnels, on the steps and against the perimeter fencing. This was one of the worst disasters in Britain's sporting history. The organisers and promoters of the event had a duty of care to ensure that all visitors, staff and players were in a safe environment. This was obviously not the case.

Try to obtain some video footage of news reports about this disaster – your tutor will help you with this. Search through past newspaper articles – you can usually do this on the internet. Again, ask you tutor for help if you need it.

Now answer the following questions.
1 Identify the injury risk factors.
2 In what ways could these have been minimised or prevented?
3 Discuss this incident within your group once you have gathered all of the necessary information.

Assessment activity 6: Rules and regulations

Look at the list of sports activities given below, which usually have a high number of participants, both children and adults. Choose two different activities.

- Over 18s football match using facilities of a local sports club.
- Ice hockey practice at the Nottingham Ice Arena.
- Under 13s basketball practice in a sports centre.
- Under 16s swimming club at a local council-run swimming pool.

To achieve a Pass:

1 *Describe* prominent rules, regulations and legislation relating to health safety and injury in sports participation. (P2)

To achieve a Merit, you must first achieve the Pass criteria and:

2 *Explain* prominent rules, regulations and legislations relating to health, safety and injury in sports participation. (M2)

Key point

Don't forget to include rules that are not legislations, but are to maintain good practice. For example, in a swimming pool you will often see a sign which says 'No diving' or 'No running'. This is not legislation but a rule of the centre that will ensure sports participants are safe. Rules laid down by sporting governing bodies should also be included in this assessment activity.

2.4 Be able to undertake a risk assessment relevant to sport

Purpose

It is essential that at any sporting venue, facility or stadium any hazards that could cause harm to participants, staff and visitors be identified. The risks must then be dealt with to prevent injuries occurring. It is the responsibility of the owner, manager and coach to work together to assess health and safety hazards and risks.

There are many potential health and safety hazards within all sporting environments, which, if not dealt with promptly, could cause serious injury to others or could even be life-threatening.

What is a risk assessment?

A risk assessment is an inspection carried out to identify hazards and to prevent accidents or injuries occurring within a facility or environment in which you are working or playing.

The purpose therefore is to:

■ ascertain or determine the level of risk
■ minimise injury
■ maintain a safe environment
■ protect participants and those people leading activities.

This can be undertaken by carrying out a risk assessment.

There are six steps to a risk assessment.

1 Identify the hazard.
2 Identify who will be harmed.
3 Give a risk rating.
4 Record existing measures being taken.
5 Suggest other measures that could be taken.
6 Record, review, monitor and evaluate.

Step 1: Identify the hazard

Be observant and alert to anything that could possibly cause harm to others. Identify possible risks involved and the level of risks to others. If a hazard is reported, ask people what they saw, when and where. If an accident occurs due to a hazard, report it and put measures in place to ensure that it does not affect anybody else.

Step 2: Identify who will be harmed

State who uses or works in the facility and who may come into contact with the hazard. Those persons who may be harmed will normally be staff, visitors and users of the facility.

Step 3: Give a risk rating

In this section, the severity of the risk and the probability that the risk could occur need to be identified.

Severity of risk, rating 1–3:

1   High risk – where the outcome would be death or serious injury.
2   Moderate risk – where the outcome would be an injury requiring hospital treatment.
3   Low risk – where the outcome is a treatable injury, which would not incapacitate.

Probability of risk, rating 1–3:

1   Good chance of it happening.
2   Could occur.
3   Not likely to happen.

Step 4: Record existing measures taken

Identify any existing measures that are currently in place, if any. Note what is already in place to stop the hazard from harming others. If there is currently nothing in place, then state that on your risk assessment form.

Step 5: Suggest measures that could be taken

In this section, state what can be done to prevent an injury occurring, or what further actions are required to control the risk.

Step 6: Record, review, monitor and evaluate

Everything recorded on a risk assessment must be reviewed, to ensure that the suggested measures are being effectively employed and are still working. Risk assessments must be reviewed and evaluated on an on-going basis.

Risk assessment procedure

Risk assessment procedure will always be the same, whether it is conducted by a sports coach or a duty officer. The completed risk assessment must be shown to the relevant person or people (for example, a manager or health and safety officer) who will then work with a team of people to reduce the likelihood of the risk occurring. The sporting activity should not commence until the risk is eliminated.

Certain rules or procedures may be implemented by an organisation to try to eliminate risks occurring. These must be monitored and reviewed regularly, to ensure they are effective.

The use of specialist equipment and contingency plans to minimise the risk of injury

Throughout this section there are tables which give suggestions for how the risk of injury could be minimised. These could be through using basic signs such as the 'wet floor' sign or posters which will alert others to potential dangers. However, it is important for anyone involved in sports, from coach to participant, to be aware of how they can prevent injuries from occurring, and this could mean the participant using specialised equipment or the coach having a contingency or back-up plan. Let's look at both of these areas.

 Key point

The benefits of maintaining a safe working environment are:

- repeat business
- good reputation
- happy customers
- smaller risk of accidents
- no fines.

Date of risk assessment: 01 July 2006					
Step 1 Identify the hazard	Step 2 Who will be harmed?	Step 3 Risk rating (severity/ probability)	Step 4 Existing measures	Step 5 Suggested measures	Step 6 Record, review, monitor and evaluate
Broken bottles, litter, cans	Sports participants Staff Spectators	Risk rating 2 – moderate risk of someone becoming injured and requiring hospital treatment Probability of risk = 1	Two litter bins around grounds. Notices encouraging people to use the bins.	More litter bins around grounds/ facility required (ca. 6-8). Notices warning of hefty fines for throwing litter on the ground. Ground monitors who check the ground regularly throughout the day. Letters to users advising them to ensure their participants do not throw litter on the ground.	Review in 1 month (01 August 2006). Users have agreed to discuss issue with participants. Ground monitors have noted a reduction in litter. More notices required around facility by 20 August 2006.

Notes:
Date of next review
1 September 2006

◼ An example of a risk assessment taken at a local council run outdoor park which has been hired for sports

Let's do it!

Possible health and safety hazard	Environment	How to minimise risk of injury	Purpose
Faulty equipment	Leisure and sports centres; gymnasiums	Report faulty equipment to a duty manager or health and safety officer as soon as it is identified. Record the fault in a log book. Withdraw the equipment, or display a notice on it stating that it is 'out of order'	■ To minimise the risk of injury to users ■ To protect participants ■ To maintain a safe environment ■ To protect those leading the activity
Misuse of chemicals/ Chemical spillages	Swimming pools (pool plant chemicals); cleaning agents in sports and leisure centres	Train staff who use chemicals in COSSH procedures. Ensure staff know how and where to use specific chemicals properly. Regular staff training and observations are required. Report chemical spillages or misuse of chemicals immediately to a superior	■ To protect the users and staff from chemical burns and/or inhalation of dangerous chemicals ■ To maintain a safe environment
Wet floors	Around swimming pools; in changing rooms; in the case of spillages	Display appropriate signs, warning that the floor is wet. Mop or dry area	■ To ensure that all staff, users or visitors are aware of the dangers ■ To prevent slips or falls ■ To maintain a safe environment

The table above shows some potential health and safety hazards within leisure, recreation and sporting environments. Extend the table, using the same headings, for the following hazards:

- *fire*
- *electricity*
- *fumes*
- *equipment falling from shelves*
- *ventilation*
- *protective headgear and clothing.*

Specialist equipment

Many sports require specialist equipment which, when properly used, can protect sports participants from accidental or routine injuries associated with a particular sport.

Protective equipment

Sport	Protective equipment
Rugby	Gum shield/Head guard
Football	Shin pads
Cricket	Helmet/leg pads
Boxing	Gloves
American football	Shoulder pads

Let's do it!

The table above lists some of the specialist protective equipment required for some sports. Pick three different sports and do the following.

1   List the protective equipment required to be worn according to the rules of the sport.

2   List the optional protective equipment, if any, which is worn for safety but which is not a requirement of that particular sport.

Contingency plans

Contingency plans are back-up plans which outline a number of decisions or measures which are required if there has been a change in circumstance. For example, if you have arranged a football match outside and there is a thunderstorm with heavy rain and lightning, it will be impossible to carry on as play will become dangerous. So what do you do? The contingency plan will help you to decide the best measure to take, if it is planned in advance.

Circumstances where you may need a contingency plan include:

- changes in weather
- a change in the number of players or participants
- insufficient or damaged equipment
- differing skills or abilities within a group.
- fire
- power cut or failure.

A contingency plan must be achievable and include the following.

- A brief description of the event.

- Use of original venue.
- Use of back-up venue – this must be arranged prior to any event.
- Transportation – how to get to the back-up venue.
- Original start time delayed or new start time.
- Numbers of people expected/participants.
- Equipment required.
- Any other risks or issues.

Key point

Football clubs and large events organisers will have to have contingency plans in place as part of the requirements of the Safety at Sports Grounds Act 1975. These will include contingency plans for the following areas/incidents:

- fire
- bomb threat/suspect package
- buildings and services
- adverse weather conditions
- damage to structures
- power cut or failure
- gas leak or chemical incident
- safety equipment failure
- turnstile counting mechanism failure
- stewards' radio system failure
- crowd control: surging or crushing; pitch invasion; late arrivals or delayed start
- disorder inside the ground
- large-scale ticket forgery
- emergency evacuation
- abandoned fixture.

Source: Football Licensing Authorities website
(see www.heinemann.co.uk/hotlinks for more information)

Let's do it!

You have organised a sporting event: a football tournament. The weather suddenly turns very bad and, if play isn't stopped, could lead to serious injuries. You have also noticed that players are missing or haven't turned up.

Your task is to prepare a back-up plan just in case this scenario happens. Write a brief but clear logical plan.

Let's do it!

1 Using the risk assessment layout in the table below, conduct a risk assessment for the following sporting situations (ensure that you identify all possible risks).

- A crowded swimming pool with one pool attendant.
- A football match on Astroturf with inadequate lighting.
- A 60 year old joining the gym, with no health screening undertaken.
- A boxing participant without the correct PPE (personal protective equipment).

Step 1 Identify the hazard	Step 2 Who will be harmed?	Step 3 Risk rating (severity/ probability)	Step 4 Existing measures	Step 5 Suggested measures	Step 6 Record, review, monitor and evaluate

2 Arrange to visit a sporting facility, swimming pool, leisure centre, gymnasium or sports stadium. Working in pairs, conduct a thorough risk assessment. Record your findings as well as your suggested measures, and present this to the rest of the group.

Assessment activity 7: Risk assessments

1 Choose a sport from the following list:

- football
- hockey
- netball
- karate
- ice skating
- weight lifting.

Independently complete a risk assessment relevant to this sport. (P6)

2 *Describe* contingency plans that can be used in a risk assessment. (M5)

3 *Analyse* specialist equipment that can be used to minimise the risk of injury. (D2)

Summary

In this unit we have established that health and safety awareness is an important factor in reducing the risk of injuries to those taking part in sporting activities. We have identified different types of injuries associated with sports participation, the ways in which sporting injuries can occur, and the ways in which to manage them. We have also looked at common illnesses associated with sports participation, such as asthma, signs and symptoms, and management.

We have also identified the importance of undertaking risk assessments before any sporting activity takes place. Checking for risks and eliminating these as they occur will greatly reduce the likelihood of someone becoming injured.

Check what you know!

Look back through this unit to see if you can you answer the following questions.

1. Briefly give details of three causes of sports injuries.
2. What type of injury is shin splints and how does it occur?
3. What are the signs and symptoms of an asthma attack?
4. Give two examples of minor injuries that can be dealt with on site.
5. Define the following terms: health, safety, risk, hazard, risk assessment.
6. What are the key intentions of the Health and Safety at Work Act 1974?
7. Identify five risk factors which can cause sporting injuries.
8. If a sports facility maintains good practice, what do you think the benefits are to that organisation?
9. What are the key intentions of the COSSH regulations?
10. What are the key intentions of the Children Act?
11. What are the risk factors associated with a busy swimming pool?
12. Describe the steps of a risk assessment, and state why it is important to carry out a risk assessment before any sporting activity.
13. Describe two common sporting injuries and the immediate basic treatment for them.
14. Name two methods of alternative medicine.
15. Why is it important to have a qualified first aider at sports events and training sessions?

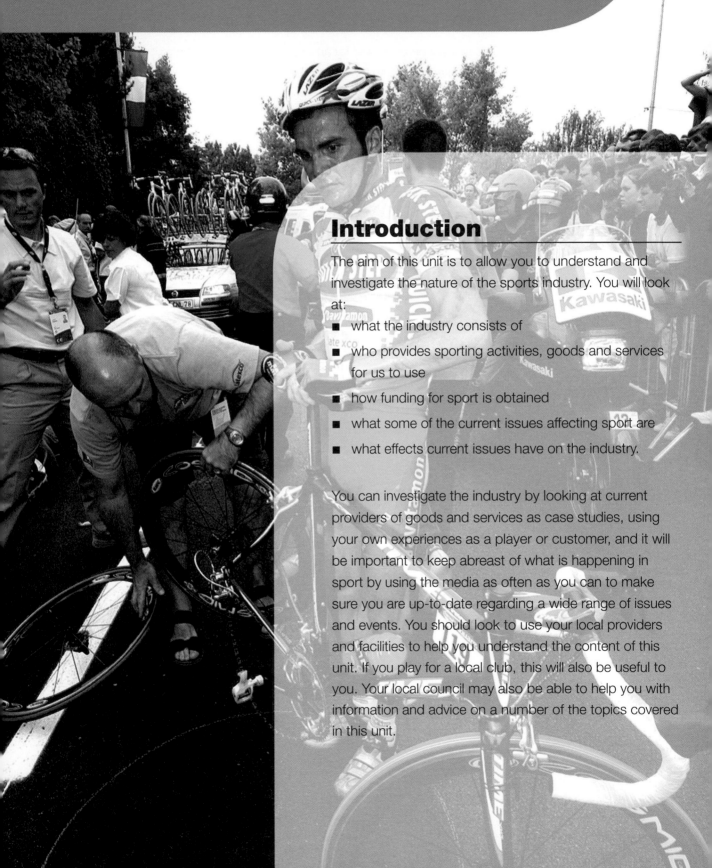

3 The Sports Industry

Introduction

The aim of this unit is to allow you to understand and investigate the nature of the sports industry. You will look at:

■ what the industry consists of

■ who provides sporting activities, goods and services for us to use

■ how funding for sport is obtained

■ what some of the current issues affecting sport are

■ what effects current issues have on the industry.

You can investigate the industry by looking at current providers of goods and services as case studies, using your own experiences as a player or customer, and it will be important to keep abreast of what is happening in sport by using the media as often as you can to make sure you are up-to-date regarding a wide range of issues and events. You should look to use your local providers and facilities to help you understand the content of this unit. If you play for a local club, this will also be useful to you. Your local council may also be able to help you with information and advice on a number of the topics covered in this unit.

▶ Continued from previous page

How you will be assessed

This unit will be assessed by an internal assignment that will be set and marked by the staff at your centre. It may be sampled as well by your centre's External Verifier as part of Edexcel's on-going quality procedures. The assignment is designed to allow you to show your understanding of the unit outcomes. These relate to what you should be able to do after completing this unit.

Your assessments could be in the form of:

- video recorded presentations
- case studies
- role plays
- written assignments.

After completing this unit you should be able to achieve the following learning outcomes.

1 Understand the nature of the sports industry.
2 Understand how and why people participate in sport.
3 Know how the sports industry is funded.
4 Understand the impact of different key issues upon the sports industry.

3.1 Understand the nature of the sports industry

The sports industry

The sports industry is part of the overall leisure industry, which provides a wide range of products and services. Sport and other recreation activities employ 412,000 people in the UK. Can you define the word leisure?

The Concise Oxford English Dictionary defines leisure as, 'time spent in or free for relaxation or enjoyment.' How did your definition compare with this? Were there any key points that appeared?

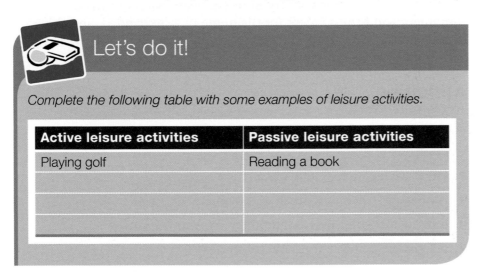

Let's do it!

Complete the following table with some examples of leisure activities.

Active leisure activities	Passive leisure activities
Playing golf	Reading a book

The *Concise Oxford English Dictionary* defines sport as, 'an activity involving physical exertion and skill in which an individual or team competes against another or others for entertainment.'

It is generally accepted that to be called a sport, an activity must:

- be competitive
- have rules and regulations
- require skill and fitness if the participant is to be successful.

The sports industry is one of the most important sectors of the leisure industry and provides a wide range of products and services including:

- sports to take part in
- sports to watch
- activities to maintain health
- sports clothing and merchandise
- sports-related gambling.

It also includes the sports retail industry (for example, sports shops) and the rapidly-emerging extreme sports industry. The sports industry employs a large number of people.

Statistics from the Office of National Statistics (www.statistics.gov.uk) show that in 2005 the following numbers of people were employed in different areas of the sports industry:

- 47,000 as sports coaches and officials
- 32,000 as fitness instructors
- 54,000 as sport and leisure attendants
- 94,000 in general sport and fitness occupations.

There has also been a huge increase in the number of fitness centres and health clubs around the country in recent years. Sales of fitness equipment and fitness videos for the home have expanded, and there are large numbers of fun runs and similar events organised every week to help and encourage people to get fit.

Activities

The many different types of sports available to each of us can be categorised in many ways, for example:

- target games such as golf and archery
- team games such as football and netball
- individual sports such as mountaineering and running
- net games such as tennis and badminton
- motor sports such as Formula One and motorcycling
- outdoor adventurous activities such as canoeing and skiing
- 'bat and ball' games such as rounders and baseball.

Sports can also be classified as:

- indoor or outdoor (basketball is an indoor game while football is an outdoor sport)
- summer or winter sports (athletics or skiing)
- contact or non-contact (rugby or netball)
- net games such as table tennis and badminton
- invasion games where the aim is to go into your opponents' 'space' to score.

Football is an invasion game since players must find space in their opponents' half of the pitch to score, while volleyball is not an invasion game because you must play on your own side of the net.

■ *Sports can be classified as indoor or outdoor*

Key point

In the UK there are:

- 2328 public fitness facilities
- 1943 private health clubs
- 5,839,565 public and private health and fitness members in total
- 933 clubs under development or in planning in the private sector, and 641 sites in the public sector
- 3621 public sports centres.

Nobody really knows how many football or cricket pitches there are!

Let's do it!

List ten sports you like and try to categorise them in a range of different ways.

Provision

There are three main providers of sport in this country.

- **public sector** – organisations such as the national government, and local authorities who provide services to the people in their area.

- **private sector** – organisations that aim to make a profit for themselves or other people. These include private clubs providing facilities and services for the benefit of members.

- **voluntary sector** – generally, local people and organisations that provide activities for the benefit of local people, and to meet a local need. Often these people have a common interest or skill, or feel that the activity they do is worthwhile and important. Volunteers give up their time and energy for free.

In addition, there are other organisations, both local and national, which influence and support the work of these three main providers, such as the Central Council for Physical Recreation (CCPR).

The public sector

The public sector provides services to people through government. These services include libraries, parks, playgrounds, sports pitches, leisure centres and swimming pools. The public sector operates at different levels, from the UK government making decisions of national and international significance, to parish councils, which make decisions affecting a small local village or area.

The different levels at which the public sector operates are:

- parish councils
- town councils
- district councils
- city councils
- large unitary authorities
- national government.

Local authorities

Facilities provided by local authorities are for local people. In part, they are also paid for by local people, through the council tax or business rates levied on each house and business in an area. In addition, a local facility will make charges for the use of its facilities and services. The charge is generally not very high, in order to encourage people to take part. Facilities may not be of the highest standards but will be more than adequate for local needs. Local authority facilities and services are discretionary. This means that a local authority does not have to provide them. There is nothing to stop your local authority closing a swimming pool or sports hall if there is a shortage of money.

Since each local authority is made up of local councillors who are elected by local people, the councillors elected will have their own ideas about what is important to the area. This may or may not include sport and could affect what is provided and how. Many local facilities owned by local authorities are managed by other organisations.

The public sector can provide a range of other services in relation to sport. These include:

- hiring pitches, courts and other facilities for playing sport
- providing grants and other sources of finance to local clubs and associations
- providing other sources of help, including assistance with lottery applications, raising awareness and acting as a link between national agencies, such as Sport England, and local clubs, schools, and so on.

The private sector

Private sector businesses are involved in a wide range of activities, including selling sports equipment and clothing, gambling, and running sports you pay to watch, such as horse racing, and sports that you pay to take part in, such as golf.

This sector is concerned with making a profit from the activities and services it provides. This profit is then either reinvested in the business, or is distributed to people and organisations who have invested money in the business. Some of these businesses sell shares on the stock exchange. This allows anybody, including you, to invest money in that company. If you look in the newspapers you will be able to see how well your shares are doing. The value of these shares may go up or down: if they go up, shareholders make money; if they go down, they lose money.

Private sector organisations are accountable to their shareholders. These people and organisations have invested in the business and they have a large say in how the business should be run. For instance, if a Premier League football club is losing money, perhaps through failing to qualify for Europe or because of poor results, it may have to sell its star player to satisfy the requirements of the shareholders.

Private sector organisations must be able to respond quickly to changes in demand from customers. For example, fashions in sports clothing change quickly. If a sports clothing company is not flexible enough to respond, it could lose a lot of money.

Private clubs

Another type of private organisation is private clubs. These are often provided by companies for the benefit of their staff, to improve motivation and working conditions. Other private clubs are set up to meet a particular need. Such clubs include golf clubs, racket clubs or health and fitness facilities.

Facilities are often of a very high standard but membership is usually expensive. As a result, the club may only be available to those with sufficient personal wealth. Many people feel the exclusive nature of these organisations is worth the high price. Like all sports-related organisations, private clubs and businesses are vulnerable to changes in the income of their customers. This is because:

- people spend their disposable income on sport – in other words, the money left over after all the bills and essentials have been paid for. If the cost of the weekly shopping or the mortgage on your house goes up, you have less to spend on luxuries like sport.

- fashion can affect the popularity of a club – after Christmas and before the summer holidays, people may join a fitness club to lose weight and tone up, but very often they lose interest and leave soon after. Gyms and health clubs have to work hard to attract and then keep their members, so that the membership fees keep coming in.

Case study

Ponds Forge International Swimming Centre

■ *Ponds Forge International Swimming Centre*

Ponds Forge International Swimming Centre is owned by Sheffield International Venues Ltd. It is an internationally-renowned swimming facility comprising a 50-m long by 25-m wide swimming pool, a 5.8-m square diving pool and a separate leisure pool. The centre was built for the 1991 World Student Games, which were held in Sheffield. It has a host of special features including a movable floor to the main pool, seating for 2500 spectators, plus fitness studios, a large multi-purpose sports hall, a night club and conference facilities. The facility is used by elite performers as well as the people of Sheffield. It is open seven days a week and is run by Sheffield International Venues. You can visit their website at www.heinemann.co.uk/hotlinks to find out more. Sheffield International Venues is a private company and this has a number of benefits.

■ The private sector managing agent has money to invest in new facilities – often, local authorities have more important priorities.

■ The private sector often has a better understanding of business.

■ Sheffield City Council – part of the public sector – does not have to provide finances for the pool or appoint staff to operate it. It can concentrate staff and resources on other, more pressing, issues.

■ Sheffield City Council has a major input into the range and nature of the provision made, the pricing policy in operation and the standard of service provided. Although it does not actually manage the centre, it still has a large say in what is provided and how.

■ By working in this way, Sheffield City Council benefits from a facility which helps meet their overall aims and objectives for much less money than if they ran the facility themselves.

Ponds Forge is also home to a number of local voluntary organisations that put on a variety of activities and events for local people to take part in. These include Sheffield Canoe Club, The City of Sheffield Swim squad and Sheffield Sharks Water Polo team. The clubs organise events and activities with the help of Ponds Forge. Such help may include volunteering the centre's lifeguards and first aiders, giving coaching sessions and instruction, but may also include help with funding and organisation.

Now answer the following questions.

1 How do you think the people of Sheffield have benefited from the swimming centre?

2 Why do you think the private sector often understands the sports business better?

3 What stops Sheffield International Venues only offering activities that make a profit?

The voluntary sector

The voluntary sector exists to meet local needs for little or no cost. These clubs are set up by people with a common interest, like a local netball team, or because a person feels that the activity is important and worthwhile.

Voluntary clubs often exist on members' match fees and membership subscriptions. They are often involved in fundraising activities to keep the club going. Voluntary clubs are very important to sport in the UK. Many of our top sportsmen and women started out as members of local clubs and teams.

The voluntary sector provides opportunities for people to play a sport they like, and also provides the volunteers that are needed for coaching, refereeing, organising and running local clubs and sports associations. It is almost impossible to calculate the value and amount of time given up by volunteers. People who cannot afford to join a private club to play tennis or squash might join a local club run by volunteers. This promotes social inclusion, ensuring all members of society have access to sporting opportunities.

Assessment activity 1: Sports provision

To achieve a Pass:

1 Gather together information on sports provision made by the public, private and voluntary sectors in your area. In small groups, *describe* your findings. (P1)
2 Once you have finished, look at the national provision of sport and *describe* how this is structured across the UK. Record your findings in writing or by videoing your group discussion. (P2)

To achieve a Merit you must achieve the Pass criteria and:

3 Now you have identified the provision of sport both locally and nationally, *compare* the two sectors and identify areas for improvement. Consider the number and range of facilities. Are there areas in which there is too much or too little provision? For instance, there may be a large number of golf clubs but very few indoor tennis courts. Present your findings as a chart or a display. (M1)

To achieve a Distinction you must achieve the Pass and Merit criteria and:

3 Look at your local area and compare the facilities available in other parts of the UK. *Evaluate* how your area compares with national averages. Suggest ways in which local provision could be improved. (D1)

Organisation

Sport has important benefits for both individuals and the country as a whole. The sports industry is important to the many people who work in it and to those people who use the products and services it offers. This section will look at how the industry is organised and the strengths and weaknesses of its various providers.

Structure and function

For sport to take place there must be organisations that give it structure and carry out a range of activities to develop and promote either sport generally or a specific sport. The organisations controlling football are a good example of how a sport is organised. The Football Association (FA) is the sole organisation that governs football in England. From this one body derive a number of regional football authorities that take responsibility for football in a region. Within each region there are a number of local bodies that govern football in a particular local area. See the diagram below – the wider the pyramid gets, the more individual organisations there are at that level.

FIFA –
The World
Football
Governing Body

UEFA – An international
football organisation. Controls
football in EUROPE

The Football Association – A NATIONAL
football governing body. Controls football in
England

Regional Football Associations – Organise football within a
county

Local Football Associations – Organise football within a town or district

■ *The organisations controlling football*

■ *Do you recognise these organisations?*

Sporting organisations

There are other organisations that are involved either directly, or indirectly, in sport. Some of these are national organisations, like Sport UK or the British Olympic Association. Some are regional, for example, a county Football Association or Netball Association, and others are local, for example a local sports group or committee. Some are international, for example FIFA, the governing body for world football.

Some organisations are sport specific. This means they are only concerned with one particular sport. Some are involved with a specific competition, such as the Olympics. Some are concerned with sport in general. Each has a specific role or aim within sport. This could be to increase participation, to get more people playing a particular sport, or to select and organise a team for a particular event.

Governing bodies

There is generally only one world governing body for each sport, but there are many national bodies (England, Scotland, Ireland and Wales, for example), and numerous local football associations – the town where you live, for instance, may well have its own local football association. Each body is a member, or is affiliated to, the body above it. So the FA is affiliated to UEFA, which is affiliated to FIFA.

In a few sports, such as boxing, a number of world governing bodies exist. Boxing, for instance, has the World Boxing Organisation, The World Boxing Council, The World Boxing Association and The International Boxing Federation! The ability to have large numbers of 'world' title fights plus a great deal of rivalry amongst boxing promoters and organisations has resulted in this situation.

Governing bodies carry out a number of tasks. They:

- organise the sport within their region
- decide on rules and regulations

Let's do it!

Discuss in small groups why sports governing bodies are important. What would happen if they did not exist?

Let's do it!

Choose one sport and investigate how it is organised locally, nationally and internationally. Produce a poster which shows this information and gives examples of what each level of organisation does.

Assessment activity 2: Organisation of sport

Choose one sport and investigate how it is organised locally, nationally and internationally.

To achieve a Pass:

1 Produce a poster, or PowerPoint presentation, *describing* how the sport is organised and funded (P3).

To achieve a Merit you must achieve the Pass criteria and:

2 Using your poster or presentation, *explain* to your group how it is organised and funded and identify areas for improvement. (M2)

To achieve a Distinction you must achieve the Pass and Merit criteria and:

3 Develop your identified areas for improvement, *evaluating and suggesting* ways in which these could be achieved. (D2)

- organise competitions
- are responsible for player discipline
- are responsible for training coaches and officials
- promote the sport within their jurisdiction.

Some bodies are responsible not for a particular sport but a range of sports or an event. For instance the IOC (International Olympic Committee) is responsible for promoting and organising both the summer and winter Olympics, deciding who is allowed to organise an Olympic games and dealing with other problems involved in running the Olympics, such as ensuring standards are met in terms of facilities. Go to www.heinemann.co.uk/hotlinks to find out more.

Development

Developments concerning the growth of the sports industry involve this country's changing population. The last census has shown that the population of this country is getting not only bigger but older. Thus the sports industry will need to cater for this emerging 'grey' market.

As more and more people enjoy the goods and services offered by the sports industry, so more people will be employed. Currently there are nearly 500,000 people working in the sports industry in a wide variety of positions including life guards, fitness instructors, coaches, etc. This does not include the many thousands of volunteers who work in the many local clubs and associations that sport depends on. In addition, thousands of people regularly take part in a wide range of sporting activities.

The 2012 Olympic Games in London

The success of the Games will very much depend on a range of developments both within the capital and the country as a whole. Over the coming months and years there will need to be developments in:

- transport systems so that competitors and spectators can move easily around the venues, etc.
- training and competition facilities to allow our athletes to reach a high standard of performance so that they are able to challenge for gold medals in a wide range of events
- education so that the country produces young men and women who want to be world champions and medallists in a range of sports
- financial and other support systems to help a variety of sports develop their most talented men and women into potential winners.

Without all the developments mentioned in this section, sport as an industry will not be able to meet the needs and expectations of its customers and participants in the coming years.

Growth

The sports industry is becoming an increasingly more important part of the country's economy. More and more people are gaining employment in the industry in a wide variety of roles, including not only sports provision but other services such as diet and nutrition. The growth in the sports industry can be explained by a number of different factors. These include:

- increased amounts of free time
- increased amounts of disposable income
- fashion.

Free time

As technology changes, so it makes our life generally easier and, as a result, affords us more free time in which to take part in activities. Television has made us all more aware of sporting activities that we had previously been unaware of. Many extreme sports owe their growth to being shown on television, especially satellite television which allows us to view sports from almost anywhere in the world at any time of the day.

Disposable income

As the general level of wages has risen, many prices of the goods we buy have dropped in relative terms, so we have more money that we are free to spend on luxuries and those products and services that we wish to consume. This is known as 'disposable' income. You decide on what you will spend it on.

Let's do it!

In small groups, discuss the ways that the sports industry encourages you to spend money on its goods and services.

This country is becoming one where more and more people are 'consumers' – we look to buy products and services that are made available to us. The sports industry has responded by offering a greater range of products and services to us as consumers. Health club membership, foreign holidays, timeshare properties and so on have all seen a massive growth in recent years as people look to spend their spare income on a variety of goods and services.

Fashion

In addition, the increased coverage of sport on television and in the media has made many sports much more fashionable than a few years ago. Many people now wear sports clothing as fashion wear – replica football shirts, branded shoes and clothing are all big business today.

■ *Many young people wear sports clothing as fashion wear*

 Let's do it!

How many of the people in your class are wearing sports-related clothing? Make up a table. Count how many people are wearing a particular brand or make, like Adidas or Nike. Count how many are wearing a particular sports item, such as a baseball cap or sweatshirt. Ask them why they are wearing these items.

3.2 Understand how and why people participate in sport

Ways

To look at the ways that people can be involved in sport, let us look at one of the most famous sports teams in the world – Manchester United Football Club!

The club employs a number of *players* who are paid large sums of money each week to play for the club. These people are therefore known as *professional players* – their job is to play football.

For the team to be successful, Alex Ferguson is employed as the *manager*; he decides who will play, how the team will play particular games, and he looks to sign or release players during a season. To help him make the team successful, he works with a number of *coaches* who are there to develop the skills and fitness of the players, and to devise team tactics, etc. These coaches work with the first team and reserves while other coaches look after the youth team, etc.

When players get injured, they need the help of a range of specialist *medical staff*. These include a club doctor and a physiotherapist, both of whom provide expert advice and treatment of injuries as they occur so that players get back to playing quickly; and a nutritionist, who advises the players on eating the right types of food to ensure that they perform at the highest level.

Away from the playing side of the club, many people are employed in what are called *administrative* roles. This means they are involved in supervising wages and salaries, liaising with people who contact the club for information, tickets, etc., and dealing with many other issues that the club must attend to if they are to operate successfully and safely. The club also has a large club shop where people are employed as retailers – they sell a wide variety of club merchandise such as replica kits and memorabilia to fans from around the world!

The Manchester United Museum also employs people who act as guides on tours of the ground, reception staff to welcome visitors and issue tickets, and waiters and waitresses to serve food and drink in the club café and restaurant. The Club Museum is open every day except Christmas Day!

The club also employs people to organise football in the local community as *sports development officers*. Their role is to take football out to local schools and children to encourage more boys and girls from all walks of life to take part in the sport. Hopefully, many will then play football in their spare time and play for a local team.

Think about it

Think about a local club you play for or support. How many different ways of being involved can you identify?

Outside of the club, very many people are involved in sport because they support Manchester United FC as *supporters*. As supporters, they will have to buy tickets and perhaps a programme on match days, they may buy goods from the club shop, such as a scarf or team shirt, and while in the ground they buy food and drink at half-time. These people are described as *consumers*. They purchase the various goods and services that the club offers. The club can therefore be described as a *retailer* – they sell goods and services to people who want to buy them.

In local clubs, many people fill the same roles but are not paid. Thus, as a player they would be classed as an *amateur* – they play for enjoyment not money. In roles such as managers and coaches, these people would be referred to as *volunteers*.

Let's do it!

In pairs, list all the different ways that you might take part in sport. Be ready to discuss your ideas! Did you think of these?

■ Player or performer.

■ Referee, umpire or other match official.

■ Coach or instructor.

■ Club officer – treasurer, secretary, etc.

■ Spectator or supporter.

■ Sports masseur, therapist, nutritionist, etc.

■ Someone who buys sports equipment and clothing.

■ A sport development officer for a sport, facility or other organisation.

■ Running a sports shop or business – a soccer coaching school, for instance.

■ Playing a sport is not the only way to be involved in the sports industry

Assessment activity 3: Sports participation

To achieve a Pass:

1 *Describe* some ways in which people participate in sport. At a football match it is not just the players who are taking part! (P4)

To achieve a Merit you must achieve the Pass criteria and:

2 Produce a spidergram *explaining* all the different roles of participation you would expect from a football match or tennis tournament. (M3)

Reasons

It is generally accepted that sport is good for:

- **health** – it provides exercise which keeps us fit and helps us to live healthy lives

- **society** – it brings people together in a common cause and reduces crime and anti-social behaviour

- **the country** – it earns the country a great deal of money through taxes and sports tourism. For example, Euro 96 generated £118 million from 250,000 foreign visitors. The Millennium Stadium in Cardiff generated, in one year, £18.5 million from just seven high-profile football matches, including the FA Cup final and the divisional play-offs. In 2012, London will host the Summer Olympic Games. It is estimated by the Olympic Games Impact Study (Price Waterhouse Coopers, December 2005) that this one event will result in:

  - An extra 38,000 jobs in London, plus another 8,000 in the rest of the country

  - A 'very positive' effect on health during the event, plus a 'positive' effect after the Games

  - An extra 439 new businesses in London alone as a result of the Games.

- **employment** – sport provides jobs and careers. There is a wide range of courses offered by schools, colleges and universities, and qualifications that can be gained.

- **character building** – sport teaches us values such as teamwork and playing by the rules. These lessons are important throughout our lives.

When the Sports Council was formed in 1972, its aims were to encourage more people to play sport and more places to be built to play sport in. Its goal was to raise the performance of our best sportsmen and women so that they would win more medals and championships on the world stage. In addition, in the last few years people have become much more aware of their health and fitness.

Why individuals participate in sport

You can see that a great many people regularly take part in sport. But why is this encouraged by a wide range of organisations including the British Heart Foundation, the many sports governing bodies and even the government? It is generally accepted that sports participation on a regular basis holds many benefits. These include:

- **health and fitness benefits** – reduced levels of heart disease, obesity

- **social benefits** – community spirit, less anti-social behaviour

- **economic benefits** – jobs and careers, income for businesses

- **national benefits** – national success, sports tourism, pride.

Some people take part in particular sports and activities because they want to adopt a particular image. Others participate in a sport because it has a cathartic effect on them. In recent years, extreme sports, such as snow boarding, mountain biking, paragliding and so on, have become more and more popular. These sports:

- help people forget the strains and stresses of their normal life

- provide the 'adrenalin buzz', which for many is missing in today's society

- allow people to get back to nature and feel alive.

For some people, playing sport is part of their daily life either because they are professional sportsmen or women, or because they have developed a love of sport at an early age and have retained this throughout their lives. For other people, taking part in sport allows them to:

- meet new people

- learn new sports skills and activities

- put something back into their community

- improve their personal health and fitness.

For others, sport is now a means of recovery after medical treatment. The twin issues of obesity and stress are often treated with exercise programmes rather than pills and operations. GP referral schemes involve local GP practices working with local fitness clubs. Patients who have suffered a recent heart attack, for instance, will be offered the chance of a planned exercise programme at the local gym to help them recover.

Factors that affect participation

One of the most important factors in encouraging people to participate in sport is the range of facilities provided. Nearly every town and city has sporting facilities provided by a number of different organisations, offering opportunities to play and to watch sport both indoors and outdoors. But before a provider can make activities available, it is important to understand who they are trying to make provision for.

Different groups

It is helpful to be able to place people into different groups in order to help as many as possible to participate in sport. This is so that you can identify what these people want to do, why they might want to do it and the typical reasons why they cannot do it at present. These groups might include:

- teenagers
- adults
- the elderly
- families
- people from different cultural groups, such as Muslims or travellers
- the unemployed.

Case study

Matthew

Matthew is 15 and attends the local grammar school in the town of Bourne, in Lincolnshire. He is preparing for GCSE exams next year. Bourne has fairly good sports facilities. The school has a sports hall and playing fields and runs clubs at lunchtimes and after school. Teams from the school play matches against other local schools. In the town there is a large leisure centre, with a leisure pool, sports hall and fitness club. The town also has a tennis club, a semi-professional football team and an outdoor swimming pool, which opens in the summer months from May to September. There are clubs for netball and rugby, keep fit classes and playing fields with football goals where people can go and have a kick-about. The nearest big city is Peterborough, 15 miles away. Bus services are available every 30 minutes most days.

Now answer the following questions.

1 What factors in the case study will have a positive effect on Matthew's participation in sport?

2 What factors do you think will have a negative effect?

All of these different groups will have different factors which will affect their participation in sport. These factors might include:

- the need for child care
- the price charged
- the time activities are made available
- whether the requirements of a particular religion or culture are catered for.

Other factors, such as race, culture and disability, will also affect participation.

Location

Where you live has an important part to play in the type of sport you might choose. It goes without saying that the UK does not produce very many top skiers, because we do not get much snow. In Switzerland and Austria the winters are much colder, with plenty of snow on the mountains. Similarly, it would be difficult for Matthew, in the case study above, to take up rock climbing, since there are no mountains in Lincolnshire.

The area in which you live is a factor. For example, some parts of the UK are very rural or very remote, and people may live a long distance from a sports club or facility. Providers may need to go to the people instead, offering activities which may take place in village halls or community centres.

Many factors can affect what is offered to local people and how it is delivered to customers. Some areas of the UK suffer from high social deprivation. This might mean, for example, that facilities are old and run down, or that unemployment is high amongst the local population. These areas may be eligible to receive a wide variety of funds from the government and from Europe to assist in regeneration.

Regeneration involves building new facilities to help attract new business and people to an area. Sheffield is a good example. Once known for producing high-quality steel products, the city is now a centre for sporting excellence thanks to the development of a wide range of elite sporting facilities.

Barriers to participation

There are some groups of people who, for various reasons, do not or cannot, take part in sport. In the past these have included:

- disabled people
- ethnic minorities
- mothers of young children
- the elderly
- females aged 16–25.

The reasons why these groups of people are unable to take part are referred to as 'barriers', and one of the roles of people and organisations involved in sport development is to remove these barriers. Barriers might include:

- racism – people being discriminated against because of the colour of their skin

- poor access to facilities – the person may not have access to a car, or public transport may be infrequent or non-existent

- no facilities allowing babies and toddlers to be left in safety (if a parent has nowhere safe to leave a baby or toddler, then she or he will be unable to take part in sport themselves)

- the attitude of society – for example, society may not like the idea of women being sweaty or aggressive!

- activities offered at the wrong time, in the wrong place or at the wrong price – because of any or all of these reasons, they may not interest the particular person at whom they are aimed.

To try to remove barriers, a local authority might, for example, employ a disability sports officer to develop and organise sport for those people with some form of disability, such as cerebral palsy or a sensory disability.

Another barrier is cost. Some people may not be able to afford the cost of using local facilities. Thus, many local authorities make provision for people on low incomes by reducing the charges made at certain times.

Religion or culture could also be a barrier. Muslim women who might be interested in swimming cannot be seen in a swimming costume by men. A local pool could make provision by covering all windows to prevent other people looking in, and using only female lifeguards. There are many other ways that barriers can be removed and overcome.

 Case study

Matt Gill

Matt Gill is employed as a disability sports officer by the Peterborough City Council's Leisure Department. His role is to improve sporting opportunities for disabled people. His salary is funded by the Children's Fund, which obtains its funding from the National Lottery. Matt's role involves him finding out what disabled people would like to do and comparing this with what is currently available. He can then suggest what opportunities could be provided. The post Matt fills lasts for three years. At the end of this time, the results of Matt's work will be reviewed to decide if the post

should remain. The council will also have to decide if they wish to fund Matt's salary themselves.

Now answer the following questions.

1 What examples are there of partnership working (two or more organisations working together towards the same aim or objective)?

2 Why does Matt concentrate on only one particular group of people?

3 Why do you think Matt's job is important to Peterborough City Council?

■ *Ladies-only swimming sessions encourage participation*

Assessment activity 4: Sports participation

To achieve a Pass:

1 Look at each of the categories in the table below. Try to identify why these particular groups of people may be unable to take part in sport. (P5)

Group	Reasons why they do not participate in sport
Disabled people	
Ethnic minorities	
Mothers of young children	
The elderly	
Young women aged 16–25 years	

2 What other barriers to participation can you think of? Fill in the table below with your answers and reasons why they affect participation. (P5)

Barrier to participation	Reason

Strategies to encourage participation

In recent years, sports development has emerged as the main strategy for helping to encourage more participation and provision of sport. A strategy is a plan that is drawn up to achieve a particular goal over a period of time. But how are people encouraged to take part? Perhaps the main way is to increase people's *awareness* of the availability of sport in their area, the *benefits* that exist to those who take part and by *making it easier* for all people to participate by addressing the barriers that exist which prevent people from taking part.

There has been a large number of campaigns and strategies which have targeted either the population as a whole or focused on specific groups of people in an effort to increase participation. This is generally part of the sports development industry.

Government strategies

The drive to increase participation generally comes from the government, which regards sport as important because:

- it keeps people healthy – this means that people need to see the doctor less frequently, and so the demand on the National Health Service is reduced
- the nation looks good when it does well in a particular sport or competition – for example, the success of the England Rugby Union team in winning the World Cup in 2003
- it helps to reduce antisocial behaviour – if people have more opportunity to take part in sport, they are less likely to spend their spare time behaving in an antisocial manner such as becoming involved in vandalism or other forms of crime.

Much of the work is carried out by:

- regional Sport England offices – look up the details of yours!
- the sports development team of your local authority
- sports development officers employed by a governing body of a sport.

Let's do it!

1   *Contact your local authority leisure department and find out how and why it tries to increase sports participation.*
2   *Visit the Sport England website at www.heinemann.co.uk/hotlinks and learn about Active Sport, Active Schools and Active Communities.*
3   *Visit the website of a sport of your choice. What does the governing body do to increase the numbers of people playing that sport?*

■ *Sporting success is good for the nation*

Much of the work is carried out in partnership – this is where two or more organisations get together and work towards one common goal. For example, Sport England and a local authority may share the salary of a sports development officer to undertake a particular role.

Volunteers

Playing, watching, coaching and officiating are all ways of encouraging people to participate in sport. Local clubs depend on volunteers who take on positions such as manager, treasurer or chairperson. These people give up their time for free but might need help and guidance about what to do, and how to do it. Sport development officers might put on courses to help improve the way people run clubs or coach teams.

The sports continuum

The work of sports development is based around the sports continuum. This is a model which shows the different levels at which people can participate in sport. The arrows on the diagram (page 129) show how a person might progress through the various levels.

■ **Foundation** level – learning the basic skills needed for sport, such as catching, throwing, passing and so on. This is generally covered in schools through timetabled physical education lessons.

■ **Participation** level – playing a sport for enjoyment and fun, at a local club or leisure centre. Results and performance are not critical – people participate at this level to have fun, meet friends and keep fit.

- **Performance** level – playing for a club in leagues and competitions. Players at this level train hard to improve their skills and abilities. This level includes not only local but regional competition. A player may play in a semi-professional manner and represent a district or region.

- **Elite** level – playing at a national or international level. Players at this level are engaged full time in their sport. They may be paid for this and will receive support from a number of different organisations, sponsors and so on, to help them develop. Top sportsmen and women, like David Beckham, Paula Radcliffe and Jonny Wilkinson, are at this level.

- Levels of participation

Case study

Encouraging people to get involved in sport

Sport England is a government agency tasked with developing sport at all levels. One of its aims is to get more people active in England. The Get Active initiative is one way that is currently being used to achieve this aim.

Sport England's aims in sport are to help people:

- **Start** – to improve the health of the nation, particularly for disadvantaged groups.

- **Stay** – through a thriving network of clubs, coaches and volunteers, and a commitment to equity.

- **Succeed in sport** – via an infrastructure capable of developing world class performers.

Sport England distributes funding to achieve these objectives. Visit the Sport England website at www. heinemann.co.uk/hotlinks and find out about how they are trying to get more people active in your area.

Sport development officers

In many sports, sport development officers are employed to develop that particular sport rather than sport in general. Also, people are employed to develop sport for a particular target group. This is a group of people who participate less than the rest of the population; for instance, women and those with a disability of some description.

Award schemes

Many sports encourage people to start playing by having award schemes, where people can collect badges and certificates by completing a series of tests and exercises to show they have attained a certain level of skill. It is hoped that as people become more proficient at a sport, they will want to keep taking part.

The 2012 Olympic Games

All these various schemes and strategies have had an effect on sports participation and success. With the 2012 Olympic Games coming to this country, there will be the need for plans to be made to ensure that as many of our sportsmen and women as possible are successful. But how might this be achieved? For instance, there will be the need for top-quality facilities. This will cost many millions of pounds. But what will happen to them once the Games have finished? Where will the money come from? Should it be spent on other things such as hospitals and schools? How can we encourage people to get involved now and possibly win that Olympic Gold medal?

Let's do it!

Contact a local leisure facility and find out how they make provision for different groups within the community. Bring the information you gather back to your group to discuss.

Let's do it!

In small groups find out about the following.

- *The work of Sport England in developing sport.*
- *The work of your local Sports Development officers in developing sport locally.*
- *The work of the governing body of a sport of your choice in promoting your chosen sport.*

1. *Now try to explain how the sport/target group/participation generally is encouraged.*
2. *What methods are used? Give examples.*
3. *Describe the success of the various schemes to date. How much has it cost? What champions/medals, etc., have been won? What about world rankings, etc? What targets have/have not been met? What new or additional facilities have been built?*

Sport England

There are those who argue that you cannot develop the very best sportsmen and women and at the same time develop more participation by the general public.

Sport England is involved in both areas. They promote campaigns and schemes designed to encourage as many people as possible to participate in sport. At the same time, they make facilities and services available to allow the best sportsmen and women the chance to reach the very top. As a result, the country has a number of National Sports Centres, a variety of sports institutes, and a World Class programme designed to help sporting stars win gold medals and world championships. This costs a great deal of money. How do we decide if this is money well spent, when it could be used to improve schools or build new hospitals?

Since the early 1970s, there has been a vast increase in the number of sports facilities available for people to access. There are now many more swimming pools, leisure centres, outdoor pursuits centres and so on. These offer a vast range of activities and pursuits, but at a price. It is a fact of life that people earn different amounts of money and have different priorities when spending that money. Taking part in sport is an everyday occurrence for some and a luxury for others. Is this right? Should certain activities only be available to those who can afford to pay? Or should everyone have the right and opportunity to take part in whatever they want?

Let's do it!

Now choose one way of being involved in the sports industry. Draw up a case study for a person in one of the jobs in the sports facilities above. List the types of activities they undertake on a day-to-day basis. Give examples of the benefits their role offers to others.

Assessment activity 5: Sports participation

To achieve a Pass:

1 In small groups draw up a list *describing* ways in which participation in sport is encouraged. (P6)

To achieve a Merit you must achieve the Pass criteria and:

2 Again in your groups, pick one sport and discuss the strategies used to encourage participation. Present and *explain* these strategies to another group in your class. (M3)

To achieve a Distinction you must achieve the Pass and Merit criteria and:

3 Once you have gathered the information on your chosen sport, think about its good points and bad points. Produce a SWOT analysis of the strategy (see page 308), *evaluating* its effectiveness. (D3)

3.3 Know how the sports industry is funded

Sport costs money! Whether you are buying a replica shirt, watching your favourite team or going for a relaxing swim, you will have to part with some cash. Where do organisations and businesses involved in the sports industry get the money they need?

Funding

There are very many sources of funding available, depending on whether you are an individual sports person, a local club or association, or a large business with a new product or service to offer. This section will first consider the main available sources of funding, and then look at how they apply to the main providers of sport.

■ *Sources of funding*

The above diagram shows the main sources of funding for sport. Each of the main providers of sport uses a different combination of these sources of income.

Government funding

Government funding comes from a number of sources, the main two being taxes that people and business pay, and the National Lottery. We have seen in a previous section why the government thinks sport is important. In support of that, the government provides funding to local authorities and other sports organisations to help:

- to encourage more participation. This might be done through the building of new facilities.
- to increase the success of our teams and athletes in terms of world rankings and medal tables at the major championships.

The National Lottery

The first ever National Lottery draw took place on Saturday 19 November 1994 and since that date total ticket sales have reached £54 billion. The proceeds of the National Lottery support 'good causes'. These include:

- the arts
- heritage
- sport
- charities
- community and voluntary groups
- supporting projects concerned with health, education and the environment.

As of January 2006, over £18 billion had been raised by the Lottery for good causes, and 224,000 grants had been made.

More than half of all the Lottery grants made have been grants of less than £5000, bringing benefits to communities across the United Kingdom. Many of our new national sports facilities, such as the Manchester Velodrome and the new Wembley, have been financed with lottery funding.

Sponsorship

Sponsorship is another important source of funding not only for small local clubs and associations but also for national governing bodies and clubs like Chelsea and Manchester United. Sponsorship is where a business or other organisation provides money or goods-in-kind in return for linking the name of the business or a particular product with an individual, team, sport or competition. Sponsorship is a very important source of funding for many sports teams and competitions. Without it, many sports would find it difficult to continue in their present form, and many competitions would struggle to continue at all. Sponsorship is becoming increasingly popular in certain sports and has a number of benefits.

Now, spectatorship and viewing figures are increasing. Potential sponsors know that many millions of people worldwide are likely to see brand names on players' shirts, for example, or on the 2005 Formula 1 world champion, Fernando Alonso's, Renault F1 car. Current sponsorship deals are huge. The latest Sky deal to show Premiership football is worth £1 billion allowing Sky to broadcast live Premiership league football and highlights from the 2004/2005 season for three years.

As certain sports have increased in popularity over recent years, they have attracted an increased level of sponsorship. Other sports find it difficult to attract sponsors.

Case study

Wayne Rooney and Coleen McLoughlin are heading for the financial big league – and could end up earning even more than Posh and Becks, it has been claimed. The Manchester United star and his fiancée are in talks with supermarket giant Asda about an advertising deal reputed to be worth £3.5m. Rooney, signed by the Reds for £30m, has already secured a £5m deal with publisher HarperCollins to write a minimum of five books, the most lucrative sports-book deal in history. The 20-year-old striker is due to finish the first book – on his life so far, including the 2006 World Cup – by the end of July.

Other big-money sponsorship deals include a £1m-a-year contract with Coca-Cola and a £5m deal with Nike for the next ten years.

A good example of the link between sport and sponsorship is provided by football. In the 1970s, football was declining in popularity. The game was not as attractive to sponsors as it had once been, because its image was linked with hooliganism. Steps were taken, successfully, to reduce the problem of hooliganism. This, together with increased media coverage of football through radio, newspapers and terrestrial and satellite television, encouraged sponsors to invest in football once again.

However, not all sponsorship is considered desirable or acceptable. Many countries now ban sponsorship by tobacco and alcohol companies as they feel it is not right to allow producers of goods that we know are harmful to our health (cigarettes) to be associated with sport.

Advertising

Advertising is another popular means of raising funds for sport. This includes adverts in club programmes or advertising boards around a football ground in the Premier League.

Broadcast rights

For many big sports clubs or competitions, one of the very key funding sources is selling the rights to a television company such as Sky or the BBC to broadcast matches and events. The 2012 Olympic Games to be held in London will aim to earn huge amounts of money by selling these rights to television companies in many countries around the world.

The media plays a key role here. Many sports, like squash for example, are not well-suited to television because of the nature of the game. Others, like archery or lacrosse, are simply not very popular with the public and are rarely seen on television or in the newspapers.

Grants

Another source of income for sport is grants. This is a payment made to a club or organisation for a specific purpose, such as improving a club's changing facilities so that the availability of the sport can be improved. Examples of grant-aid organisations include:

- the Football Foundation
- Sports Match
- the Sports Aid Foundation.

Visit www.heinemann.co.uk/hotlinks to find out more about how they can help with funding.

Funding for the public sector

Local authorities have a number of sources of funding available to them, which they use to provide services and facilities for local people.

- The council tax – this is the main source of funding and refers to charges made to all local residents. The amount is based on a number of factors, including the value of the house in which you live, whether you are in work or full-time education, and your age.
- Money from central government.
- Money from charges made to use local authority facilities like sports halls, swimming pools and car parks, and from selling merchandise such as squash balls or swimming goggles.
- Money borrowed from banks, for example to build new facilities.
- Local authorities may also apply to the National Lottery for funds.

Funding for the private sector

National and local businesses and clubs have a number of sources of income available.

A business can raise money by selling shares on the stock exchange. This is where people and organisations, who want to make money, buy shares in other businesses in the hope and belief that the business will be successful. This can be quite risky because if the business doesn't do well the investor will lose money. A number of Premiership football clubs, such as Manchester United, Leeds United and Tottenham Hotspur, sell shares on the stock exchange.

The private sector also generates money through fees and charges made for its products and services. A replica football strip costs nearly £40, but it does not cost this much to produce: the price includes a profit for the seller. Health and fitness clubs raise money through membership fees. All Premiership sides earn money in this way, to a greater or lesser degree. For some clubs, the amounts of money involved are huge. Other sports are not as fortunate as football. Lack of popularity means they find it more difficult to generate income and attract sponsorship.

Funding for the voluntary sector

This sector can find it very difficult to generate funds. Since the organisations are usually quite small, there are limits to the amounts of money they can raise. There is a variety of sources of income that voluntary sport organisations can access.

The National Lottery

A certain percentage of the cost of each ticket bought goes to good causes. It has so far contributed £1.6 billion towards the arts, heritage and sport. Organisations involved with sport can make an application to the Lottery for funding to help improve facilities such as changing rooms and pitches. One difficulty is that an organisation must raise the same amount of money itself – the Lottery will only match funds. This can be a problem for small local organisations.

Fund raising

This is often the most popular way for voluntary sports clubs to raise funds. Activities may include raffles, car boot sales, sponsored events, or entertainment such as a disco. A proposed development at the club may require a number of events and activities to raise the required sum of money.

Local authority grants

The local council may give a local club or association a sum of money to help with their activities, or they may give help in other ways, such as reduced costs for using facilities owned by the council. The local council will also help with Lottery applications in some cases.

Sponsorship

Another popular way for local clubs to raise money is to approach a local business for help. In this situation, the club would receive money or goods in return for promoting the business by, for instance, wearing the name of the business on their team strip.

■ *Premiership football teams raise money through sponsorship*

Sport-specific funding

There are various sources of funds of this sort that a local sports club could tap into. A football team, for example, could apply for funding from the Football Association via the Football Foundation. Find out more by visiting the FA website at www.heinemann.co.uk/hotlinks to look at the grass-roots work that is being undertaken.

Membership fees

Nearly all local clubs, whatever the sport, will raise income by charging a membership fee to join the club. Match fees may also apply, to help cover, for example, the cost of administration, washing kit or replacing damaged equipment.

Grants and donations

A club may benefit from the generosity of local people who donate money to local good causes. This money might be left as part of a person's will. There are also funds which exist to remember a local dignitary or benefactor, to which clubs and individuals can apply for financial assistance. In some situations there is a number of criteria that must be met before an award can be made.

Problems with sponsorship

Although many sponsorship deals have been very important to the continued existence of some sports and sporting competitions, it is not all good news and there is often a price to be paid. Let us look at some examples.

Dependency on a source of income

The collapse of the ITV digital agreement with the Nationwide Football League caused problems for many clubs, which suddenly found that money they had already spent was now not going to be forthcoming. By being dependent on a large, single source of income, they found themselves at the mercy of factors outside their control. In the same way, a local club may enter into an agreement with a local business which then fails, and can no longer provide the funding it promised.

The influence of the source of income on the sport

Some sports have changed a great deal as a result of entering into deals with other companies. Football provides a good example. In the 1970s and 1980s, football was played on Saturdays and Wednesdays. Saturday games kicked off at 3.00 pm. Now, with the control that Sky television has as a result of its huge financial commitment, matches are played seven days a week at a variety of times, to suit the broadcasting schedules.

Sometimes, rules are changed to make games more telegenic. For instance, cricket has seen the emergence of the Day–Night game, and certain finals at the Olympics are run at times to suit US television companies no matter what the local time is. In bowls and cricket, players now wear clothing in a variety of colours instead of traditional white. How far do you think this should be allowed to go?

Assessment activity 6: Sports funding

To achieve a Pass:

1 Choose a sport you participate in. *Describe* how it is orgnised and funded. (P3)

To achieve a Merit you must achieve the Pass criteria and:

2 In small groups complete the table below for a local sports club. *Explain* how it is organised and funded, identifying areas for improvement. (M2)

Source of funding	Administration and paperwork	Amount of money available	What can money be spent on?	Any conditions attached?
The National Lottery	Large amount of paperwork required		Buildings and facilities – not kit, etc.	
Sponsorship from a local company		Usually smaller amounts		Regular mention in club publicity
Fund raising			Anything	Clashes with other similar events
Membership and match fees	Setting charges and recording payment			Different rates for unemployed, school age players, etc.
Grants and donations	Letters to be drafted and sent	Various		
Funding from a National Governing Body		Often set limits	Often decided by NGB	

3.4 Understand the impact of different key issues upon the sports industry

Issues

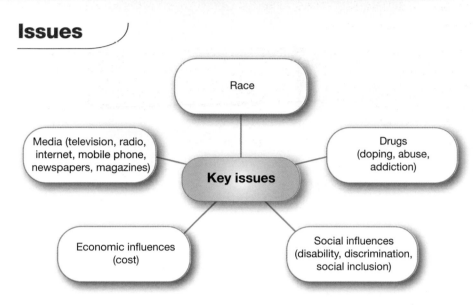

■ *Impact of key issues*

Sport is faced with a number of key issues, some of which have been present for a long time and others which have arisen recently. As society changes, so do the expectations that people have of sport and the role it plays in people's lives.

The society we live in today includes many different types of people – people of different ages, different ethnic backgrounds, different religious beliefs, and people who have special needs because of a physical or mental disability. In the past, little or no sports provision was made for people who were outside the norm.

Today, the belief is that all members of society should have access to the same opportunities in relation to sport. Values in our society have changed gradually over the years. For instance, in the 1968 Olympic Games, there was no track event over 800 metres for women because it was still believed, in some circles, that racing over longer distances might damage a woman's ability to bear children.

Today women compete in exactly the same programme of events as men. The only differences are the heights of equipment such as hurdles and the weights of equipment such as shot-putt and javelin.

It is now accepted that all people have the same rights and should have the same opportunities, and this includes access to sporting opportunities and facilities. Legislation now makes discrimination on

■ *Everyone should have equal access to sporting opportunities and facilities*

the basis of sex, ethnic background or disability against the law. Sports halls are now designed and built with the needs of the disabled in mind.

Sports centres also try to encourage all members of society to use a centre, by offering the elderly, the unemployed and the under-fives a concession on the entry price. All these measures help to include everyone in the community and offer everyone the same opportunity to participate in sport and reach their full potential, at whatever level that may be.

Racism

Racism is an important issue in sport at the moment. Racist behaviour gives sport a bad image, which has the effect of turning off both spectators and sponsors.

Sexism

This is where a person is discriminated against because of his or her gender. Usually, the discrimination is against women.

Ageism

This is where a person is treated differently because of their age. In sport, many activities are considered to be for young people. Many older people are still fit and healthy, however, and there is no reason why they should not continue to enjoy many of the activities that younger people participate in. The population of this country is getting older as people live longer, so it makes financial sense for companies to cater for older people, too. For example, many travel companies now design holidays specifically for the older customer.

Let's do it!

Look through the newspapers in your college or school library, and search for any articles concerned with drugs in sport.

- *How is the issue reported?*
- *What do you think this issue does for the image of the sport?*
- *Do you think that drugs in sport should be allowed?*

Drugs

Another important issue is the use of drugs in sport. These drugs are illegal substances designed to artificially improve performance. There are many types available to sportsmen and women. Anabolic steroids help athletes to train much harder and recover more quickly. Blood doping allows the body to carry more red blood cells and thus improves its ability to carry oxygen around the body. Diuretics reduce the water content in the body, so reducing body weight.

Cheating

One of the factors that make an activity a sport is that it has rules and regulations. Drug taking is very often described as cheating. Cheating in sport might include deliberate diving in football or tampering with the ball in cricket, as well as the use of illegal substances.

Part of the appeal of sport is that an individual or team wins because of superior skills, technique or tactics. If the team or individual has deliberately broken the rules, this is no longer the case.

The problem is that there is a very fine line between cheating and gamesmanship. Gamesmanship is defined as the art of winning games by using various ploys and tactics to gain a psychological advantage, which many be regarded as unfair but which are not against the rules.

Think about it

Where do we draw the line? Is sledging in cricket (where fielders and bowlers make a variety of often unpleasant comments to the batsmen) cheating or gamesmanship? When Dwayne Chambers deliberately takes his time when called to his starting blocks by the starter, is he using gamesmanship to unsettle his opponents? When the New Zealand rugby union team perform the Haka before each game, is this a tactic designed to gain a psychological advantage?

Let's do it!

In small groups, discuss the following questions.

- *What is the difference between cheating and gamesmanship? Give further examples.*
- *What are your own attitudes to cheating and drug use in sport? Does it really matter?*
- *How would you feel if sport allowed competitors to take drugs openly?*
- *Would you take drugs to perform better?*

The 2012 Summer Olympic Games

A number of issues have also been raised in relation to the 2012 Games. Consider the following.

The cost for the Games is estimated at £2.375 billion. What else could £2.375 billion buy?

- A new hospital in Manchester, a so-called 'super hospital', was estimated to have cost £400 million in 2001.
- The cost of building a new primary school in Worcestershire was estimated at £1.5 million; the capital cost of a new secondary school in Wales, £13 million.
- The average cost of constructing one mile of a dual three-lane motorway in 1998 was estimated at £17.1 million.

Using such information we can look at the 'cost' of staging the Games as follows:

- We could build nearly 6 new 'super hospitals'.
- We could build 158 new primary schools around the country or 18 new secondary schools.
- We could construct 140 miles of new motorway.

Think about it

What do you think? Do you think that the country should be hosting this very expensive event? Why? Are there ways at looking at the benefits other than in money terms? What could they be? What about health benefits? Consider the benefits for national prestige, and the facilities that will be left for people in this country to use.

The media

The mass media exert an enormous influence on sport and its supporters and spectators, and can be a power for both good and bad. It can have long-lasting effects on the reputation of a sport and on how the public views that sport, as well as seriously affecting the lives of those people who play sport and are in the public eye.

Newspapers

In recent years, sports coverage in the newspapers has increased enormously. Sport sells newspapers, but how is sport portrayed and which sports are covered?

Newspapers fall into two main groups: tabloids and broadsheets. The tabloids, sometimes called the red tops, include the *Sun* and the *Daily Mirror*. They tend to be more sensational in their coverage of a story, with less emphasis on facts and more on gossip and rumour. The language used is simpler, and tabloids often use headlines that deliberately attract attention.

The broadsheets, such as *The Times*, the *Daily Telegraph*, and the *Guardian*, are much less concerned with gossip and more concerned with reporting the facts accurately. The range of sports covered is much wider and the language used is more complex.

The media can have a huge effect on people's opinions. When Wayne Rooney starred in the European Football championships in 2004 at the age of only 18, he became a superstar overnight. He is an idol for many young people and, as a result, is a role model for many young players. This has led to a huge increase in the amount of media interest in anything that he does, especially if it is of a negative nature. The ESFA recently withdrew an invitation to attend an ESFA soccer course because they felt that Rooney had become an unsuitable role model for young players due to the amount of negative press reports that had appeared in the press. Was the amount of media interest in all that Wayne Rooney does partly to blame for the poor behaviour that Rooney has demonstrated at times?

Pressure from the media

Sportsmen and women are in the media spotlight more than ever before, and the increased pressure on sportsmen and women has seen an increase in the number taking drugs to improve their performance. Player behaviour both on and off the field is under much closer scrutiny than ever before.

Many sports personalities are seen as much on the front pages of the papers as they are on the back pages, where sport is traditionally covered. Their private lives are regarded as public property. The public knows which player is dating which pop star, which player is going to which club, and what players' latest hairstyles are.

■ *Sports personalities are celebrities and their private lives are regarded as public property*

Assessment activity 7: Key issues in sport

To achieve a Pass:

1 *Describe* four key issues that you think currently affect sport. These might be issues that you have seen in the news or on the television or may come from personal experience.

2 Complete the table below for these four issues. (P7)

Issue	Why does it affect sport?	What impact does it have?

To achieve a Merit you must achieve the Pass criteria and:

3 Using the information above, create a PowerPoint presentation or poster display explaining the impact of each of the four issues you have identified. Look in your local newspapers or national press – can you find a recent example of each to illustrate your findings? (M4)

Impacts

Increase in sports coverage in the media

The increase in coverage has had many effects.

- Sponsors have been attracted to a number of sports because of the amount of media coverage they receive.

- The dress and language of many people is influenced by what their sports heroes wear and say.

- The opinion of millions of people can be influenced by what they read about sport in newspapers and magazines, and what they see and hear on the television and radio.

- Sports have changed their rules and competition format to accommodate the needs of the media. Football has done this for Sky, due to the amount of money the company has put into the game.

- Many sports are now seen as fashionable. Players in such sports have become role models for young people who often try to emulate their heroes. This is fine if the role model presents a positive image, but what if a sports star displays some form of negative behaviour? How might this effect the behaviour of young people? Can you think of an example?

- Sports that receive increased media coverage also enjoy increased numbers of players and spectators.

- How have sports that have been overlooked by the media been affected? Since they receive less media coverage, they struggle to generate and attract sponsorship and so find it hard to develop.

There is no doubt that the coverage of sport by the media has greatly changed people when it comes to their behaviour, opinions and attitudes.

 Let's do it!

In small groups, discuss the effect of the media on a sport of your choice.

1 *Do you think the effects have all been positive, or are there some negative effects?*
2 *How far should the media be allowed to change the nature of your chosen sport?*
3 *Now choose a sport that struggles to gain any significant media interest. What have the effects of this been on the sport?*

Technology

The rapid developments in technology over recent years means that we can now watch sport from any part of the world at almost any time. For instance, the Commonwealth Games that recently took place in Melbourne, Australia, could be seen live on TV if you were prepared to get up early enough!

Interactive TV allows you to choose the sport you want to view, while 'player cam' and a wide range of camera angles plus instant replays and slow motion coverage allow viewers to really appreciate the skills and techniques involved. However, it might be argued that we have become 'armchair' referees, and every decision is analysed and picked over to decide if the ref was right or wrong. It is a pity the referee has to make an instant decision without the benefit of all this technology! The media openly criticise players' and managers' decisions and actions and encourage us to debate their performances in minute detail.

Financial benefits

For players, the financial benefits have been staggering. An average Premier league player will earn £250,000 to £500,000 per year. Prize money in sport is increasing, sponsorship deals get ever larger. Transfer fees for top football players are measured in tens of millions of pounds. However, there has been a price to pay. Sports stars have become celebrities.

But away from the world of top flight sport, what about the small, local club or semi-professional or amateur player? Have things changed for the better for them?

Summary

In this unit you have examined a wide range of factors concerned with the sports industry, looking at:

- definitions of various terms
- the main providers of sports activities and facilities
- the organisation and structure of sports governing bodies
- the development, growth and trends within the sports industry
- the importance of sport to individuals, communities and the country
- how and why people participate in sports and the factors that affect participation
- the funding of sports clubs and organisations
- the effects of the media on sport
- the key issues which currently affect sport in the UK.

Let's do it!

Discuss the effects of the various changes in sport over recent years on the following. Draw up a poster to show your thoughts.

- *Your nearest professional football team.*
- *Facilities for sport locally.*
- *Sports coverage in the media.*
- *The range of sports available to you personally.*

Check what you know!

Look back through this unit to see if you can you answer the following questions.

1. What is the difference between amateur and professional sport?
2. What are the factors which have led to the growth of the sports industry?
3. Which factors can affect participation in sport?
4. What are the benefits of taking part in sport?
5. How is sports development carried out, and for what reasons?
6. What can be done to overcome barriers to participation in sport?
7. What are the three main sectors in sports provision? Give local examples of each.
8. Give the main reason why each of these three sectors makes sports provision.
9. Describe a local example of how each sector is involved in the provision of one sport of your choice.
10. Why is it important that people are encouraged to participate in sport?
11. How might you encourage groups of people to take part, who traditionally do not do so?
12. When England won the Rugby World Cup, what resulting effects might you have expected to see locally in each of the three sectors?
13. Name three of each of the following:
    - local sports organisations
    - regional sports organisations
    - national sports organisations
    - international sports organisations.
14. How does the amount of coverage that a club or sporting figure receives in the media affect it?
15. What are the key issues affecting sport, and how could they be tackled?

4 Preparation for Sport

Introduction

In this unit you will gain a better understanding of how the body is affected by various factors in training and performance. You will look at lifestyle and its relevance to training and performance, and analyse changing training practices. You will also find out how knowledge of nutrition and psychology can improve performance if it is included in the training programme.

How you will be assessed

This unit will be assessed by an internal assignment that will be set and marked by the staff at your centre. It may be sampled as well by your centre's External Verifier as part of Edexcel's on-going quality procedures. The assignment is designed to allow you to show your understanding of the unit outcomes. These relate to what you should be able to do after completing this unit.

▶ Continued from previous page

Your assessment could be in the form of:

■ video recorded presentations

■ case studies

■ role plays

■ written assignments.

After completing this unit you should be able to achieve the following learning outcomes.

1 Understand the fitness and lifestyle of an individual sports performer.

2 Be able to plan a simple fitness training programme for an individual sports performer.

3 Understand the nutritional requirements of effective sports performance.

4 Understand the psychological factors that affect sports training and performance.

4.1 Understand the fitness and lifestyle of an individual sports performer

Components of physical fitness

Physical fitness is having the minimal level of fitness in order to have good health.

There are a number of components that make up physical fitness.

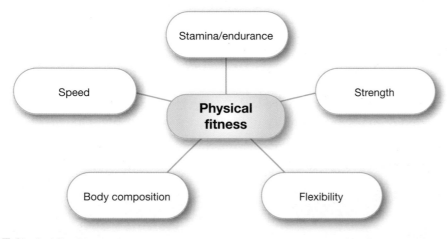

■ *Physical fitness*

These help in everyday activities as well as in sport.

Key point

- There are five major components of fitness – strength, flexibility, speed, body composition and endurance.
- The amount of each component that a person possesses will vary. Some people are born with more flexibility than others and will develop this component through maturation. This will obviously help in following certain sporting careers, for example, gymnastics.

Strength

Strength can be defined as the maximum force a muscle, or group of muscles, can produce in a single movement or contraction. There are three categories of strength.

Think about it

Can you think of examples of three sports which use the three different types of strength described here?

Write your examples down.

1 **Maximum strength** – needed to produce a single movement against a resistance, for example, power lifting.
2 **Elastic strength** – needed to produce movements that are very close to each other in time, such as floor routines in gymnastics, or the triple jump.
3 **Strength endurance** – needed to produce repetitive movements of a muscle, or muscle group, and not to get tired while doing so.

Flexibility

Flexibility is the range of movement that a joint or series of joints can perform. There are many factors that can determine the range of movement around a joint, including:

■ the elasticity of the ligaments and tendons at the joint

■ the strength of the opposing muscle group (antagonistic muscle group)

■ the shape of the surface of the bones that make up the joint.

The degree of movement is also associated with the type of joint at which the movement is taking place. Joints are designed for stability, movement, or both. The hinge joint at the knee, for example, is designed primarily for stability; therefore, the movement that can be produced in flexion and extension only.

■ *Many sports require flexibility*

Speed

Speed is required in many sports and can be defined as the ability to move the body or body parts quickly over a set distance. It is important to note that speed is not only concerned with running, but also the speed at which other body parts can move. For example, you need to move your arms quickly when you catch and pass a ball during a game of rugby, to avoid it being lost in a tackle.

Endurance

Endurance of the heart and lungs (cardio-respiratory endurance) is the ability to continue exercising for a long period of time. To do this, the body needs to transport and use the oxygen that is breathed in during exercise. Cardio-respiratory endurance relies on the efficiency of the cardiovascular system to deliver oxygen. All long-distance sports depend on this component of fitness to supply and maintain the energy that is required.

Muscular endurance is the ability of a muscle or muscle group to sustain repetitive contractions over a period of time. There is an oxygen-rich blood supply to the muscles that helps to delay the onset of tiredness.

Body composition

The study of body composition looks at the difference between the body's fat mass and its non-fat mass, and where they are around the body. It is very important to think about body composition, not only for sports but for health and well-being.

A body that contains more fat mass than lean or skeletal muscle mass can suffer from severe health problems, such as obesity, cardiovascular disease and other associated complications. For sportspeople, a high fat mass can result in the reduction of muscle mass. This will lead to a reduction of performance due to the drop in efficiency of skeletal muscle, because more energy is required to move a greater mass. In other words, more energy is being used to move the mass than to perform.

Components of skill-related fitness

Skill-related fitness

Skill-related fitness can be defined as the ability to carry out day-to-day activities and extra activities for exercise without the onset of unnecessary fatigue. This encompasses sportspeople and non sportspeople.

There are different components that make up skill-related fitness. These components contribute towards the different needs of sport, but they also require the help of physical fitness components.

Agility

Agility is the ability to change the direction of the body as a whole at speed. Therefore, it also consists of other components such as speed, balance, power and coordination.

Agility is an important factor in many activities, including football, badminton, basketball and skiing. As with other components, agility can be improved by training specific tasks set in the environment that relates to the sport. It is essential that the other components highlighted (speed, balance, power and coordination) are also developed as this will affect the efficiency of agility.

Balance

Balance is a basic skill needed in almost every sport. Changing your centre of gravity to match your moves is the key to efficiency in sport.

Coordination

Coordination refers to the efficient way that you move and can therefore be defined as the ability to carry out a number of movements effortlessly and efficiently. Some of the methods that are used to assess levels of coordination include:

- hand-eye coordination
- foot-eye coordination
- whole-body coordination.

Power

Power is the ability to produce a large amount of force in a short period of time. It is the result of strength and speed. The amount of power required by different sports varies. A rugby player, for example, requires more strength and speed than a 1500-metre runner, although both sportspeople will need to include strength and power training in their training programmes. Most sports need strength and power for optimum performance, but in many actions it is power that is more important.

Reaction time

Reaction time is the time it takes to respond to an event. There are different types of reaction time:

- simple reaction time
- choice reaction time.

Simple reaction time
Simple reaction time is the time taken between an event and the start of an action, for example, starting a 100-metre sprint on hearing the gun.

Choice reaction time
Choice reaction time is the time taken between an event and an action that requires a choice being made, for example, deciding what to do when receiving a pass from a team mate during a game of rugby. Do you pass? Do you go into contact? Do you try to run around the opposition?

Fitness tests

Fitness levels

Fitness is a term that has different meanings for different people, depending on the goals they set themselves to become fit. Fitness levels vary, and getting fit could mean anything from attending exercise classes twice a week, to training for running a marathon.

The current fitness level of an individual needs to be established before any improvements can be made.

The best way to measure an individual's fitness level is to carry out field tests of physical fitness. Fitness tests are designed to measure changes in the body through the stresses that exercise places upon it. The two changes that need to be defined are:

- **response to exercise** – the short-term changes that occur when the body exercises. (In other words, the immediate change in the body's systems to maintain a balance of the internal environment when required to exercise after a period of rest.)

- **adaptation to exercise** – the long-term changes that occur in and to the body when it has been exercised over a period of time.

Changes last only as long as the exercise or training continues. It can take up to six weeks to change your fitness level, and only two weeks to lose those changes.

Think about it

What is your idea of 'fitness'? In a group, discuss the goals you set yourselves and your training regimes for a typical week.

Let's do it!

Consider the list of sports given below. Rank the components of fitness that each sport requires, in order of their importance. Give reasons for your choices.

- *Weightlifting.*
- *Parallel bars in gymnastics.*
- *Shot putt.*
- *1500 metre running.*

Fitness tests help to assess the various components of fitness. Some of these tests are complex to administer, others are easily carried out.

Two tests for strength

The table below shows two tests for strength.

1 The dynamometer test is specific to one muscle group.
2 1RM (one repetition maximum) tests various muscle groups. For this test, only one repetition can be completed for the weight that is being lifted.

■ *Hand grip dynamometer*

Strength tests				
Test	**Muscle group being measured**	**Description of protocol**	**Advantages**	**Disadvantages**
Hand grip dynamometer	Muscles in the forearm	Three attempts of the test from each hand (left and right), keeping the hand by the side of the body	A simple test; an objective measure	Not a total measure of strength because it is a measure of the forearms only
1RM (1 rep max)	Various, depending on exercise being performed	One possible maximum force to lift free weights or other gym-based equipment	Accessible equipment	Greater possibility of injury due to the maximum weights that are required

Hand grip strength scores		
Classification	**Non-dominant hand (kg)**	**Dominant hand (kg)**
Woman		
Excellent	>37	>41
Good	34–36	38–40
Average	22–33	25–37
Poor	18–21	22–24
Very Poor	<18	<22
Men		
Excellent	>68	>70
Good	56–67	62–69
Average	43–55	48–61
Poor	39–42	41–47
Very Poor	<39	<41

Fitness testing for speed

The 30-metre sprint			
Test	**Description of protocol**	**Advantages**	**Disadvantages**
30-metre sprint	To run as fast as possible along an obstacle-free distance of 30 metres on a non-slip surface, from the call of the timer '3, 2, 1, GO!'	A simple test; easy to administer	Timing can be affected by error. Condition of the running surface can affect speed

Sprint test scores		
Time (in seconds) Male	**Time (in seconds) Female**	**Rating**
<4.0	<4.5	Excellent
4.2–4.0	4.6–4.5	Good
4.4–4.3	4.8–4.7	Average
4.6–4.5	5.0–4.9	Fair
>4.6	>5.0	Very Poor

Two tests for aerobic endurance

Multi-stage shuttle run test

This test is used to predict the maximum amount of oxygen that a person can take in and use during exercise. This test requires participants to complete 20-m shuttle runs in time to a pre-recorded cassette. As the test goes on, the speed at which they are required to run gets faster each minute. The test stops when the participant cannot keep up with the speed. At this point, you can record the number of levels and shuttles completed. This gives an indication of aerobic fitness.

Multi-stage shuttle run test			
Test	**Description of protocol**	**Advantages**	**Disadvantages**
Multi-stage shuttle run test	Individuals must line up on the 20 m mark. On hearing the triple beep that starts the test, the subjects must start to run to the other line 20 m away. The subjects must reach the 20 m target before or on the single beep that signifies each shuttle run. Subjects must continue to run, arriving at each line on the beeps. Each subject can be given three chances before they either stop running or they are pulled out. Subjects must run until they feel they can not run any further.	Comparisons can be made with published data Large numbers can be tested at once Limited equipment is required	Relies on the subject's motivation and honesty to perform the test until exhaustion Not an absolute measure, only a prediction A running test, so may favour subjects who participate in activities that involve running

Three-minute step-up test

This looks at the recovery rate of the heart rate, which can also determine aerobic fitness.

The three-minute step-up test

Test	Description of protocol	Advantages	Disadvantages
Three-minute step-up test	Step on and off a 45-cm-high box or bench at a rate of 30 steps per minute. The speed can be set with a metronome. The test should last three minutes. Heart rate is taken before the test starts, to establish resting heart rate, and on three occasions during recovery phase of the test Heart 1 @ 1st min ⎤ each for 15 seconds then rate 2 @ 2nd min ⎬ multiply each time by 3 @ 3rd min ⎦ 4 to gain a minute value	Requires minimal equipment; easy to administer	Taking the heart rate at the set times; may rely on the experience of the experimenter to find the pulse rate at each stage Relies on other experimenters to monitor the accuracy of the steps

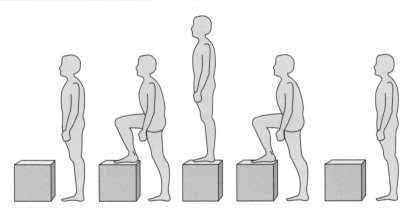

■ The three-minute step-up test

Three-minute step-up test scores

Classification	Male	Female
Superior	<118	<121
Excellent	119–133	122–136
Good	134–143	137–154
Average	144–166	155–175
Poor	167–193	176–205
Very Poor	>194	>206

Two tests for muscular endurance

Press-up test

The press-up test				
Test	**Muscle group being assessed**	**Description of protocol**	**Advantages**	**Disadvantages**
The press-up test	Pectorals, triceps and deltoids	To perform as many press-ups in a minute as the subject can manage. The body must be lowered to approximately 5 cm away from the ground	Easy to administer Limited equipment Not time consuming	Level of accuracy of the press-ups and body position that is required relies on the motivation and honesty of the subject

Press-up test scores		
Classification	**Male**	**Female**
Excellent	>45	>40
Good	41–45	35–40
Average	31–40	25–34
Fair	21–30	15–24
Poor	10–20	5–14
Very Poor	<10	<5

Curl-up test

Curl-up test				
Test	**Muscle group being assessed**	**Description of protocol**	**Advantages**	**Disadvantages**
The curl-up test	Abdominals	To perform as many curl-ups in a minute as the subject can manage. The upper body must be raised off the ground to an angle of 30–40 degrees with the knees bent at 90 degrees and feet on the floor. Place your arms across your chest or by the side of your body	Easy to administer Limited equipment required Not time consuming	Accuracy of the curl-ups and body positions relies on the honesty and motivation of the subject

Curl-up test scores		
Classification	**Male**	**Female**
Excellent	>50	>40
Good	45–50	36–40
Average	35–44	26–35
Fair	25–34	16–25
Poor	15–24	10–15
Very Poor	<15	<10

■ *Curl-up test*

Fitness testing for flexibility

The sit-and-reach test				
Test	**Muscle group being assessed**	**Description of protocol**	**Advantages**	**Disadvantages**
Sit-and-reach test	Hamstrings and lower back	Subject sits with both legs flat against the floor and feet against the sit-and-reach box Subject then stretches arms forward to push the cursor on the box as far as possible, in a smooth action This stretch must be held for two seconds	Easy to administer	Limited area of muscle being tested; muscle temperature can affect the scores

Sit-and-reach test scores		
Classification	**Male**	**Female**
Excellent	>35	>39
Good	31–34	33–38
Fair	27–30	29–32
Poor	<27	<29

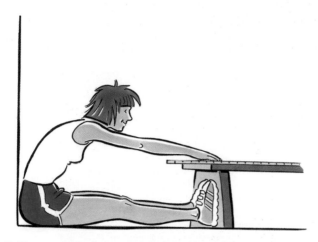 

■ *Sit-and-reach test*

Fitness testing for body composition

The BMI (Body Mass Index) test				
Test	**Considerations being measured**	**Description of protocol**	**Advantages**	**Disadvantages**
BMI (Body Mass Index)	Weight against height	Take measurements for subject's height and weight: BMI = $\dfrac{\text{weight in kg}}{\text{height in m} \times \text{height in m}}$ The higher the score, the greater the level of body fat	Simple and easy test	It does not always apply to sportspeople; not an accurate test to distinguish between fat and lean mass

Ratings for BMI	
Classification	**Rating**
Healthy	20–25
Overweight	25–30
Obese	>30

Another way you can calculate your Body Mass Index is to use a chart such as the one below.

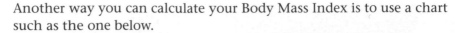

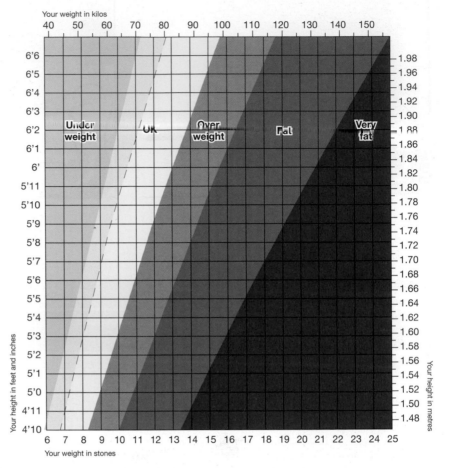

■ *Are you the right weight for your height?*

The skinfold test

There are four basic sites that can be used to establish body fat percentage in individuals. These measurements can be gained by using skin callipers.

The four sites are:

■ biceps (front of the upper arm)

■ suprailiac (immediately above the hip)

■ triceps (back of the upper arm)

■ subscapular (just below the shoulder blade).

Biceps (front of the upper arm)

With the arm resting comfortably at the side, take a vertical fold on the front of the upper arm, over the bicep muscle using the index finger and thumb. Place the skin fold in the callipers and take the reading. Ensure that the elbow is extended and the arm relaxed.

■ *A skin fold test*

Suprailiac (immediately above the hip)
Take a diagonal fold of skin just above the iliac crest. Place the skin fold
in the skin callipers and take the reading.

Body Fat %						
Skin Fold thickness (mm)	17–19		20–29		30–39	
	Boys	Girls	Boys	Girls	Boys	Girls
10	0.14	5.34	0.04	4.88	5.05	8.27
12	2.46	7.60	2.1	7.27	6.86	10.85
14	4.21	9.53	3.85	9.30	8.40	12.68
16	5.74	11.21	5.38	11.08	9.74	14.27
18	7.10	12.71	6.74	12.66	10.93	15.68
20	8.32	14.05	7.96	14.08	12.00	16.95
22	9.43	15.28	9.07	15.38	12.98	18.10
24	10.45	16.40	10.09	16.57	13.87	19.16
26	11.39	17.44	11.03	17.67	14.69	20.14
28	12.26	18.40	11.91	18.69	15.46	21.05
30	13.07	19.30	12.73	19.64	16.17	21.90
32	13.84	20.15	13.49	20.54	16.84	22.70
34	14.56	20.95	14.22	21.39	17.47	23.45
36	15.25	21.71	14.90	22.19	18.07	24.16
38	15.89	22.42	15.55	22.95	18.63	24.84
40	16.51	23.10	16.17	23.67	19.17	25.48

Triceps (back of the upper arm)
With the arm resting comfortably at the side, take a vertical fold on the back of the upper arm, over the triceps muscle using the index finger and thumb. Place the skin fold in the callipers and take the reading. Ensure that the elbow is extended and the arm relaxed.

Subscapular (just below the shoulder blade)
Take a diagonal fold of skin just below the shoulder blade. Place the skin fold in the callipers and take the reading. Compare your readings with those in the table on the previous page.

Fitness testing for power

The vertical jump test				
Test	**Muscle group being assessed**	**Description of protocol**	**Advantages**	**Disadvantages**
Vertical Jump Test	Legs	Place belt around the waist of the subject. Ensure the string attached to the foot mat (which stays on the ground) is taut. The subject bends the knees and jumps upwards in a smooth action. Score appears in centimetres on the electronic clock on the belt. Can be repeated three times with the best score taken. If a vertical jump belt is not available, the procedure can be carried out using a wall, metre ruler and chalk. Stand side on to the wall, arm closer to the wall stretched above head. Mark the wall with chalk. Place chalk in hand again and jump to the highest point; at the same time, mark it. Measure the distance between the reach and jump points.	Simple and easy to use	None

Let's do it!

With the help of your tutor, describe a fitness test for each of the following components of fitness. Ensure it is suitable for the fitness component and also for the area of the body you wish to test.

Vertical jump test scores		
Classification	**Male Distance (in cm)**	**Female Distance (in cm)**
Excellent	>60	>47
Good	51–59	36–46
Average	41–50	29–35
Poor	27–40	25–34
Very Poor	<26	<24

Case study

Robin

Robin is training to be a fitness instructor. She needs to gain a client base on which she can practise her planning and implementation of fitness tests.

Robin has covered the areas of health, fitness and fitness testing and now needs to produce written advice for at least two different clients. The following clients have volunteered to receive help from Robin to improve their health and fitness levels.

Client one:
A 19-year-old female, who visits the gym three times a week, for an hour each time. She wants to improve her levels of endurance, and lose some weight.

Client two:
A 30-year-old male, who smokes 20 cigarettes a day. He plays rugby for the local team each Saturday and

trains once a week. Client two plays on the wing for the team but would also like to start playing squash. Now answer the following questions.

1 Robin needs to ensure that she has all of the details for each component of fitness. Provide a booklet that contains all the health-related and sports-related fitness components that Robin can easily access to explain to each client what each component is.

2 Highlight the components of fitness that each of Robin's clients needs to work on to maintain both their health and sports fitness levels.

3 Identify and explain the tests that Robin needs to carry out for each of her clients so that they can start working towards their targets.

Protocol

The way you carry out a test can be classed as a procedure or the protocol. The protocol that is used should have been tested for validity and reliability.

Valid

If the test is classed as valid, it should measure what it is supposed to measure. If a test is considered to measure cardiovascular endurance, then it is essential that it does.

Accepted and standard

It is essential that testing is carried out in the same way for each individual and under the same conditions if any comparisons are to be made between individuals. This will limit factors that could explain differences between individuals.

Method

The method should be consistent. The method is what you did as a tester to complete the test or investigation. This section can be divided under three headings.

Key point

If a test is reliable, it is said to measure what it is designed to measure with some level of consistency.

1 Subjects
All of the subjects that were used for the test should be listed. Details of where they were from, their gender, age, height, weight, fitness and health levels. NOTE: names should not appear in this section.

Method

2 Equipment
All of the equipment that was used for the test must be listed.

3 Procedure
Details of what was done to complete the test or investigation should be written in such a way that any reader could follow and repeat the test accurately.

■ *Method of testing*

Results

It is important to write up the test results as soon as possible after testing, as this allows for further investigations (testing) to be carried out or conclusions to be made.

The results section should include the results of the tests in an at-a-glance format, by using graphs, charts and tables. Ensure that each graph, chart and table has a title and description of what it is attempting to show the reader.

Conclusion and evaluation

This is a summary of what the investigation has found, making reference to what you were aiming to do when you started. You should ensure that any statements that you make about the results gained are referred back to the results section (add any data where necessary). You should evaluate your results.

Assessment activity 1: Components of fitness and the use of tests to determine fitness levels to improve performance

To achieve a Pass:

1 *Describe* the components of fitness and their effects on sports performance. (P1)
2 Work with a sports performer and your teacher. Select and conduct three tests related to different areas of fitness. Record your results accurately. (P3)

To achieve a Merit you must achieve the Pass criteria and:

3 Working independently, select and carry out three appropriate tests from different areas of fitness to gain the results of a sports performer. You must accurately record the results and assess the fitness levels of your sports performer. (M2)

To achieve a Distinction you must achieve the Pass and Merit criteria and:

4 Working independently, select and carry out three appropriate tests from different areas of fitness to gain the results of a sports performer. *Analyse* the fitness test results, *drawing suitable conclusions* to make recommendations for future sports performance. (D2)

Informed consent

When carrying out any testing or investigations on individuals, consent should be obtained. Full details of the test, the results and the expectations of the individuals should be given prior to starting any testing.

Calibration of equipment used

Calibration of the equipment is essential. All equipment should be in full working order as this could affect the test results.

Lifestyle

There is a variety of lifestyle factors that affect our fitness levels. These factors need to be considered if we are to perform to the best of our ability. Understanding the factors that affect out fitness level can help to increase our quality of life and, in some cases, increase our life-span.

We should follow a lifestyle that helps to maintain our health and fitness levels at their optimum to ensure that we can fulfil both our daily tasks, and activities for sport. We should therefore avoid a lifestyle that increases the possibility of ill-health or injury.

■ *Lifestyle factors*

Stress

Stress is an emotional response to situations that we experience. Stress has been related to health problems such as heart disease, high blood pressure and lowered efficiency of the immune system. The body needs time to relax from day-to-day stresses to allow it to recover before the next demanding situation. Exercise has been found to be a beneficial method of reducing the effects of both stress and health-related illnesses.

The effects of alcohol

Alcohol has both short-term and long-term effects. The short-term effects include:

- dizziness
- loss of motor control
- reduced ability to make decisions
- reduced perception of movement.

These symptoms will increase as more alcohol is consumed, eventually leading to unsafe, even life-threatening, behaviour.

The long-term effects of regular drinking beyond the recommended amounts can increase blood pressure and reduce the efficiency of the heart. Symptoms that may be experienced include:

- breathlessness
- swelling of the legs
- muscular fatigue
- an increase in body weight
- joint problems
- liver damage
- heart failure (in extreme cases).

The effects of smoking

Aerobic fitness can be reduced by between five and ten per cent due to smoking. Smoking introduces carbon monoxide into the body. This is an odourless gas that takes space from oxygen in the blood. A smoker, therefore, has less oxygen available during exercise. Smoking can also increase the risk of cancer, heart disease and respiratory disease.

The effects of drugs

Fitness levels can be increased by removing harmful substances from a lifestyle. Harmful activities include smoking, drinking alcohol and taking drugs for recreational use. Banned substances are used to increase capabilities for training and rapid recovery between exercise sessions. However, they can be harmful to health. If drugs are abused or incorrectly taken, they can reduce fitness levels.

Sleep patterns

These may vary due to the pattern of training or other external demands on life, such as family and work. Younger people commonly need at least eight hours sleep per night. As you get older, the amount of sleep that that you need usually decreases. However, as training intensity increases, the need for sleep will increase accordingly. If sleep is not balanced with work, then the positive effects of training will not be seen.

Work demands

In modern society, work hours have increased and the time available to relax or partake in non-work activities has decreased. As a result, stress levels have risen, leading to more and more instances of stress-related diseases.

Medical history

Our fitness levels are inherited partly from our parents, as are some of the health-related problems that may be experienced through the years. Training can increase levels of fitness but only to the capacity that has been passed down from generation to generation.

Level of activity

The more active an individual, the greater the level of fitness they will possess. Non-active lifestyles are related to many diseases, such as obesity, heart disease, high blood pressure and joint and bone problems. An active lifestyle can help reduce these problems and increase the quality of life.

Diet and weight

A healthy diet will ensure a balance between the nutrient value that you consume and the energy that you use for muscular activity. Two results are possible if there is an imbalance between these two factors:

- less food and more exercise will result in weight loss
- more food and less exercise will result in weight gain.

■ *Doing exercise later in life helps improve your quality of life*

Gender

The fitness level of males and females differs due to the structures of their bodies. These differences are most noticeable after puberty. The two genders are also psychologically different. They cope differently with the stresses of physical demands made by work and exercise. There is a high drop-out rate in physical activity in females aged between 16 and 21 years old. This could be due to social pressures, for example, to succeed in personal relationships and careers, or financial pressure.

Culture

Fitness levels are different for individuals from a variety of cultures for many reasons. For example, exercise may be seen as a lower priority than pursuing a career or developing a family, or exercise and an increase in fitness levels may be perceived as a predominantly male activity.

Sports participation

Participation in competition and sports activities can overtake the importance of maintaining fitness levels. Too many competitions hinder fitness levels and stress the body without providing adequate recovery. Exercise can be become an addiction, where increasing participation can reduce the effects of training, resulting in reduced fitness levels.

Assessment activity 2: Lifestyle factors that can affect sports performance

To achieve a Pass:

1 *Describe* four different lifestyle factors that can affect sports performance. (P2)

To achieve a Merit you must achieve the Pass criteria and:

2 *Explain* the effects of fitness and the lifestyle factors of sports performers on sports performance. (M1)

To achieve a Distinction you must achieve the Pass and Merit criteria and:

3 *Evaluate* the effects of lifestyle factors on sports performance providing recommendations for changes. (D1)

4.2 Be able to plan a simple fitness training programme for an individual sports performer

Fitness training methods

Flexibility training

Training for improvements in flexibility includes:

1 **Static flexibility training**, involving slow, sustained stretching of a joint – stretches can be classed as:

   ■ *active* – where a muscle is lengthened in a position without assistance but requires the strength of other muscles to hold the position

   ■ *passive* – where a muscle group is assisted through the stretch by an external force, such as a partner or physical object.

2 **Dynamic flexibility training**, involving stretching during active contraction of the muscle tissue. This includes ballistic stretches, which are performed using a fast, bouncing action so that the momentum of body weight can assist in taking the joint beyond its range of movement. This method of stretching carries a high risk of injury to the muscle group concerned and is not recommended. However, it is still used in specific sports, such as dance and karate, to gain a greater range of motion to the joint area.

 Key point

Stretching to warm up and cool down
There is a difference between stretches used as part of the warm up and cool down of a training session and a flexibility training session. The stretches used in a warm up are to prepare the muscle groups that will be used for performance. The stretches used in cool down are primarily for relaxation and the reduction of muscle soreness after performance. Neither of these types of stretches is for the improvement of flexibility.

■ Maintenance stretches are held between 6–20 seconds, usually during a warm up as part of a training or competitive session.

■ Developmental stretches are usually held between 15–30 seconds during the cool down section of performance training.

Strength and power training

Training for improvements in strength

- **Circuit training** – can be designed to improve general and/or specific strength. Circuits are ideal for people new to strength training because they use body weight rather than external loads and are therefore safer. Work periods are short but at a high intensity and the rest periods are longer. To improve strength, intensity needs to be greater than 80% of the maximum effort.

- **Weight training** – this is carried out using weights equipment or machines.

- **Specific strength training** – this includes exercises that are specific to the sport, for example slinging a medicine ball in shot putt.

- **Plyometric training** – this improves either the strength or the speed at which a muscle contracts (shortens). After undertaking plyometric training, performers in sports like rugby and football will observe improvements in sprinting, throwing and jumping movements.

Training for improvements in muscular endurance

- **Circuit training** – for this component, the exercises need to be carried out over a set period of time, during which as many repetitions as possible are carried out.

- **Resistance machines** – these can place further intensity on an exercise but should only be used when the exercise can be performed over a period of 30 seconds or more.

- **Reps** – between 12 and 15 reps will improve muscular endurance.

- **Sets and resistance** – between three and five sets at approximately 60–75% of the maximum effort will improve muscular endurance.

Training for improvements in speed

Repetitive short bursts of maximum effort for set periods of time.

- **Hollow sprints** – these consist of two sprints divided by a recovery period of walking or jogging. For example, you might sprint for 30 metres, jog for 30 metres and then sprint again for a further 30 metres. You would then finish with a recovery period for a distance of 100 metres, before repeating the sprints. This is ideal for games players.

- **Acceleration sprints** – these gradually increase in pace from a rolling start, to jogging, to striding out and then to maximum effort. Rest intervals, either by walking or jogging, should be included to ensure that full recovery has occurred. The runs can be completed in repetitions of about 3–6 and grouped in sets, for example three sets over a given distance on a sports pitch or court.

- **Interval training** – this is the most common form of training to improve speed endurance. There needs to be a balance between the intensity of the exercise and its duration. There also needs to be an adequate recovery period integrated into the training. You need to take into account the work length and pace/rest ratio. If the length of work is longer than in competition, the pace of the exercise needs to be slower. Decreasing the number of rest periods and decreasing the work intensity will develop the endurance component. Increasing the number of rest periods and increasing the work intensity will develop speed.

Endurance training

The following are forms of training for improvements in cardio-respiratory endurance

- **Distance training** – slow but over long distances.

- **Interval training** – set periods of work at high intensities with incorporated recovery periods (the work time can vary from 30 seconds to 5 minutes and the recovery phase can be complete rest, walking or jogging).

- **Fartlek training** – continuous intensity maintained for a period of time and then varied, for example, running continuously but at varying speeds. There is no complete rest period and the activity is continuous.

- **Continuous training** – exercising for a period beyond 30 minutes at a steady pace, during which time the intensity of exercise keeps the heart rate between 130–160 beats per minute.

- **Heart-rate training zones** – calculating heart rate percentages allows the body to work in different heart rate training zones, which helps affect long-term changes. To improve cardio-respiratory endurance, an individual must attempt to train at close to 75% of their maximum heart rate. This can be done by swimming, running or cycling at an intensity that increases the heart rate to this zone.

■ *Swimming can provide opportunities for heart-rate training*

Training programmes

Principles of training

The major principle of training is to stimulate the adaptations that the body and mind go through during participation in sport, with the aim of improving performance. These adaptations must be controlled through the specific principles of training. Individuals react differently to training programmes, due to the differences in physiological, psychological and inherited factors. The design of the training programme should allow the body and mind of the individual to cope with the demand of the sport during participation.

Some of the key principles of training are:

- Specificity
- Progression
- Overload
- Frequency, Intensity, Time and Type (FITT).

Specificity

A training programme should be specific to the sport that it is attempting to improve. It should be closely related to the activities that the sports performer will experience on the field. If not, the programme will be irrelevant, and the required changes to the body may not occur.

Progression

If there is too sharp an increase in the demands made on the performer, the overload principle could result in injury. The higher levels of challenge should be organised in progressive steps, to allow the body to cope with the increased intensity of the demand placed upon it.

Overload

If an athlete's body experiences the same intensity or stress each time they train, their performance will not improve. The body learns to cope with stress over time. As a result, it is necessary to keep increasing the level of challenge, in order for changes to occur and improvements to be made. Overloading the body encourages these further developments.

Frequency, Intesity, Time and Type (FITT)

Strengths and weaknesses need to be highlighted before any training programme is designed, as these give the basis for the frequency of training sessions, the intensity of the work that needs to be carried out, the type of exercises that should be included, and the time that is required for the session (FITT).

- Frequency
- Intensity
- Type of exercise
- Time needed

Key points

- Reversibility – a training programme needs to be exciting to keep the performer motivated. If the performer stops training, all the hard work in building up fitness will be reversed, that is, lost.

- Tedium (variation) – a training programme also needs to have varied activities, to maintain the performer's interest and enjoyment. This will ensure the performer is applying skills and fitness in a variety of ways.

Highlighting strengths and weakness can contribute to identifying areas for improvement of fitness levels, which in turn can help to highlight the areas of improvement in the training programme, so that changes can be made.

Think about it

- *Get together with other members of your group.*
- *List the times when you have pushed yourself in training. Give specific examples.*
- *Write down the times when you have carried on with the same routine for too long. Discuss your experiences with your tutor.*

Evaluate

To make clear and appropriate evaluations of training programmes, testing before and after a training programme must be carried out. This will give a starting point for any training programme design. It is important to evaluate the strengths and weaknesses of every training programme. Try to identify areas for improvement within the training programme, and where modifications or changes could be made.

Specific training programmes and evaluation

All training programmes must include the principles of training discussed in this unit. Every training programme should include sufficient warm ups, including exercises that work on the larger muscle groups with lighter weights, and then moving on to heavier weights. It is helpful to spread the exercises so that the different muscle groups are being worked.

Strength training programme – chest press:
10 reps at 75% of max effort (10 × 75%)

8 × 80%

5 × 85%

3 × 95%

1 × 100%

This can be repeated 4–5 times for leg press, rowing, shoulder press and bicep curls.

Speed programme
3 sets of 6 × 60 m at 90-100% effort

5 minute rest period

3 × 100 m acceleration runs (25 m jog, 25 m striding, 25 m at 75% and 25 m at 100% effort)

3 × 100 m hollow sprints (30 m sprint at 100% effort, 30 m jog, 40 m at 100% effort).

Let's do it!

Choose a sport that you regularly participate in. Write down the exercises that your coach encourages you to do as part of your training programme. Can you think of other exercises that might be specific to the sport?

Key point

There are two types of strength programmes that can be followed: 3 sets of 6 repetitions and pyramid training. The number of repetitions in each set during pyramid training is decreased as the weights used are increased.

Continuous programme

Maintain a steady pace (walking pace) for about 40 minutes. The pace should be at a level where the time can be completed. The distance should be monitored so improvements can be recorded. The same distance can then be completed in less time or the distance can be increased.

Circuit training for muscular endurance

1	Bicep curls	**4**	Press-up	**7**	Step-ups
2	Sit-ups	**5**	Squats	**8**	Lateral raises
3	Shuttle runs	**6**	Back extensions	**9**	Dead lifts

1 × set 60 seconds with 20 seconds rest between each station

1 × set 45 seconds with 10 seconds rest between each station

1 × set 30 seconds with 60 seconds running between each station.

Let's do it!

Describe a training programme you have taken part in. Can you identify the principles of training integrated into it?

Assessment activity 3: Training programme design

To achieve a Pass:

1 *Using teacher support*, plan a training programme for a specific sports performer. Design the programme to be carried out over a six-week period. (P4)

To achieve a Merit you must achieve the Pass criteria and:

2 *Working independently*, plan a training programme for a specific sports performer. Design the programme to be carried out over a six-week period. (M3)

4.3 Understand the nutritional requirements of effective sports performance

The subject of nutrition looks at the components of the food that we eat and how these components affect our everyday activities. A diet can be described as the pattern by which we eat the food, for example, a wheat-free diet or vegetarian diet. The way that a diet is organised can affect how fast and how well an individual will develop.

Our reasons for eating can be:

■ **physical** – our bodies need food to function and develop. Food is necessary for muscle contraction, cell function, brain function, muscle development and growth, repair and recovery of tissues and to satisfy hunger

■ **psychological** – we eat because it makes us feel safe and because it is a pleasurable experience

■ **social** – the environment in which eating takes place is also important; we often eat because others are eating.

Think about it

- *List all the occasions at which you have eaten over the past two days.*
- *When did you eat for physical reasons, or in other words because you were hungry?*
- *When did you eat for psychological or social reasons?*

Nutrients

Each food component is called a nutrient. Each of these nutrients is essential to the diet and has a main function or role in the body.

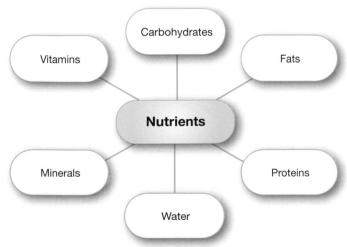

■ *Nutrients*

Carbohydrates, fats and proteins are called the energy nutrients because they are used as food fuels during metabolism.

Carbohydrates

The main role of carbohydrates is to provide the body with energy. Carbohydrates are stored in the muscles and liver as glycogen, and can be found in the blood as blood glucose. The body uses glycogen and blood glucose as its food fuels.

Carbohydrates are broken down by the body to a simple form of glucose. This is then stored as glycogen in the muscles and the liver, along with about three times its own weight in water. There is approximately three times more glycogen stored in the muscles than in the liver. The body can only store a small amount of glycogen – glycogen stores are very limited compared with fat stores found in the body.

The body can only hold a certain amount of fuel, just as a car can only hold a certain amount of petrol. The total store of glycogen in the average body is 1600–2000 kcal. This is enough energy to last up to one day if nothing else is consumed. There are small amounts of glycogen present in the blood and brain and the concentrations of these are kept within a very narrow range, during rest and exercise. This allows the systems of the body to continue to function.

There are two types of carbohydrate:

- **simple sugars** – found in sweet foods such as jam, confectionary, fruit and sugar
- **complex sugars** – found in wheat-based foods such as pasta and bread, and also potato- and rice-based products.

Dietary fibre

This is essential for the regulation of the gut. Dietary fibre is not digested by the body but is used to maintain the function of the gut. Most of the foods that contain dietary fibre are also rich in carbohydrates.

Fats

Fat can be divided into two categories:

- **stored fats** – found in a layer underneath the skin. The supply of this store of fat is much greater than the stores of glycogen. A small amount of fat is stored in the muscle tissue, but the majority can be found around the organs and beneath the skin.

■ *Excess fat*

- **essential fats** – needed for the healthy function of the body. These fats are not stored and so need to be consumed.

The amount of fat that is stored around specific areas of the body is mainly determined by your genes and hormonal balance. Your fat deposits will generally be in line with one or both of your parents. Males usually take after their fathers – hormones tend to favour fat storage around the middle. Females usually take after their mothers – their hormones tend to favour fat storage around the hips and thighs. This explains the pear shape of females and the apple shape of males.

Fats are stored in the body in the skeletal muscle and fat cells underneath the skin. Fats are a form of fuel and have many functions in the body.

- They help the absorption of the vitamins A, D and E.
- They regulate body temperature.
- They encourage brain growth.
- They are the main source of energy for cell function.

Fats provide almost twice as much energy for one gram compared with the same amount provided by either carbohydrates or proteins.

Energy supplied by different nutrients		
Amount of nutrient	**Nutrient**	**Unit of energy supplied (in kcals)**
1 gram	Carbohydrate	4 kcals
1 gram	Fat	9 kcals
1 gram	Protein	4 kcals

Fats can be divided into saturated and unsaturated fats.

- **Saturated fats** – these are found in many animal products and can be harmful to health if consumed in large amounts on a regular basis. Foods in this category include meats, dairy produce, cakes, pastries and confectionary.

- **Unsaturated fats** – these are less harmful and many foods in this category can help us absorb the essential fats that are necessary for many of the bodily functions. Foods in this category include oily fish, such as mackerel, sardines and salmon. For those following a vegetarian diet, foods such as flax seed, pumpkin seeds, walnuts and dark green leafy vegetables contain smaller amounts of unsaturated fat.

Proteins

Protein is not stored by the body in the same way as fat and carbohydrates. Protein forms muscle and organ tissue. It is predominantly used as a building material rather than an energy store but proteins can be broken down to release energy if required. The muscles and organs, therefore, represent a large source of potential energy.

As with the previous nutrients, proteins can also be divided into two categories:

- **high value** or **animal** proteins
- **low value** or **plant** proteins.

All animal products, such as meat and dairy, contain the essential amino acids that form proteins. These amino acids are the building blocks of proteins, and are essential for their function in the body. The low-value proteins are important but they do not include all of the amino acids in one food. If you do not eat meat and dairy products you need to eat a careful combination of low-value proteins to ensure that all of the essential amino acids are obtained. Low-value proteins include beans, lentils, peas, nuts, seeds and soya bean products.

Vitamins and minerals

These are essential for all bodily functions. The majority of the fruit and vegetables that make up the western diet include most of these vitamins and minerals. The exceptions are certain vitamins, for example Vitamin B12 and Vitamin D, which are obtained from animal products.

Vitamins

There are two types of vitamins: **fat-soluble** and **water-soluble**.

Vitamin A
Helps to develop eyesight, especially night vision. Helps in growth and aids in healthy skin.

Foods rich in vitamin A
Eggs, milk, apricots, nectarines, carrots, sweet potatoes, spinach and liver.

Vitamin E
Vitamin E is needed to maintain most of the body's tissues. It helps protect the lungs from polluted air. It helps in the formation of red blood cells.

Foods rich in vitamin E
Whole grains (e.g. wheat and oats), wheat germ, leafy green vegetables, sardines, egg yolks, nuts.

Fat-soluble vitamins are stored in body fat, until they are needed

Vitamin D
Vitamin D is needed for strong bones. It is also useful for forming strong teeth. Vitamin D helps the body to absorb calcium.

Foods rich in vitamin D
Milk and other dairy products fortified with vitamin D, fish, egg yolks.

Vitamin K
Vitamin K is needed for the formation of blood clots. This process helps the body to repair itself when damaged.

Foods rich in vitamin K
Leafy green vegetables, liver, pork, dairy products like milk and yogurt.

■ *Fat-soluble vitamins*

The B vitamins

There are several B vitamins: B1, B2, B6, B12, niacin, folic acid, biotin and pantothenic acid.

The B vitamins are important in making and releasing energy. This group of vitamins is also involved in making red blood cells, which carry oxygen around the body.

Foods rich in vitamin B

Whole grains (e.g. wheat and oats), fish and seafood, poultry and meats, eggs, dairy products such as milk and yogurt, leafy green vegetables, beans and peas, citrus fruits such as oranges.

Water-soluble vitamins travel around the body to where they are needed. If they are not used, the body disposes of them.

Vitamin C

Vitamin C is important for keeping body tissues (e.g. gums and muscles) in good shape. This vitamin helps you to heal when you cut or wound yourself. Vitamin C helps your body resist infection, or helps in the recovery process.

Foods rich in vitamin C

Citrus such as oranges; strawberries, tomatoes, broccoli, cabbage.

■ *Water-soluble vitamins*

Let's do it!

Make a list of all the food that you have eaten over the last two days.

Minerals

There are many vital minerals that the body requires for everyday life, but the ones that we will focus on are calcium and iron.

Calcium: Calcium is the top macro mineral (large mineral) when it comes to bones. Calcium helps to build strong bones and healthy teeth. It is essential that sportspeople take in enough calcium for the purpose of maintaining bone strength.

Foods rich in calcium include:

■ dairy products (e.g. milk, cheese and yogurt)

■ canned salmon and sardines with bones

■ leafy green vegetables (e.g. broccoli)

■ calcium-fortified foods (e.g. orange juice, cereals and crackers).

Iron: Every cell found in the body needs oxygen to work and iron helps the body to get this oxygen. The body needs iron to transport oxygen from the lungs to the rest of the body. Iron helps because it is important in the formation of haemoglobin, which is the part of the red blood cells that carry oxygen throughout the body.

Foods rich in iron include:

- meat, especially red meat (e.g. beef)
- tuna and salmon
- eggs
- beans
- baked potatoes with skins
- dried fruits (e.g. raisins)
- leafy green vegetables (e.g. broccoli)
- whole and enriched grains (e.g. wheat or oats).

Water

Water is one of the most important nutrients that the body requires. This is because many functions in the body rely on the presence of water. These include:

- cell function
- maintaining body temperature through sweating
- transportation of nutrients and the movement of blood
- removal of waste products via urination and breathing
- lubrication of the joints.

Water is found in many of the processed foods that the western diet is made up of, as well as in fresh fruit and vegetables. It is important to ensure that sufficient amounts are consumed to avoid the body deteriorating.

Healthy diet

Recommended nutrient intake

Not all nutrients are taken in the same amounts, as this could have a detrimental affect on health and physical fitness. For example, fat provides the most concentrated form of energy to the body but it is not necessarily the best form of energy. Most of the energy provided by fats in the western diet is supplied by saturated fats that are harmful to health. There are national recommendations that encourage individuals to consume a balanced diet encompassing all of the necessary nutrients in the correct amounts.

Eating patterns before and after competitions, events or training

Your body uses most energy when the muscles are working during breathing, digestion, circulation and exercise. A balanced diet will be different for each individual. The amount of energy, and therefore food,

Key point

The body can survive longer without food than without water.

Let's do it!

Look at the list you made of all the occasions at which you have eaten over the last two days. What foods did you eat? List them and categorise them into the different food groups. Don't forget to make a note of drinks too. Compare your list with others in your group.

Fruit and vegetables

Bread, other cereals and potatoes

Milk and dairy foods

Meat, fish and alternatives

Foods containing fat

Foods containing sugar

■ *Pie chart to show a balanced diet*

you need will depend on your age, gender and body build, and also your activity level.

If you are preparing for a competition your diet must be a planned part of your training regime. Your programme should include what you should eat and when you should eat it, and this will be different for training and competition. If this part of your programme is planned for carefully, it should result in optimum performance during training and competition.

Nutrition strategies

Recommended dietary guidelines

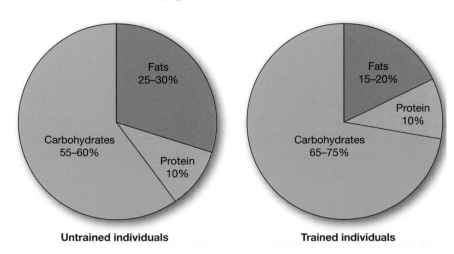

Fats
25–30%

Carbohydrates
55–60%

Protein
10%

Fats
15–20%

Protein
10%

Carbohydrates
65–75%

Untrained individuals

Trained individuals

■ *The percentage of different nutrients that should be consumed by trained and untrained individuals*

Timing of food intake

Imagine that your body is like a car. A car must have a full tank of fuel in order to reach the end of its journey. If it doesn't, it may stop before the destination has been reached. Similarly, your body needs a full tank of fuel before starting a training session. You will then be able to maintain the intensity of the training and complete the task. If your tank is only half full, you are likely to reduce the training intensity or stop before the task is completed.

The primary fuel that the body requires is the energy gained from carbohydrates. As you know, carbohydrates are stored as glycogen, which is found in the muscles, blood and liver, and fats are stored in the tissue found beneath the skin. The stores of glycogen are limited compared with fat stores.

It is important to refuel after exercise to ensure that the body maintains good levels of glycogen. The best time to refuel is directly after exercise has stopped, and for up to two hours afterwards. The refuelling process is faster during this time. It then starts to slow down, making the refuelling process less efficient. The body needs to recover from exercise – eating after exercising helps this recovery process, even if it is late at night.

Key point

The efficiency of refuelling carbohydrate can be improved by training and increasing fitness levels.

Eating for competition

Eating strategies should change in the lead up to a competition, in order for the sportsperson to reach optimum fitness. A high carbohydrate diet should be maintained to ensure that the glycogen stores remain full. Tapering, or reducing, training days before a competition can help to maintain glycogen stores for competition day. This strategy is especially important for athletes competing in events that may last for 60 minutes or more, and athletes competing in a number of heats over a short period.

Hopefully, by the morning of the athlete's competition, the previous day's eating will already have filled his or her glycogen stores. The pre-competition meal should be high in carbohydrates, low in fat, low in protein, low in fibre (i.e. not too bulky and filling), enjoyable and familiar.

Complex carbohydrates

Complex carbohydrates should be eaten as part of the pre-competition meal as these release energy slowly. Simple carbohydrates should be avoided as these release energy quickly but also stimulate the release of insulin, which can soon make the athlete feel tired.

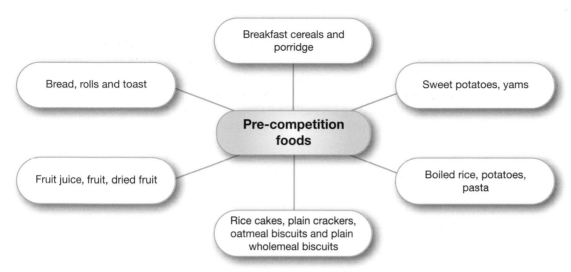

■ *Pre-competition foods*

Eating before a competition

There are many myths regarding eating before a competition. You may feel nervous on the day of the competition and not want to eat. If you avoid food altogether your liver glycogen stores will be low. These provide the body with fuel before the activity starts, so you will be starting the journey without a full tank of fuel. This could affect your performance, especially in the latter stages of an endurance event (or in one that lasts over one and a half hours).

Key points

- The liver can only store enough glycogen to last 12 hours. Eating nothing after the previous day's evening meal can result in the liver glycogen stores being depleted.

- Studies have shown that eating certain types of carbohydrates just before competition helps to delay fatigue and improve endurance. If exercise starts within about five minutes of eating, an increase in insulin will be prevented and your blood-sugar levels will remain slightly raised for longer.

- Studies have also shown that if you exercise for more than an hour, taking extra carbohydrates during training or competition may help delay the onset of fatigue and maintain exercise intensity.

Eating after a competition

After the competition or event, it is important to refuel the body with the energy that has been used for the activity. Glycogen and water stores need to be refilled for the next training session or competition.

Immediately after exercise has finished, the performer should eat foods high in complex carbohydrates. The optimum time to eat is within two hours of the exercise stopping. Foods such as baked potatoes and pasta

Let's do it!

Design a pre-competition meal for an individual who will be competing throughout the day in heats. The first heat will start at 11 o'clock. Consider the types of nutrients, the foods and the size of the meal that will make up this pre-competition feast.

dishes are great meals to eat after exercise, as long as the fat content is not too high.

It is also vitally important to ensure that the fluid that has been lost during exercise is replaced. This can be done by drinking isotonic drinks. The body can then replace its carbohydrate and water content rapidly. If water only needs to be replaced after exercise, however, then a hypotonic sports drink would be more beneficial.

Key point

If you feel thirsty you are already dehydrated.

Hydration

Hydrating your body means ensuring it has enough water for its needs. Keeping your body well hydrated can help prevent muscle fatigue and problems with health after exercise has finished. Hydration should be maintained during training sessions and for competition. The body needs to be trained to cope with continuous hydration and exercise.

Sports drinks

Sometimes glycogen levels can be best replenished through consuming carbohydrate drinks. There are various carbohydrate drinks that serve different purposes.

Sports drinks		
Type of drink	**Amount of glucose**	**Purpose of drink**
Hypotonic drinks	Low levels of glucose	Replenish fluids – hydration
Isotonic drinks	Same amount of glucose to fluid	Replenish fluid and carbohydrates
Hypertonic drinks	High levels of glucose	Replenish carbohydrate levels

Nutritional requirements for different sportspeople

Individuals following different types of sports will have different nutritional requirements.

Let's do it!

Find one example of each of the sports drinks listed above.

Endurance sportspeople require a mixture of fuels to supply the body with energy. The fuels that are supplied predominantly come from fats and muscle glycogen (carbohydrates). Due to the limited supplies of glycogen stores in the body, as exercise continues energy must be supplied by fats as well. As exercise intensity increases, there is a greater demand on energy being supplied by glycogen stores; this results in the glycogen store depleting faster as this intensity is maintained.

Nutritional requirements for different levels of intensity		
Exercise intensity	**Main fuel source**	**Percentage of the fuel being used**
Low intensity	Fat	Approximately 80%
Moderate intensity	Carbohydrate	50%
	Fat	50%
High intensity	Carbohydrate	80%

Power athletes participate in activities that last for short periods of time, lasting no longer than four minutes, with effort being close to maximum. It is very important to ensure that muscle glycogen stores are full before exercise or competition. Power events predominantly use glycogen to provide the body with energy, and this needs to be replenished after activity, especially if the training session has been hard. It takes longer to replenish the stores if muscle damage has occurred. Therefore, sufficient time is needed between events for the body to recover fully.

Nutritional supplements

The best nutritional advice is to make sure your diet is varied and balanced, and to ensure that you are consuming all the nutrients in the correct amounts. However, some groups of people are at risk of nutritional deficiencies. Such groups include:

- **athletes** – if training is not balanced with food intake, or if injury is experienced and inadequate recovery has taken place

- **young adults** – because of the social influence of fad foods, the image of certain foods, or lack of money

- **females** – because of the changes taking place during adolescence, with the onset of periods

- **vegetarians** – due to a lack in vitamins B12 and D, iron and possibly zinc. (If the diet is not balanced there will be a risk of replacing proteins with high fat foods)

- **the elderly** – may have deficiencies in vitamins and minerals due to a lack of fruit and vegetables in the diet

- **those on a low income or with a low social status** – may not be educated about balanced diet, may lack a variety of methods to cook foods and may be unable to afford certain foods (especially organic foods). This group is also more likely to smoke and drink heavily.

- **people with eating disorders** – reducing the intake of nutrients will inevitably increase the risk of disease and deficiencies

- **people who suffer from illness** – because the immune system is low, and replacing nutrients is difficult when the appetite is suppressed

- **people with allergies or intolerance to certain foods** – alternatives must be found with which the body can cope and which have the same nutritional value

- **people following calorie restricting diets** – such individuals will be consuming fewer calories than are recommended by national organisations such as the British Nutrition Foundation

- **pregnant women** – the unborn baby is feeding from the mother so the mother must replace these nutrients, to supply her own body and that of her baby.

There are different types of supplement that can be taken, and these are summarised in the table below.

Types of supplement	
Supplements	**Description**
Energy bars	A convenient way to obtain further carbohydrates during endurance exercise and immediately after exercise
Vitamin and mineral supplements	Usually taken to maintain the immune system rather than for energy during exercise – for example, vitamin C tablets
Creatine powders	Creatine is naturally produced by the body – it is used for high-intensity exercise and is stored as phosphocreatine in the muscles. It enables the body to perform maximal exercise for longer. It also speeds up recovery between exercise bouts, which results in an increase in lean muscle mass
Protein powders	These can be mixed with water or milk and are usually used by power or strength athletes during very heavy training. Protein powders stimulate the immune system and can spare the use of muscle tissue during heavy exercise

Before taking a supplement, take the following factors into account.

- Think of food first – is there any way you can supply the deficiency within your diet?

- Choose a supplement that is closer to 100% of the recommended value for the day's intake.

- Avoid supplements that have excessive amounts of vitamins and minerals, as this can offset the benefits of other minerals in the body.

- Make sure the supplement has not expired.

- Ignore claims for 'natural vitamins' as they may have been produced using synthetic ingredients.

- Avoid any vitamin or mineral that does not state on the label that it has passed the 45-minute dissolution test. This may mean that it will not be absorbed by the body.

- Optimise the absorption of the supplement by taking it just before a meal or immediately after.

Assessment activity 4: Dietary guidelines

Choose a sports performer from the categories below or use yourself to complete this activity.

■ Hockey midfielder – endurance athlete.

■ Hammer thrower – power athlete.

■ Speed skater – speed athlete.

To achieve a Pass:

1 Prepare and present dietary guidelines for your chosen sports performer with suitable meal plans over a two-week period. (P5)

To achieve a Merit you must achieve the Pass criteria and:

2 Prepare and present dietary guidelines for your sports performer with suitable meal plans over a two-week period. *Explain* the dietary guidelines and meal plans that you have selected for this sports performer. (M4)

4.4 Understand the psychological factors that affect sports training and performance

Factors

Motivation

The term motivation describes the level at which an individual is directed and influenced to complete a task. Motivation can be:

- **intrinsic** – which means coming from within yourself
- **extrinsic** – which means coming from someone or somewhere else
- **arousal and anxiety** – which means affected by the energy with which a task is carried out; the stronger the arousal, the greater the effort put into the task.

Intrinsic and extrinsic motivation

Intrinsic motivation	Extrinsic motivation
Performer works hard and motivates him- or herself to develop the best-possible performance; self-directed or determined	Performer works hard to achieve the best possible performance because of rewards that come from external sources Rewards can be tangible (i.e. things you can touch) and non-tangible (i.e. things you can't touch): - tangible rewards include trophies, money, medals, badges and certificates - non-tangible rewards include positive comments (from teacher, coach, peers, spectators) media recognition, winning/glory and social status

Extrinsic motivation can be both useful and harmful to performance. Rewards may become meaningless or worthless if they are over-used. On the other hand, if there are not enough rewards, the sports performer may no longer see the worth of performance.

There is a link between intrinsic and extrinsic motivation. A sports performer may think of extrinsic rewards as a way of controlling his or her behaviour, rather than praising or rewarding it. Good behaviour does not necessarily lead to successful performance.

If you are planning to increase intrinsic motivation through the use of extrinsic rewards:

- make sure that rewards are dependent on performance
- give praise both verbally and non-verbally

- provide a variety of rewards during training and competition-type situations

- provide opportunities for the sports performer to make decisions on performance

- encourage the negotiation of goals, to match up with a performer's skill level.

Let's do it!

List all the reasons why you started to participate in a particular sport. Then list the reasons why you have continued with the sport. Have your reasons changed?

■ *A sports performer's desire to win may be a strong motivator*

Arousal and anxiety

Taking part in a competition can give you a mixture of feelings that either excite you or cause you to become anxious. Placing stress on your body, either mental or physical, changes your arousal levels. This in turn affects the way you process incoming information and the quality of your output, or final performance.

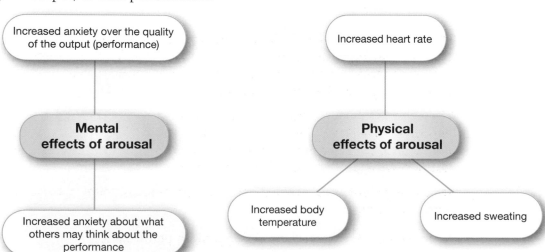

Increased anxiety over the quality of the output (performance)

Increased heart rate

Mental effects of arousal

Physical effects of arousal

Increased body temperature

Increased sweating

Increased anxiety about what others may think about the performance

■ *Effects of arousal*

Think about it

Get together with your group. Discuss your personal experiences of taking part in competitions. How did you feel? Did you suffer from any of the mental or physical effects described? How did this affect your performance?

Personality

Personality is a major influencing factor in sport. This does not mean to say that an individual must fall into just one category to become a top sportsperson. The traits that make up different personality types are relatively stable for each individual but they could change in a changing environment, even though personality traits are said to be innate.

Individuals can be divided into two groups according to the personality traits that they show.

■ **Introverts** (or type A) are more inward in their behaviour, and do not require high levels of arousal to achieve optimum performance. Introverts often favour sports that are classed as individual, and that require precision for success. Introverts often have low pain thresholds.

■ **Extroverts** (or type B) require high levels of stimulation to achieve the optimum performance. They thrive in highly competitive situations, where there is a great amount of noise and input from the audience. Extroverts often favour team sports rather than individual sports. Extroverts often have high pain thresholds.

Let's do it!

Look at the list of athletes below.
■ *Jonny Wilkinson – rugby.*
■ *Andrew Flintoff – cricket.*
■ *Paula Radcliffe – athletics.*

Consider the sports that they are involved in and the media attention that they may experience. What personality type do you think each has? Explain your choice, giving examples of their behaviour to justify your reasons.

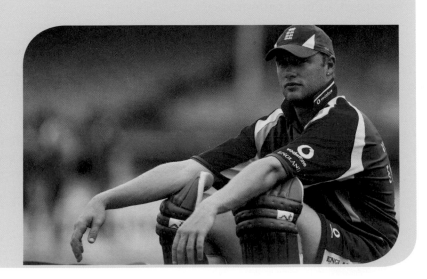

Concentration

Any performer participating in sport is constantly being bombarded with different information. A performer's ability to cope with this depends on his or her experience, either in performance or through training under similar conditions.

When a performer processes information, he or she has to do two things:

1 make sense of it
2 decide on the best action to take.

To carry out these two tasks, the incoming information first has to be filtered. Irrelevant information is discarded, leaving only relevant information to be dealt with. If this process is not carried out efficiently, it can hinder decision-making. Each of us can only handle one thing at a time – this is termed limited channel capacity, or limited concentration capacity. An overload of information will hinder performance.

A sports performer will go through different phases to achieve efficiency in the execution of a skill. When you learn a new skill, concentration on all aspects of the skill may be given equal billing. With practice, each part of the skill will become second nature, and more concentration can be placed on the performance of the skill. Experienced players perform skills automatically. This means they are able to attend to other information, such as changes in the opposition's performance, more efficiently than a beginner.

Let's do it!

List the tasks or skills that you perceive to be strongest in your performance. Then list the tasks or skills that you think are weakest. Discuss these lists with your coach, teacher or team players.

Effects

Short-term effects on training and performance

Targets should be set during each session by both the coach and the performer. These targets should be realistic and achievable, but also challenging. This will help increase the motivation of the sports performer to move towards improvements.

Long-term effects on training and performance

The small steps that are used during each session should aim towards the long-term plan of the performer. These goals should be set from the testing that occurred before training started and measured during each session for progress. The principles of training highlighted earlier on in this unit (see pages 171–6) will help provide a good base to see changes in performance occur.

Case study

Kerry has been coaching a women's rugby team for the past seven years. The team is facing relegation if it does not win their last game of the season. The team has lost quite a few key players over the season due to injury, work commitments, and pregnancy. However, Kerry has two weeks to build the confidence of individual players as well as the team as a whole to ensure that they achieve their goal of staying in their current league. Kerry also needs to be thinking of the plans for the next season, whether the team goes down to the next league or stays up in the current league.

Kerry has had ladies joining the team at the start of the season but they are new to the game of rugby and have only played about four of the league games over the course of the season. There is good news: two new but experienced players have joined the team over the last week. Both players are a little nervous about joining a new team, as they would not like to push any current players out of position and upset the spirit of the team.

Now answer the following questions:

1 What methods can Kerry use to motivate the following players to perform in the last game of the season?

Inexperienced players	Experienced players	New players

2 List three short-term goals that Kerry can set for each of the following groups of players in the team:

Inexperienced players	Experienced players	New players
1		
2		
3		

3 Set three long-term goals that Kerry can use for each of the following groups of players in the new season:

Inexperienced players	Experienced players	New players
1		
2		
3		

Assessment activity 5: Psychological factors that affect performance

To achieve a Pass:

1 *Identify* the psychological factors that can affect sports training and performance and what the effects on sports training and performance could be. (P6)

To achieve a Merit you must achieve the Pass criteria and:

2 *Describe* the psychological factors that can affect sports training and performance and what the effects on sports training and performance could be. (M5)

To achieve a Distinction you must achieve the Pass and Merit criteria and:

3 *Analyse* the psychological factors that can affect sports training and performance. (D3)

Summary

Preparing for sport and training can be a big commitment, and life-changing. Changes to your sleeping, drinking, eating and training patterns need to be planned and implemented over a prolonged period of time – optimum performance does not happen by accident!

Understanding the factors that affect performance is essential to ensure proper planning and training, bringing you that one step closer to achieving your highest potential.

Check what you know!

Look back over this unit and see if you can answer the following questions.

1. Flexibility is one component of fitness. What are the other components of physical and skill-related fitness?

2. Identify a test for each of the components of fitness highlighted in question 1.

3. Explain what the terms validity, reliability and standardisation mean.

4. Explain the lifestyles factors that affect training and sport performance.

5. Evaluate the effects of lifestyle factors on sports performance.

6. List the considerations that must be taken into account when designing a 12-week training programme.

7. List the six principles of training.

8. Name the two main fuels that are used for energy in the body.

9. Give three examples of foods containing the following nutrients: proteins, fats, carbohydrates, vitamin A, C and K, and iron.

10. Explain what dietary guidelines are, and how they can be used to design meal plans.

11. Explain what is meant by anxiety and arousal.

12. How can anxiety and arousal affect sports performance during competition?

5 Planning and Leading Sports Activities

Introduction

A good sports leader can direct certain sporting situations or sports sessions to help guide and motivate groups of people on skills, regulations and health and safety for example. Sports leadership is how a sports leader achieves their aims of a session or competition.

Successful sports leaders combine good performance and leadership skills. This helps achieve both personal and team goals. Sports leaders possess common factors as well as specific skills and qualities that make them successful in sporting situations. A good sports leader will show leadership qualities through their planning, delivery and evaluation of each sports session.

This unit looks at ways you can prepare for leading a group in a practical sports session. It suggests ways to improve your delivery and looks at how you can evaluate your own performance as a leader once the session has finished.

▶ Continued from previous page

How you will be assessed

This unit will be assessed by an internal assignment that will be set and marked by the staff at your centre. It may be sampled as well by your centre's External Verifier as part of Edexcel's on-going quality procedures. The assignment is designed to allow you to show your understanding of the unit outcomes. These relate to what you should be able to do after completing this unit.

Your assessment could be in the form of:

- video recorded presentations
- case studies
- role plays
- written assignments.

After completing this unit you should be able to achieve the following learning outcomes.

1 Understand the skills, qualities and responsibilities associated with successful sports leadership.

2 Be able to plan and lead an activity session.

3 Be able to review your planning and leadership of sports activities.

4 Be able to assist in the planning and leading of a sports event.

5 Be able to review your planning and leadership of sports events.

5.1 Understand the skills, qualities and responsibilities associated with successful sports leadership

All sports require leaders. Good sports leaders inspire and encourage the team at vital moments in a game and provide a good role model. As an effective sports leader, it is part of your role to develop the performance of each individual in the group. It is also important to encourage cohesion, so that your group of individuals works well as a team.

Skills

People who develop and encourage sports at grass roots level, helping coaches and teams, are also sports leaders in their own right. The role of these sports leaders is to develop and encourage young people and adults to participate, and continue to participate in all types of sports. Sports leaders need to possess certain skills to help in leading groups:

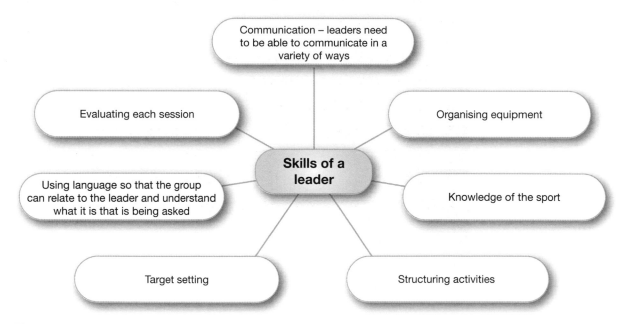

■ *Skills of a leader*

Communication

If you can communicate at various levels you will be able to bridge the gap between players, other coaches, the opposition and officials. You can communicate:

■ using verbal language

- using non-verbal language, such as facial expressions and bodily gestures
- by listening.

Communication skills are essential for any leader to have, develop and use. A sports leader must have a clear voice and a command over the language that dominates the performers in the sport being delivered. Many people are chosen to be a captain or a coach in their sport due to their experience as a player at a very high level. However, although they may have an excellent understanding of the sport, if they cannot communicate effectively they will not be able to pass this knowledge on.

Delivering information effectively is important, but to do this, you must also listen. Listening carefully to performers as they acquire skills may help you to improve the performance of the player. Listening to performers' experiences of playing may clarify areas of difficulty that you, as a leader, may not be able to see. Communication is a two-way process for the improvement of performance.

■ *Non-verbal communication*

Key points

Effective communication skills are essential to:

- pass on information about what players must do for each skill
- use appropriate language to direct players to improve performance
- provide further information that helps the organisation of the sport to run smoothly off the training or playing ground.

Organisation of equipment

Organisational skills are essential to the sports leader. As a sports leader or member of a coaching team, it will be your responsibility to organise:

- each training session (including facilities and equipment)
- competitions
- paperwork, which may be essential if performers are to compete
- health and safety
- the evaluation of each meeting for the performer and their parents.

Key point

Time-management skills are essential for a good sports leader. You need to allow time to plan your session. Also, your plan needs to include:

- the time the session starts
- the duration of the session
- the duration of each component activity or task.

During the session, you then need to stick to your plan as far as possible, to ensure you cover everything and achieve your aim.

Knowledge

A good sports leader should have detailed knowledge of the sport that they are involved in. This will help in guiding others through the sport when they experience various situations, whether it be as a sports leader who is performing alongside other players or as a sports leader who guides through coaching.

It is essential that you master the tactical and technical aspects of the sport being delivered, these include:

- a good understanding of its laws and rules
- sport-specific knowledge
- knowledge of basic fitness training and health and safety issues
- knowledge of current first aid techniques, and, if possible, an up-to-date qualification
- basic knowledge of the care and prevention of sports injuries.

As more coaching experience is gained, a personal 'knowledge bank' is created. This will help when making decisions. Playing experience is also important – it will give you, as a sports leader, a vision for the game or sport that cannot be taught in a classroom environment. As a performer, you have an understanding of what it is like to be a player and what it is like to be coached – in other words, you will be able to put yourself into another performer's shoes.

Activity structure

It is obvious that some of the knowledge you will need as a sports leader will be gained through experience. This experience can be specific to the sport, or may be gained through coaching and leading other groups. Some elements of coaching remain the same in any sport for example, planning, preparation, organisation, evaluation and review of the session or programme.

Target setting

It is very important that a leader sets targets that the team or an individual can follow. This should be done in conjunction with the individuals involved, for example, the performer, the coach, the captain, and possibly parents for performers who are under sixteen years of age. These targets should be designed so that they challenge the performer in a realistic manner. They should be aimed at the correct level of the performer or the team, and be specific to the sport, position or the competition. Targets should also have a purpose, such as to improve performance.

Use of language

Effective leaders are usually confident and this can be seen through the language they use. Language can influence how a performer behaves.

Language is a positive tool, and if used well can help to:

- demonstrate respect for performers
- develop an understanding of what is being set
- expand the knowledge of the sport
- explain rules and regulations for a sport or organisation/club
- increase self-esteem of others in the group
- show the value of others.

The language should be appropriate for the group, as inappropriate language could offend. The level of the language used should also be set at the appropriate level for the group. For example, it should not be too technical for a group of beginners in a sport, but neither should it be aimed at a level that the group, team or individual feels that they can not understand. The use of appropriate language can enable performers to understand their role.

Evaluation of each session

A good leader always evaluates a session that he or she has led. The evaluation of a session helps to highlight what was successful about the session as well as what was weak.

The evaluation should be carried out soon after the session has been completed so that essential information is not lost for the planning of the following session. All information, whether good or bad, should be used to help the success of the next session. (The evaluation of each session is discussed later in this unit.)

Let's do it!

Using the information about the skills of a leader, briefly explain the headings that have been used for the spidergram of 'Skills of a leader' (page 199). Give your own examples of where you may have seen these skills being used by a sports leader in your sport.

Think about it

Get together with other members of your group. Can you think of an occasion when:

■ *you had to change your plans when you were leading a session*

■ *you attended a session where the leader had to change his or her plans?*

1 *Discuss your experiences.*
2 *Why were the plans changed?*
3 *How were they changed?*
4 *Did the changed plans work? If not, why not?*

Qualities

■ *Qualities of a leader*

Appearance

A good standard of appearance will gain you the respect of the group. However, it is essential to wear appropriate clothing for the activity that you are involved in, to ensure that you are safe. Wearing baggy clothes or large jewellery that could hinder your movements can be a hazard in some sports. Your appearance as a sports leader is not only dependent on what you are wearing but how you present yourself to your group. For example, you need to show your confidence without being a show-off.

Leadership style

The way you approach specific tasks will determine how effective you are as a leader. Such tasks include planning your activity, delivering it and providing opportunities for feedback. Your success as a sports leader will be measured in terms of your team members achieving a set goal.

Leaders in sport all have different styles. These styles vary because of the personality of the leaders and also because of the demands and requirements of the sport.

There are many different ways that sports leaders can be effective and successful. Different types of leader suit different situations. The table below lists some of the factors that you need to consider when you lead a team.

Task	Team	Individual
What needs to be done?	How do the group interact as a team?	How are the needs of each individual being met?
	How does your team benefit from your leadership style?	

Three leadership styles have been identified: autocratic, democratic and laissez-faire.

Leadership style	Description	Benefits	Disadvantages
Autocratic	Does not involve others in the decision-making process. Task oriented rather than team oriented	Decision making can be carried out quickly. Effective in team sports with large numbers.	Task becomes leader centred rather than performer centred. May not bring out full potential of individual team members Can be very inflexible
Democratic	Involves others in the decision-making process. Is interested in the team members as individuals, developing close personal relationships	Less formal approach to leading a team. Team members more likely to develop	Decision making is time consuming, and may not be quick enough under pressure. Problems may occur in teams of large numbers
Laissez-faire	Acts as a consultant rather than a decision maker – the initiative is left to others	Flexible approach. Encourages others to take the initiative	Lack of structure to the task. Lack of direction or co-ordination. Risk of poor decision making

Case study

Leilah

Leilah is eight years old and has been swimming for the last 18 months for the local swimming club. At present she is attending her club twice a week, at the weekends. Leilah enjoys all sports and participates in gymnastics and football at school. Leilah strives to be the best in any activity she gets involved in, and enjoys the praise that comes with her successes.

During training for swimming, Leilah's coach:

■ does not dress in the formal club uniform

■ praises the children in every attempt that they make in the tasks that are set

■ does not highlight the mistakes that the children may make

■ allows the children to dictate what they will do for the session.

Leilah enjoys the sessions and always comes back very happy. However, there has been no evidence of improvements in Leilah's performance in the time trials that she enters.

Now answer the following questions.

1 Describe the leadership style of Leilah's swimming coach, giving examples from the case study as evidence to support your description.

2 Working in pairs, develop a role play situation where you are the mother of Leilah and your partner is the swimming coach

■ Leilah's mother would like to know the reasons why Leilah is not making progress.

■ The swimming coach will defend the approach that he is using to coach Leilah.

Let the rest of the group observe the points that you have made and place their comments beside yours for comparison.

Personality

Sports leaders are usually confident in their approach to the sport that they are involved in. They are also confident about organising others and giving advice and guidance.

Introvert and extrovert personality types

Personalities fall into two categories, extrovert and introvert (for a description of these two personality types, see Unit 4 Preparation for Sport, page 149). There is a strong link between an individual's personality type and the type of sport he or she is attracted to. Extrovert personalities are often found in team-based sports, where situations are unpredictable and can change quickly. Introvert personalities tend to be found in sports that require low levels of stimulation but require high levels of accuracy in delivery. (This does not mean, however, that introverts only participate in individual sports and extroverts only stay in team game sports.)

Your personality type can be a key factor to success as a sports leader. Your leadership style will be determined by the type of personality you possess – you are likely to lead in a way that suits your personality type. Additionally, the personality types of the individuals you are leading will influence your leadership style.

Think about it

1 List the common factors for each of the personality types, introvert and extrovert.

2 State which personality category you think you fall into, giving sporting examples why.

3 Explain why different personality types may be attracted to different sports.

To be a good team leader, you need to be positive. Leaders need to motivate their teams and a positive approach is the best way to achieve this. Team members feel more comfortable with a leader who is easy to get along with and pleasant to be around. A sense of humour can help to keep players interested and focused during practice sessions and matches. It also helps to ease the tension that can arise from intense sports sessions.

As a sports leader, part of your role will be to impart knowledge and advice to team members. In order to do this, you need to have a positive relationship with your team mates. You also need to be positive about the area of delivery you are commenting upon but remember that this does not mean only offering positive comments. The team will not be able to improve if you concentrate only on their strengths and neglect to highlight weaknesses. Such comments can be put in a positive way, by giving constructive advice and offering solutions.

A further role of a sports leader is to help other performers to achieve their goals. You can directly influence a team member's performance by discussing it with them. You can also influence performance by being a role model or inspiration in their sport. For example, Pelé (in football) and Steve Redgrave (in rowing) were the world's best in their sports. Each continues to be an ambassador for his sport, showing great commitment and the positive attitude that is required for all sports.

Leaders can be chosen either by the management structure of the club or by the players and are usually the captain of the team. However, other senior players within the team can also be leaders. For example, Martin Corry was the captain of the English rugby team in the Six Nations in 2006, but the selection of experienced players such as Lawrence Dallaglio and Matt Dawson provided good support, advice and leadership to help Martin Corry.

Remember that as a captain of a team you can be influential as a leader but this may only be on the playing field and not in the area of planning and delivery of a sports session.

Enthusiasm, motivation, humour, confidence

Being enthusiastic and motivated is contagious! These qualities rub off on sports performers, other leaders, members of the coaching team and spectators. The coach or sports leader often creates the 'spark' that keeps the team members moving and creative. Motivating performers can be very difficult at times but there are a number of ways sports leaders can help this process.

Some of the ways that performers can be motivated are:

■ setting challenging but realistic goals for individuals and the team

■ measuring targets, so that performers know their achievements

■ rewarding performers for their hard work in training and competition

■ providing useful feedback at the appropriate times.

A good sports leader will enable a session to have time for laughter. Learning should be a joyful experience and having a good sense of humour is essential. You should create an atmosphere where individuals should be willing to look at their performance and not fear their mistakes. However, it is vitally important not to ridicule any group member or encourage others to do so. Having fun should never be at the expense of a performer's mistakes!

Confidence is important so that the participants trust in what is being said and what they have been asked to do.

Think about it

In pairs, discuss the sports leaders you have come into contact with.

1 *Who have you most admired?*
2 *Why?*
3 *With your partner, list the qualities that you think make a strong leader.*
4 *State why you have listed these qualities for a good leader.*

■ *Responsibilities of a sports leader*

Key point

Some of the key factors to success as a sports leader are:

■ the ability to communicate
■ a positive attitude
■ enthusiasm
■ concern for others
■ good sense of humour.

Responsibilities

Professional conduct

A sports leader will agree to a series of statements that outline the do's and don'ts of behaviour during a training session. These do's and don'ts will be set for all in the group but the sports leader will be expected to follow and reinforce them with experienced performers and newcomers. Examples of professional conduct could be sporting ethics or respecting the rules and regulations of their sport and club.

Health and safety

If sports leaders are to take responsibility for a training session then they are also taking responsibility for the group during that time. They should carry out the necessary checks of the equipment and facility to ensure that all performers are safe during physical activity.

Check equipment at three stages.

1 Before it is set up.
2 Once is has been assembled.
3 Just before it is used.

Check for the following.

1 Damage to the working parts of the equipment.
2 Missing parts of the equipment that could cause damage.
3 Lack of function.

Any damage that you note must be reported immediately. Repair should only be carried out according to the manufacturer's guidelines, or by a qualified technician. If this is not possible, the equipment must be removed from use.

■ *Damaged equipment*

Insurance

Sports leaders must possess the necessary insurance to participate in a sport as well as lead a training session. Insurance is there to protect both leaders and participants in sport.

Legal obligations

There are various legal requirements which you, as a sports leader, are required to know about. You also have a responsibility to take steps to enforce the legislation. The legislation is found in various Acts passed by Parliament, to ensure the safety of groups of individuals undertaking physical activity.

Child protection

Child protection is becoming an increasing concern for all areas of physical activity. Children need to be protected and clubs have a duty to ensure that policies and training are put in place to encourage this safety. It is recommended that all leaders in the majority of sports carry out sports-specific child protection workshops to be fully aware of the issues surrounding coaching and leading performers under the age of 18 years.

Children's Act 1989

This Act concerns any provision of leisure, recreation and play services for children. It affects planning, delivery and management of these services. The Children Act enforces duties that must be carried out by the service providers. These duties include:

- providing care services and supervised activities for children

- publishing adequate information about these services

- reviewing and monitoring these services and consulting with the appropriate bodies (i.e. those bodies that deal with the protection of children)

- ensuring that registration is completed for all day-care and supervised activities for children under the age of eight years.

Before a service can be registered, the suitability of the organisation, all its employees and its premises need to be assessed. Organisations can seek help from the Child Protection Unit of the Institute of Sport and Recreation Management (ISRM). This organisation provides practical recommendations for service providers for children.

Data Protection Act 1998

Any business or organisation that holds personal information or details on staff or individuals using its facilities may be required to register with the Data Protection Registrar. The Data Protection Registrar places the business or the organisation on a public register of data users. It also issues the organisation with a code of practice, which must be adhered to. The code of practice states that:

- information must be kept in a secure location

- information must be accurate and relevant to the needs of the organisation

- if information is requested by an individual about his or her details, it must be supplied.

Activity Centre Act (Young Person's Safety Act) 1995

This Act requires that all facilities providing adventure activities for children under the age of 18 years have a licence. The Act applies to facilities run by local authorities and commercial businesses. It sets strict guidelines about:

- the qualifications staff should hold
- operating procedures and emergency procedures
- appropriate ratio of staff to children participating in any activity.

The licence aims to give assurance that good and safe practice is followed by the organisation holding it. This has had two beneficial results.

- Facilities of this type have gained a good reputation.
- There are now greater opportunities for young people to experience adventure activities.

■ *The Activity Centre Act ensures the safety of young people taking part in adventure activities*

Equality

All performers are different and each has a variety of needs. However, whatever the differences that performers come with are, they should have the same opportunities to develop and improve in sport. Therefore, sports leaders should be working in clubs without prejudice and to eliminate discrimination.

Rules and regulations

As stated in the professional conduct of sports leaders, sports leaders should encourage all performers to learn and follow the rules and regulations of the sport, organisation and club that they have chosen to follow. Sports leaders also have a responsibility to inform the performers of the consequences if they infringe these rules and regulations.

Ethics and values

Ethics and values should be developed to enhance the participation of others. They should feel secure and happy in the club that they have joined. A sports leader has the responsibility of encouraging this in every individual in the group.

Assessment activity 1: Using skills and personal qualities to lead activities

To achieve a Pass:

1 *Describe* the skills, qualities and responsibilities that are needed by a successful sports leader. To help you, use two examples of successful sports leaders using these skills, qualities and responsibilities. (P1)

To achieve a Merit you must achieve the Pass criteria and:

2 *Explain* the skills, qualities and responsibilities that are needed by a successful sports leader. Compare successful sports leaders using these skills, qualities and responsibilities. (M1)

To achieve a Distinction you must achieve the Pass and Merit criteria and:

3 *Evaluate* the effectiveness of the skills and qualities of two different sports leaders in the same sport. (D1)

5.2 Be able to plan and lead an activity session

A successful sports session depends upon good preparation. Being prepared will help you to cope with last-minute problems with the session, such as changes in weather, lack of equipment or changes in numbers. If your sports session is well organised, your group will be able to enjoy an activity where every eventuality has been considered. The session will be fun, fluent and educational.

The lesson plan you design must be realistic and suitable for the group you are leading. At the planning stage of a session, you need to be thinking about:

- aims, objectives and target setting the purpose of the session
- the different requirements of members of the group – making sure you have information about special medical, cultural or educational needs
- the facility, and any resources or equipment you may need
- how to sequence activities
- your target group
- preparation – e.g. carrying out checks of the venue and equipment
- clothing and equipment – ensuring the athletes' clothing is appropriate and that they are wearing the required protective clothing; providing adequate and appropriate equipment.

Plan

There are several considerations that need to be made when planning for a sports session.

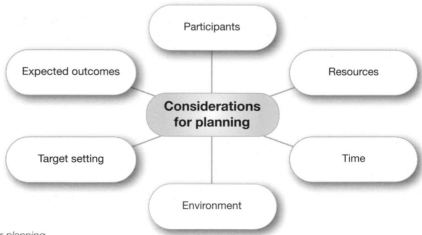

■ Considerations for planning

Participants

It is important to collect information about your group, such as:

- the age range
- gender mix
- the level of ability
- how big the group is
- any relevant medical information
- specific needs of the group or its members.

The design of the session plan must be realistic for the sport and the group that is being coached. The type of delivery and leadership style you adopt will also be affected by the size of your group and the age range you are coaching. You need to be aware that there are rules and regulations set by law that state the required ratio of leaders to children of certain ages. Some sports also require leaders to have attended a child protection course if leading children under the age of 16 years.

Sports leaders work with various groups of people, including children, the elderly, individuals with specific needs and people with different cultural backgrounds. When you are planning and delivering sports activities you will need to take the needs of the different individuals in your group into account.

There are many common factors in the development of children and many sports activities have been specially adapted to take these into account. It is important that you are aware of the limitations of the children whom you are leading, so that you can avoid unsafe practice during the session. Children's physiological make-up is different from adults, especially with regard to their body temperature regulation. For example, children need to be encouraged to drink fluids on a regular basis to avoid dehydration.

Although there are many similarities, there are also big differences between children as they develop. These differences are both psychological and physical. A sports environment will often highlight the special emotional and physical needs of individual children. When you lead children in sporting activities it is important that you are aware of each child's individual needs.

Teenagers

During adolescence, both males and females see changes in their bodies that are also visible to others.

Changes during adolescence include:

- increased muscle growth
- emotional outbursts due to an imbalance of hormones released
- bigger bone structures.

Specific changes in males during adolescence include:

- shoulders become broader
- facial and body hair growth.

Specific changes in females during adolescence include:

- hips widen to prepare for child birth
- some irrational behaviour and outbursts, due to an imbalance of hormones being released
- menstrual cycle begins
- greater deposits of fat tissue around the body
- breast development.

Not everyone develops at the same rate or in the same way. The way in which an adolescent deals with the changes in his or her body is influenced by:

- **external factors** – for example, peer group, family or coaches
- **internal factors** – for example, the hormones that are released during puberty, which can lead to emotional outbursts of withdrawal from an activity.

Children who were well co-ordinated before the onset of puberty may become less so afterwards, due to changes in their body structures. As a leader, you will need to be aware of this. Make sure you have prepared contingency plans, to ensure that all participants experience some success. This will also lessen the focus on these changes by others in the group.

You need to consider these factors when leading a group of teenagers in a sports session. Ensure that you:

- are aware of the physical differences between members of the group – don't avoid the subject but encourage tolerance of differences
- support children who show clumsy tendencies.

50+ groups

A 50 year old can often do as much as a 30 year old, depending on his or her personal level of fitness. It is important that you remember this, and treat this age group with respect. However, there are certain conditions that individuals in this age group become increasingly prone to.

Although not all individuals in this category will be suffering from these problems, you still need to consider them. Some, though not all, of your clients may need approval from their GPs to attend sports classes. This information can be gained from the medical history forms that all individuals must complete before participating in sport and exercise. Some clients may also be referred to an approved sports facility that caters for referral patients from the hospital. Facilities will have procedures in place for these types of initiative, so such information will be made available to you, as the sports leader.

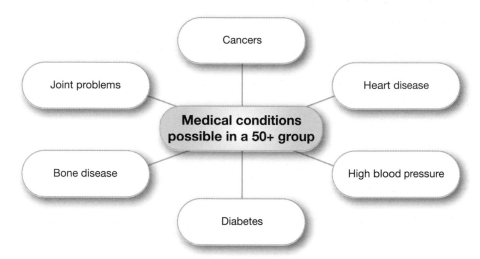

■ *Medical conditions possible in a 50+ group*

Mixed or single sex groups

The choice of an individual to attend a session that only has a single sex participating must be respected and catered for. Women-only sessions may require a female leader, as well as female-only participants.

When you work with mixed groups, you need to be aware of different considerations for males and females, especially during and after puberty. It is also important not to stereotype individuals on the grounds of their gender. Certain sports are dominated by one gender, for example football is dominated by males. This does not mean, however, that only males play football, or that all males are more aggressive and competitive than females.

Think about it

Do you think that there should also be male-only sessions? If so, why? If not, why not?

 Let's do it!

Instruct your partner in a particular sports skill. Use different methods to do this, for example, using demonstration or verbal instruction. Record how well the performance went using the different methods of instruction.

Each member of the group must complete a medical history form before participating in any activity. If the individual is under 18 years old, his or her parent or guardian must give signed permission for him or her to participate.

INCORPORATING PAR-Q
(A questionnaire for people aged 15 to 69)

Name: _____ Age: _____ Sex: _____

Address: _____ Postcode: _____

Occupation/Course: _____ Tel Wk: _____ Tel Hm: _____

Person to be contacted
in case of accident: _____ Tel Wk. _____ Tel Hm. _____

SECTION 1

Common sense is your best guide when you answer these questions. Please read the questions carefully and answer each one honestly. ✓ Tick – YES or NO.

YES	NO	
☐	☐	Has your doctor ever said that you have a heart condition and that you should only do physical activity recommended by a doctor?
☐	☐	Do you feel pain in your chest when you do physical activity?
☐	☐	In the past month, have you had chest pain when you were not doing physical activity?
☐	☐	Do you lose your balance because of dizziness or do you ever lose consciousness?
☐	☐	Do you have a bone or joint problem that could be made worse by a change in your physical activity?
☐	☐	Is your doctor currently prescribing drugs for your blood pressure or heart condition?
☐	☐	Do you know of any other reason why you should not do physical activity?

If you answered YES to one or more questions:
Talk with your doctor by phone or in person BEFORE you start becoming much more physically active or BEFORE you have a fitness appraisal. Tell your doctor about the PAR-Q and which questions you have answered YES to.

- You may be able to do any activity you like as long as you start slowly and build up gradually. Or, you may need to restrict your activities to those which are safe for you. Talk with your doctor about the kinds of activities you wish to participate in and follow his/her advice.
- Find out which community programmes are safe for you to follow.

SECTION 2

Have you ever had or do you have any of the following?		
☐ Muscular pain	☐ Diabetes	☐ Epilepsy
☐ Arthritis	☐ Asthma	☐ Are you pregnant?

Have you ever had or do you have any major injuries to any of the following areas?				
☐ Neck	☐ Back	☐ Knee	☐ Ankles	☐ Other

If you "✓" please ask instructor for exercise class or programme guidance before starting.
If your health changes so that you then answer YES to any of the above questions, tell your fitness or health professional. Ask whether you should change your physical plan.

What exercise type have you been doing recently?

Intensity: Hard – Medium – Light   How long?   How often?

Signature: _____ Date: _____

■ *Example of a medical history form*

Special needs

Special needs could refer to medical needs, for example allergies to sun creams, fluids or medication. It could also refer to any special educational needs (SEN). Some performers learn differently and, as a result, you will need to adjust the way in which you deliver information. Performers can learn through instruction, through demonstration, or through a combination of the two. Some performers learn better if a demonstration is given first, followed by instruction. Others learn better with a number of small demonstrations, followed by feedback at the end of the performance.

Resources

It is essential for a good sports leader to check the resources and equipment that will be used for a sports session. These checks are to ensure that all resources and equipment are safe to use and should be carried out before the session starts. It is also important that you have sufficient knowledge of the venue that you use, for example the location of the fire exits, toilets, first aid kit and nearest telephone. It will also be very important that you have full knowledge of the equipment that you will be using, as incorrect use can increase the risk of injury.

Time

A good sports leader will always allow sufficient time before the session begins to make the necessary checks of the area, facility and provision. Organising any complicated equipment prior to the start of the session can also save time during the session. The members of your group will want to participate, not watch their leader organising the props!

The environment

If your sport takes place outdoors, weather conditions can hinder the delivery of a session. Rain and wind can increase the risk of injury, as can performing sport in the sun. You need to consider these factors and take appropriate steps. For example, during hot weather, encourage the performers to provide their own fluids, sun cream and hats; during cold weather, ensure that performers are wearing the correct footwear and outdoor clothing.

If your sport takes place indoors, book your facility in good time. Just before the event, check again that the facility will be available. A double-booked facility at the last minute can cause real problems. Check the facility before the session, to ensure that it is appropriate and safe to use.

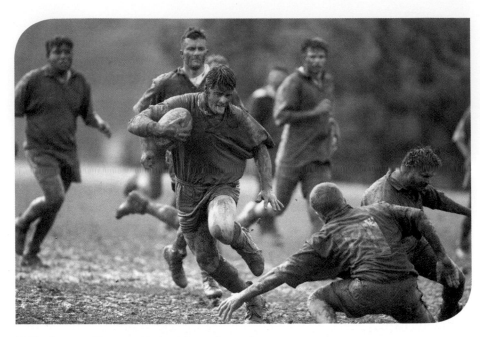

■ *Weather conditions can hinder delivery of a session*

Target setting for planning a session

The SMART model can be used for setting individual targets for performers. Each training session and competition should provide you with the information on the strengths and weaknesses of a performer in specific situations. This can be used to set targets for the performer.

Expected outcomes

Your sports session might be going to plan but then something significant changes at the last minute.

Such changes might include:

■ too many or too few members turning up to your session

■ a double-booked facility

■ an adverse change in the weather if you are working outside

■ not having enough equipment

■ equipment and facilities not being up to standard

■ the need for specialist support or help.

You need to ensure that:

■ you have thought carefully about what could go wrong

■ you have done everything you can to prevent things going wrong – for example, checking that the facility is available, or ringing up the participants the night before to check they are all still coming.

■ you have an alternative action plan – in other words, a plan to help you cope with things that might go wrong.

Let's do it!

Draw a plan of the area in which your sport takes place. Include ten unsafe obstacles and problems that would need to be considered if you were about to lead a group of children in a physical activity. Swap drawings with a partner. Try to identify the problems on your partner's drawing.

Assessment activity 2: Plan and lead a sports activity

A variety of skills, qualities and responsibilities have been discussed previously in this chapter. You now need to show your understanding by leading a skill using some of these factors.

To achieve a Pass:

Using teacher support, complete the following stages.

1 Choose a sport that you have some knowledge and experience of.
2 Now choose a skill that is used in this sport that you feel that you could help a partner learn.
3 Write down the technical information that you will need to know about the skill.
4 Write down the considerations that you will need to make to ensure that your partner will be safe when performing the skill.
5 Now lead your partner in this skill.
6 Ask your partner to make comparisons between the information from this chapter and how effective your skills, qualities and responsibilities were in leading the sports skill. (P2)

To achieve a Merit you must achieve the Pass criteria *independently*. (M2)

Lead

An activity can be led by giving verbal directions, or providing a visual guide, for example correctly demonstrating the skill or the behaviour that needs to be repeated.

An individual who leads a physical activity needs to have sufficient knowledge of the activity that is being carried out. If an individual is not the best person to demonstrate a skill there are a number of ways that the skill can still be observed.

- A member of the group demonstrates the skill.
- A guest performer demonstrates the skill.
- The skill is shown by video.
- The skill is shown on a poster, section by section.

However, it is essential that, when leading an activity, further information can be provided to reinforce the learning by the group. The information that is provided should be at the required level of the group, including the appropriate level of language. It is important that the group feel that they are lead at the appropriate level. They should not feel out of their depth due to complex instructions, or patronized by language that is considered too young.

It is not enough just to know about the sports and the activities. You also need to know how to control the group. In particular you need to know how to start and stop activities. If you can successfully control your group, you will be able to supply useful feedback after each activity and further information to enable the group to progress to more advanced tasks. During a sports session there will be lots of personal and social interaction occurring. It is your responsibility as a leader to ensure that this is a positive experience for all participants in the session.

Your session must flow or you will lose the interest of the group. If as a leader you stop an activity too frequently, because the group can't master the skill, the group may become bored and tired. This also occurs if the activity is carried out over a long period of time. Both situations can result in disruptive behaviour, after which you could lose control.

Set the rules at the start of the session and make sure everyone understands them. It is a good idea to explain the consequences if rules are broken. There is a number of ways that you could give warnings; one way is to use red and yellow cards as a quick visual way for players to recognise that they are not abiding by the rules.

It is not a good idea to allow children to choose their own teams each session. This could lead to the same individuals been left out on each occasion, resulting in low self-esteem. Teams should be chosen on your knowledge of the skills of each player gained through each session or through physical attributes such as height. It is important to remember that sports sessions are about taking part – organise groups in a swift but fair manner.

Key point

The most important thing to achieve when leading any session is maximum participation of the individuals in the group.

Activity

Activities can be designed and used:

■ for warm ups

■ as skill drills

■ for competitive situations

■ to help performers learn skills specific to the sport

■ to help performers learn the rules of the sport

■ to practise working as a team.

The structure of your session

Whether your session is for beginners or experienced performers, it will have three phases:

1 **a starter** – usually a warm up
2 **a middle or main task** – usually a skill practice and competition
3 **an end or plenary** – usually a cool down.

These three phases should be well balanced and will not all take the same amount of time. You will need to use your time-management skills to control the session. Allocate times for all your activities in your plan, and then make sure that you stick to these. In this way, you will achieve the aim of your session and ensure that the session finishes as advertised.

The activities you have chosen should be designed for the number of participants, their ability, the venue and the equipment being used. However, when delivering the actual session, you will need to be flexible. You may need to adjust your plans on the day in response to the number of participants in the group, their behaviour on the day of the session, or changes to the venue or equipment.

The structure of your session and the sequence of tasks you deliver should be directed by:

■ what you want to achieve in the session and how you want to achieve it

■ what the members of your group want or expect from the session.

Design your session to ensure that if quick progression is made by any individual, he or she can move on to further tasks. This helps small groups or individuals to progress at a faster rate than others in the group and keeps the performers physically and mentally active throughout the session.

The progression of tasks should take into account the different needs of the group, for example those who are experiencing difficulties as well as those who are gifted or talented. It is possible that you may need specialised support for certain activities, or for certain individuals. Make sure you take account of this at the planning stage.

A session plan should also carry relevant information from the previous session and have space to evaluate the current session. An example is given below.

You will need to check that equipment and resources are safe before the session starts.

Activity		Introduction to rugby	
Venue: Sportsvilla Centre		Health and Safety Checks: ladders on the wall marked area for the activities to be away from the walls	
Date: 01.02.06	Group size: 15 (4 females/11 males)	Age range: 9–12 years	SEN none
Duration (Time in mins)	Coaching element or skill	Coaching points to remember	Equipment
10	Warm up Passing skills: in a grid	Hands out: ready to receive the ball Avoid contact with other group members	1 ball per group of 3
5	General stretches	Ensure that all stretches are carried out standing up	none
15	Passing the ball backwards Line work	Ensure that the individual reaches each one before a pass is delivered	1 ball for each line of 4
10	Tag rugby game	The ball must be passed back No hand offs	1 ball, tag and belts for each team
5	Cool down and summarise the session	Question and answer to ensure the group has learned the laws of the game	
Points from previous session	None, first session in this sport		
Evaluation of the session	Quicker progression to move the individuals forward and the ball back. Bring a whistle to control the group especially during the game. Work in smaller groups so fewer people are standing around waiting for their turn with the ball.		

■ *An example of a session plan for the introduction to rugby*

The warm up

A warm up should be designed to prepare the body for more strenuous activity.

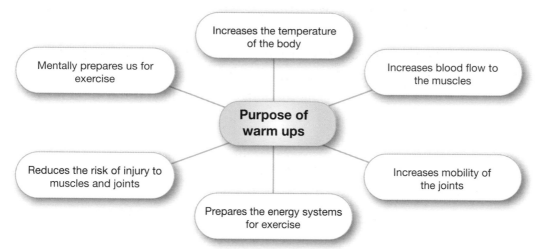

Increases the temperature of the body

Mentally prepares us for exercise

Increases blood flow to the muscles

Purpose of warm ups

Reduces the risk of injury to muscles and joints

Increases mobility of the joints

Prepares the energy systems for exercise

■ *Purpose of warm ups*

To warm the body up small games can be played, for example, 'stuck in the mud', 'cups and saucers' and 'hot rice'. You may have experience of these types of games that you played in school; they are good for all ages.

Key point

The body should be warm before any of the stretches are carried out. It is vitally important that demonstrations of any stretches are correct.

■ *It is important to warm up before exercise*

Skill introduction

Your session plan should have a purpose; this purpose is usually what you aim to achieve from leading the session. Examples of skill introduction will depend on the experience of the group in the sport, the age of the group and type of group. For example, are they attending your session to keep fit or to improve on their performance for a competition?

The introduction of a skill could be, for example, chest pass for netball, dribbling for basketball, shooting for football, or sprint starts for track athletics.

Development of the skill

The session should include a section where performers can develop their skills, whether they be from previous weeks or from that session, as some performers will develop more quickly than others.

Conditioned game

To see how your performers are really progressing, it is a good idea to use a conditioned game. That is, design a small game where they must attempt to use the skills that have been introduced during that session.

Competition

The session should end with a climax, and that climax should allow the performers to play a game where they can show off their previous skills as well as their skill learned from the session.

The cool down

The cool down is an important aspect of leading any session as it allows for the body to start returning to its resting state.

Exercise should not cease abruptly but gradually to allow for blood flow to reduce to resting levels. This helps in reducing soreness and stiffness of the muscles days after exercise.

Key point

Stretches should be held for longer during the cool down phase to allow for the muscle fibres to start to recover after exercise.

Recording

To help improve on leading sport sessions it is important to keep a record of what you have done. This can be carried out in a number of ways:

- diary
- logbook
- portfolio
- video
- audio
- observation records
- witness statements
- feedback sheets.

Let's do it!

With the help of your tutor, produce a lesson plan for a sports session.
Make sure you:

■ *identify the target group*
■ *plan the progression, timing and sequencing of activities*
■ *take account of health, safety and legal requirements*
■ *note down expected outcomes.*

Assessment activity 3: Review the planning and leading of a sports activity

To achieve a Pass:

1. Review the way you have planned and lead a sports activity, *identifying* strengths and areas for improvement. (P3)

To achieve a Merit you must achieve the Pass criteria and:

2 *Explain* the strengths from your session and how improvements could be made in the planning and leading of a sports activity. (M3)

To achieve a Distinction you must achieve the Pass and Merit criteria and:

3 *Evaluate* your own planning and leading of your sports session using the explanations from your strengths and areas for improvement. (D2)

Case study

Owen

Owen has completed his level 1 and level 2 coaching courses for rugby and plays for his team on Saturdays. He thinks that there is insufficient provision for rugby in the inner city areas for school children. He has decided to start a touch rugby session at his local school.

There are no grass fields at the school. Provision includes:

- a concrete yard about the size of a basketball court
- a hall that is also used for dinner time, morning school meetings and all PE lessons – there is also some sports equipment left out, which could be a possible hazard.

Owen asked for help from the local rugby development officer, who has provided him with rugby balls, belts and tags.

Owen planned a session for 15 children, but on his first session he attracted 25 Year 5 pupils, 9 girls and 16 boys, from a variety of cultural and social backgrounds. Many of the children came to the first session without sports kit. Owen thinks that participation is important, so he allowed them all to take part in the hope that they would enjoy the session and be motivated to purchase kit.

Owen provided a warm up designed so that everyone could participate – even children without appropriate kit could progress to more strenuous activities.

Owen started with playground games, like tag and hot rice (a version of tag using a soft ball). He then progressed to rugby activities in grids, using the concrete yard in the playground. He finished off with a

rugby game. No rugby tackles were performed because the game that Owen introduced was tag or touch rugby. He also placed conditions on the game to ensure maximum involvement. For example, he organised small sided games in which every player in the team had to touch the ball before a try could be scored.

Now answer the following questions.

1 Owen planned a session for 15 children but 25 turned up. What should he have done? Circle the correct statement.

   a Turn 10 children away.
   b Not change the plan.
   c Include the first 15 children, make the others sit out, then swap.
   d Adapt the plan to include all 25 children.

2 State three reasons why you have chosen your answer for question 1.

3 The day Owen carried out his session was a very windy day. Which factor would be the most important that Owen would need to consider? Circle the correct statement.

   a Having bright clothes on.
   b Being able to project his voice.
   c Being a good fun leader.
   d Having lots of equipment.

4 Give a reason why you have chosen your statement, and why you feel the other statements are not so important for question 3.

Key point

The most important thing to achieve during the delivery of any session is maximum participation of the individuals in the group.

5.4 Be able to assist in the planning and leading of a sports event

The different types of sporting events have increased over the years. These include:

- swimming galas
- half-marathon running events
- cross-country events
- tag rugby festivals
- softball taster days
- walk/run for life events
- cycling events
- girls' football days
- golf for beginners.

These are just a few – there will be many more around where you live.

Plan

You may be involved in the planning of some of these events but as a sports leader you will be involved on the day of the event, as a part of a team.

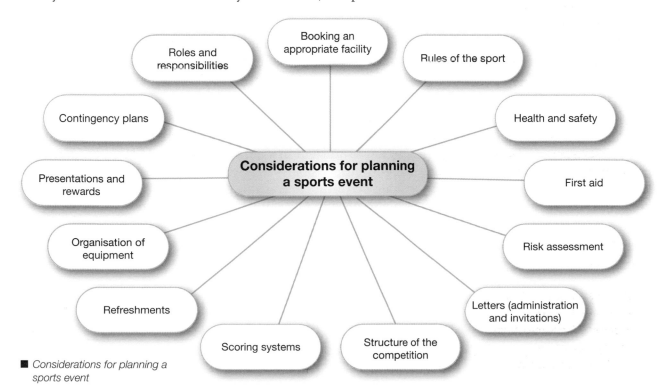

Roles and responsibilities

Booking an appropriate facility

Rules of the sport

Contingency plans

Health and safety

Presentations and rewards

Considerations for planning a sports event

First aid

Organisation of equipment

Risk assessment

Refreshments

Letters (administration and invitations)

Scoring systems

Structure of the competition

■ *Considerations for planning a sports event*

Booking the facility

The facility that you book should be suitable for the event that is being organised. It should be: appropriate in size, accommodating the expected numbers to the event; have sufficient toilets; car parking; changing areas and suitable playing areas, possibly for indoor use in case of bad weather.

Rules of the sport

As part of the organising team, people may ask you questions about the rules of the sport during the event. It is always a good idea to ensure that you up-date your knowledge of the rules. This may also come in handy if you are asked to officiate.

Health and safety and risk assessments

Health and safety is one of the most important responsibilities of any sports leader. Unit 2 of this book deals with health and safety in detail. You are recommended to read this unit to supplement the information given in the paragraphs below.

Health and safety procedures are carried out to protect the leader and the performers from harm. The assessment of risks should be carried out on a regular basis. The results of each check should be recorded. The record should be signed and dated by the person responsible, and a note made of the time the assessment was made.

You will need to complete health and safety checks for each different venue you use and every activity or event that you deliver. You will need to identify hazards and take measures to reduce them before the activity is delivered. Any changes that you make should take into account the facilities' recommendations and any relevant manufacturers' guidelines. Everything you note and decide upon must be recorded.

First aid

As a sports leader, you will need to be able to recognise various common injuries, and have sufficient first aid knowledge to help an injured person. It is your responsibility to ensure that someone holding a current first aid certificate is available during the running of your session. You also need to find out where first aid resources are kept.

A fully stocked first aid box should also be available.

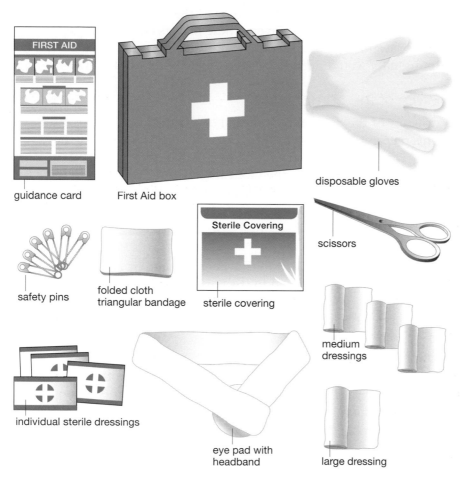

■ *The contents of a first aid box*

The facility should have guidelines on what to do in the case of any injury occurring. Make sure you know what these are and what lines of communication you should follow when an injury occurs.

Emergency procedures

As a sports leader, you must also know the procedure for evacuation of the facility and ensure that any relevant individuals know too. For example, in case of a fire drill, it is important that you know the location of the fire exits. You should also check them regularly, to ensure that there are no obstacles to prevent access.

Letters

You may be responsible for the administration of the event. This will include communicating in a variety of ways with a variety of other organisations. You will need to ensure that all of the relevant governing bodies, clubs, performers and organisations are contacted about the type of event that is being carried out, when and where. Specific information about numbers attending, type of facility being used, and health and safety procedures in place needs to be given to the appropriate organisations in plenty of time.

You may also want to increase the profile of the event by inviting the media, or high profile sports players; these players cold also be used to present the awards and prizes at the end of the event. However, this kind of responsibility would need to be agreed before the event day.

Structure of the competition

The structure of the competition should be planned well before event day. This preparation can give all participants a clear idea of the day's structure. For example, when will the first match or race take place? How will participants be placed in the race categories? What do participants need to do before they compete? Do they register for the day or each event?

Scoring system

The scoring system that is used for the event should be agreed by the organising team and distributed to the participants before the event so they have time to train for the competition. This will also help to standardise the scoring for all officials on the day of the event.

Refreshments

Whether refreshments are offered or sold will depend on the duration of the event. It is always a good idea to offer free refreshments, as both performers and spectators enjoy hydrating themselves through hot and cold days.

Organisation of equipment

It is important in your planning of any event that you have sufficient equipment that works. You will have a good idea of the number of performers that will attend your sports event as you may insist that they reply with a application form if they wish to participate in your event. This will help in organising sufficient equipment for the day.

Contingency plan

As with planning for a sport activity having Plan B is always an event saver. You need to predict possible changes in the day that could change the structure of the event. For example, more numbers attending the event, extreme hot weather or torrential rain.

Roles and responsibilities

It is vitally important that everyone involved in assisting in the planning and leading the event knows their role and responsibilities. You need to ensure that you carry out the tasks that are set out for you otherwise this could hinder the next person's job before and on the day.

Assessment activity 4: Assist in the planning and leading of a sports event

Work in groups of three or four to assist in the planning of a sports event.

To achieve a Pass:

1 *Describe* your own role within the event, producing evidence that this has been effective. (P4)

To achieve a Merit you must achieve the Pass criteria and:

2 *Explain* the strengths and how improvements could be made in helping to plan and lead a sports event. (M4)

To achieve a Distinction you must achieve the Pass and Merit criteria and:

3 *Evaluate* your own planning and leading of the sports event, commenting on strengths and areas for improvement for further development as a sports leader. (D2)

5.3 & 5.5 Be able to review your planning and leadership of sports activities and events

Review

Successful delivery of your sports session depends largely upon the quality of your organisation and preparation. Once everything is in place, it is up to you as sports leader to deliver the session with confidence. Your aims and objectives should be clearly defined, you should have prepared the tasks thoroughly and have a secure knowledge of them. As a result of this, you should find that group control is easier. It is good practice to have a whistle close at hand – you may not need to use it once control of the group has been gained, but it is a good precautionary measure.

Planning and preparation

Planning and preparation are key factors for a successful session. Before the session starts, ensure that you have the appropriate resources and equipment available, and any other facilities that you may need. Also ensure that you have the permission of parents and carers if this is appropriate.

Gathering information

As you are leading a session, you are constantly taking on board information about the session, the group and the activities. This information includes things that went well, for example, successful tasks and methods of delivery, and things that didn't go so well and that you will need to improve or change in future sessions.

There are different ways in which you can gather information about your session. For example:

- making a video of the session, which you can then play back and discuss with friends or with your tutor
- asking peers, colleagues or your tutor to watch the session – they may be able to highlight those elements that worked and those that didn't, and make suggestions for change
- compiling a questionnaire about the session and asking peers or your supervisor to complete it
- self-reflection – asking yourself questions, such as:
  - did my session plan take into account the venue, equipment, group size and ability?

- what changes did I make to the session plan during the delivery?
- how flexible was I?
- did I communicate effectively?
- did the participants understand the instructions given to them?
- did the participants understand what they were meant to learn?

Formulating a review

You need to use this information to formulate a review after the delivery has taken place. Your review should measure the delivery of your session against your original goals. Don't forget that these goals include the participants' objectives, as well as your own personal aims. The evaluation process is very important. You need to find out whether changes need to be made to improve the design of the activities or their delivery. It is important that you see these changes as positive, and of great benefit to you, as the leader, and to the group.

The spidergram below shows some of the factors involved in your review.

■ *How you will be assessed*

Setting goals

As a sports leader, you need to set goals for the short, medium and long term. This can seem a daunting task. Having an overall plan will help you to set goals over a period of time and in an achievable way. It will also help you to deal with the changes that you may come across during each session or programme.

Evaluation

After each session and programme you should carry out an evaluation. This will help you to maintain a clear and accurate account of the progress that has been made. The evaluation process can also be used to compare the results from each session with the objectives that were set at the start. The information that is gained through this process needs to be interpreted, and made relevant to future plans.

SWOT analysis

A SWOT analysis can be carried out to gain this information. This will highlight the factors that have caused problems and help you to improve the delivery of future sessions. Act on any weaknesses that you find by making changes to your original plans if necessary. If you avoid changing them now, you may find that this leads to further disappointments for both you and the performers.

A SWOT analysis looks at:

- **S**trengths
- **W**eaknesses
- **O**pportunities
- **T**hreats.

Strengths and weaknesses

Identifying strengths and weaknesses is a useful thing to do. In terms of your delivery of a session, you will probably identify your strengths in those aspects of the session which went smoothly. Your weaknesses will be identified in the areas that did not go too well, or did not work at all. Try to identify where things went wrong or right.

- Were the tasks or activities chosen appropriate?
- Was the level at which the tasks were set appropriate?
- Was your verbal delivery set at the correct level? (In other words, did you communicate effectively for the age range and ability level of your group?)

You need to have a good understanding of your strengths so that you can play to these qualities and improve them still further. It is also important to recognise areas of weakness, so that you can work either to improve them or to avoid them.

Opportunities and threats

These are factors that may not be fully in your control. Opportunities can arise unexpectedly. For example, the increased confidence of one performer may have encouraged others to come and join the sports club. Threats can be equally unpredictable; for example, if a performer is accidentally injured during play, this can affect the confidence of the team.

Unit 9 page 308 also looks at SWOT analysis as a tool.

Set targets for improvement and development

The SMART model can be used for setting individual targets for performers. Each training session and competition should provide you with the information on the strengths and weaknesses of a performer in specific situations. This can be used to set targets for the performer. Start by determining your long-term aim, and then break this goal down into smaller goals, or objectives. The goals of a sports leader must have input from the performers that he or she works with. The SMART model will help you to set these goals.

Think about it

SMART stands for:
Specific, **Measurable**, **Agreed**, **Realistic** *and* **Timed**.

Specific

This refers to the content of the goal. It must be specific to your chosen sport or event. For instance, a top 100-metre sprinter in athletics does not need a great deal of stamina. Even within a particular sport, different performers may have different aims. A football goalkeeper, like Edwin van der Sar of Manchester United, will not need to practise shooting as much as the striker Wayne Rooney.

Measurable

Your goal needs to be measurable. There must be some way to clearly see when it has been achieved. In athletics, measuring the achievement of goals can be very straightforward – you will run a certain time, or jump a particular distance, for example. The measurement is very objective. Changes in your fitness can also easily be measured by undertaking fitness tests.

■ *Sports players have different aims*

For other goals, you will need to think of other ways to measure them. For example, you might look at reaching targets by a set date. Athletes will usually try to reach their peak performance at the same time as competing in major events, for example the Olympic Games. If they are able to peak at the right time, they will hope to perform well. If they peak too early or too late, their chances of success will be reduced.

Agreed

Goals that you set must be agreed with your teacher or coach. This will involve sitting down and discussing what you might aim for, by when, and how your success will be measured. Failure to agree these points will ultimately lead to confusion, conflict and failure.

Realistic

Any goal that you set must be realistic – you must be able to achieve it. This does not mean to say that the goal set should be easy, but neither should it be too hard. It should be possible to achieve it, assuming that, for example, you stay free from injury, receive the required resources and so on. Be realistic in relation to the set timescale as well as the actual performance goal. Winning this year's London Marathon is unlikely to be realistic for you, but completing the race in an agreed time may well be.

Timed

Your goals must be time-constrained. This means that a deadline is set by which the goal should have been achieved. For instance, if you are learning to drive, the date of your exam is the deadline for learning and being able to perform all the various skills required. Deadlines should be flexible, as they may need to be changed because of injury or illness. Deadlines can also be long-term. Top athletes will often set a deadline a number of years away. For instance, a swimmer or runner may set goals for the Olympic Games four years in advance.

Keeping up-to-date

Your work as a sports leader does not stop at the end of the session. It is your responsibility to keep up-to-date with the changes in the sport or physical activity that you lead, and its health and safety requirements. There are various special educational programmes or courses that you can attend, designed to help sports leaders and coaches to develop. Examples include those organised by Sports Coach UK (National Coaching Foundation) and the Football Association, as well as more general courses on child protection and first aid.

The influence that you have as a sports leader is massive. Your responsibility as a sports leader goes beyond the demonstration of skills in sport. You must also set, and show, high moral and ethical standards. By improving the performance of young people, your aims should include:

- identifying and meeting the needs of all individuals under your supervision

- improving performance through a progressive and safe programme for sport

- ensuring that the activities set include a guided practice, that a method is provided for measuring performance and that opportunities for competition are available

- creating an environment in which participation is continuous and challenging, and where improvements can be observed.

Making changes as a result of evaluation

The spidergram below shows some of the modifications you might make as a result of your evaluation.

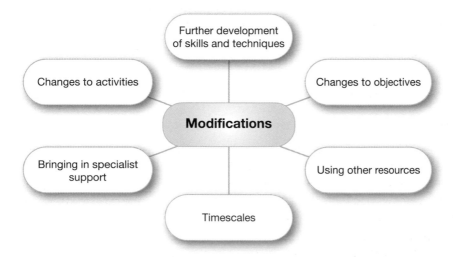

- *Making modifications as a result of your evaluation*

Assessment activity 5: Review performance in leading of a sports event

To achieve a Pass:

1 *Comment* on your own role assisting in leading a sports event.

2 *Comment* on how effective your role was in leading the sports event.

3 *Identify* the areas of strength and areas where improvement could be made. (P5)

To achieve a Merit you must achieve the Pass criteria and:

4 *Explain* the areas of strength and areas that need improvement in assisting in the leading of a sports event.

5 *Make suggestions* relating to the improvements that could be made. (M4)

To achieve a Distinction you must achieve the Pass and Merit criteria and:

6 *Evaluate* your leading of your sports event using the explanations from your strengths and areas for improvement for further development as a sports leader. (D2)

Summary

It is important to establish a leadership style that is not only appropriate to the individual or group, but also one that you are comfortable with. Leaders should not try to be someone else – you need to develop your own style.

Setting aims and objectives are also important as they guide practice and keep it focused.

There should always be a balance of knowledge, understanding, enjoyment and safety through any training session or sporting activity that you lead.

Check what you know!

Look back through this unit to see if you can you answer the following questions.

1. List five skills and qualities that a leader in sport should have.

2. Place these skills and qualities in order of importance, number one being the most important.

3. Explain how a quietly-spoken sports leader can be successful.

4. Fill in the table below by identifying three leaders from three different sports. They do not have to be captains of their teams, but your choices need to be explained in the last column.

Sport	Leader's name	Explain the type of leader

5. Whose responsibility is it to check for damage of equipment that will be used for an activity?

6. Describe the importance of having knowledge of child protection issues when leading a sports event.

7. Explain how a sports leader can keep a record of their progress in leading a sports activity.

8. Why is it important to get feedback from a variety of individuals about a leader's strengths?

9. Choose two similar sports leaders and comment on why they are effective when leading a sports session. Identify their strengths and suggest how they could make improvements.

10. List and explain the factors that need to be considered for modifications to a sports event after an evaluation.

6 Practical Sport

Introduction

In this unit you will look at a variety of aspects connected with playing and performing the two sports you have selected to study for your First Diploma qualification. This unit is very practical. It assumes that you play sport a lot! You must have access to coaching and competition, through a club, school or college, for the two sports that you offer for assessment. It will not be enough to have a go for a few weeks: you will need to be able to commit to your chosen sports for a long period of time.

The range of possible sports cannot be covered in this book. For this reason, three sports will be used as examples to give you guidance on how to collect and present your evidence and information. These sports are:

- a team sport – basketball
- a racket sport – badminton
- an individual sport – swimming.

For each sport, you will be guided through the areas that must be covered in your unit assignment. You must develop an understanding of:

- the rules that apply
- the skills required to play
- the tactics and strategies employed
- the roles of match officials.

▶ Continued from previous page

How you will be assessed

This unit will be assessed by an internal assignment that will be set and marked by the staff at your centre. It may be sampled as well by your centre's External Verifier as part of Edexcel's on-going quality procedures. The assignment is designed to allow you to show your understanding of the unit outcomes. These relate to what you should be able to do after completing this unit.

Your assessment could be in the form of:

■ video recorded presentations

■ case studies

■ role plays

■ written assignments.

After completing this unit you should be able to achieve the following learning outcomes.

1 Be able to demonstrate a range of skills, techniques and tactics in selected sports.

2 Know the rules, regulations and scoring systems of selected sports.

3 Understand the roles and responsibilities of officials in selected sports.

4 Be able to analyse the sports performance of an individual and team.

6.1 Be able to demonstrate a range of skills, techniques and tactics in selected sports

All sports require skills, techniques and tactics to succeed. This section will lead you through some definitions of the key terms and allow you to recognise the differences and similarities between them. You will then need to apply this knowledge to your chosen sports.

Skills and techniques required to perform the sport effectively

Skills

In sport, skill relates to how various movements and actions in the game are performed.

Skills are learned. When you learn a sports skill you pass through various phases, from not being able to perform the skill at all to being able to perform the skill without thinking about it.

Generally, a skilful player:

- will make the game look easy – they will often appear to be hardly trying
- will not waste either time or energy – they will always seem to be in the correct position to perform the skill or technique and will not appear to take a great deal of time to perform the skill
- will achieve a desired result with maximum certainty – they will score the point 99 times out of every 100 attempts.

Sport involves individual players and teams performing a variety of skills in order to achieve the best result. Basketball, for example, involves:

- individual skills, including shooting, passing and dribbling
- team skills, including a zone defence, a fast break attack or a set move from a jump ball.

Think about it

In small groups, discuss what you think being skilful means. Try to give examples. Bring your findings back to the class and be ready to present what your group decided.

■ *Football is a team sport*

Skills in sport can be categorised in various ways. The skills used may be:

- **complex** – for example, a tumble routine on the floor mat in gymnastics

- **simple** – for example, catching a ball in netball.

Skills can also be termed as **closed** or **open**. Closed skills are those that are not affected by the external surroundings, like the weather or other players (a serve in badminton, for example). Open skills are those that are affected by the environment (sailing a yacht, for example, because the sailor needs to react to the force and direction of the wind).

Skills can also be externally paced, where the performer has no control over when to perform the skill (the start in a 100-metre race, for example, is decided by the starter not the athlete) or self-paced, where the performer decides when the skill is performed (for example, the player decides when to serve in tennis).

Techniques

To understand the idea of techniques, choose a player you would recognise from a sport of your choice – it might be one of the sports you are using for your practical performance in this unit. Now choose a particular skill that is required to play the game. *Watch* your player perform this skill a number of times and *describe how* they perform the skill. Try to watch them perform the skill in different situations – in bad weather, when they are tired, etc. Can you see any *differences* in the way they perform the skill? Now repeat this exercise for another performer in the same sport performing the same skill. In what ways do they perform the skill *differently*? These differences illustrate differences in technique.

Let's do it!

Choose one of the sports you are going to study. Draw a table like the one below. Now choose some of the skills and techniques used in your sport and decide what type of skill they are: open or closed; self- or externally-paced and so on. Here is an example for a basketball game.

Skill/technique	Type of skill	Reasons
Chest pass	Open	Opponents try to intercept your pass
Free throw shot	Self-paced	You decide when to shoot after receiving the ball from the referee
Tip off jump	Externally-paced	You must jump when the referee throws the ball up
Dribbling	Open	You have to react to the movements of team mates and opponents

Let's do it!

1   *Working in small groups, choose a skill like bowling in cricket or serving in tennis. Look at the skill used by a number of players and discuss the differences in the technique used. Produce a display to highlight these differences.*

2   *Now repeat this exercise for a skill in one of the sports you are studying. Make notes on the technique of the performer, in other words how he or she carries out the skill. For example, look at the position of the arms, legs and so on. Look at the follow-through after the skill.*

3   *Now video yourself performing the same skill. Make notes on the differences between your performance and that of the player you have observed. Write these up in a table. Try to use these headings (your tutor can help you with this).*

   ■ *Early preparation.*
   ■ *Footwork.*
   ■ *Result of the skill.*
   ■ *Follow-through.*

The table below looks at the skill of place kicking. It looks at the technique of two players in the final of the 2003 Rugby World Cup.

Component of skill	Jonny Wilkinson (England)	Elton Flatley (Australia)
Position of ball	Very upright	Pointing at the posts Ball at a very shallow angle
Movement from the ball to kicking position	Five steps backwards and to the right	Three steps back followed by two to the left
Body position before kick	Arms held in front with elbows bent and hands together	Arms hanging down beside the body
Action before kick	Looks at the ball then the posts, then at a point high in the stands, then the posts again and finally the ball	Looks once at the posts
Kicks with:	Left foot	Right foot
Approach to ball when kicking	Four steps to ball	Two steps back and slightly left. Then four to the ball
Follow-through	Long and across to the right	Long and left

Tactics

You will also need to consider tactics in your chosen sport.

In sport, the specific end is to win the match or the race. In Formula One racing, for example, tactics will include when to pit for fuel and tyres in the race (two stops or three?). In a 10,000-metre race, for example, a runner like Paula Radcliffe needs to decide at what pace she will run each lap. In football, a Premier League manager will need to consider what formation to play. The decision might be to play a 4–4–2 line-up, or perhaps 3–5–2. The opposition the team faces might be the deciding factor. For instance, a football team wishing to add width to their attack while maintaining a strong midfield might employ a five-man midfield, with the two wing backs attempting to get forward down the wings to deliver crosses. This means that the opponent's dangerous full back has to help defend this, rather than trying to get himself or herself forward.

Tactics will relate to a number of facets of the game, such as:

- attack and defence – are you in possession or not?
- the situation in the game – are you are winning or losing? How much time is left?
- the style of play you naturally prefer – are you an aggressive player who likes to attack? Or are you more conservative, preferring to wait for your opponent to make errors?
- the opponent you are playing – what are their strengths and weaknesses?

You need to be flexible with tactics, able to change and adapt to respond to the way the game or match is going.

Case study

When the England cricket captain Michael Vaughan selects a team for a Test match, he has to make tactical decisions. All of the decisions he makes will be part of the tactics he employs to obtain the desired result.

Here are some of the questions he might ask himself.

- Am I going to play with a spinner or not?
- How many recognised batsmen are there?
- Do I need to win the match to win the series, or would a draw be sufficient?
- What weaknesses have I spotted in the opponents' batting?

- Do the opponents have bowlers who struggle when bowling to left-handed batsmen?
- When on the pitch, in what positions will I place my fielders?
- How will I use my bowlers?
- Will I declare at a particular point, to allow my bowlers time to get their opponents out?

Now answer the following questions.

1 Can you think of other questions that the England captain might ask?

2 How do you think the answers to these questions will influence his tactics?

Think about it

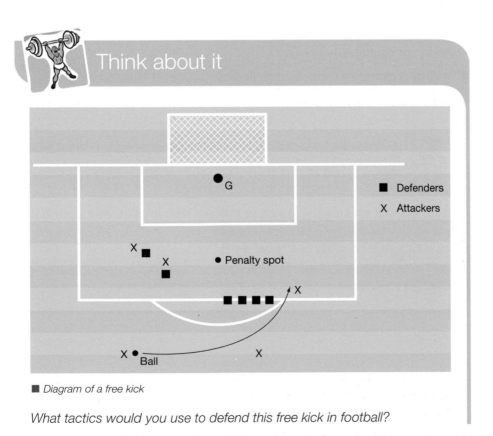

- *Diagram of a free kick*

What tactics would you use to defend this free kick in football?

Sports

You will also need to consider the types of sports you choose. They could be team sports, such as association football, basketball, cricket, hockey, lacrosse or netball. They could be individual sports such as golf, judo, trampolining, archery or table tennis.

Recording

The record you keep of your sports performance can take a number of different forms. The most effective is a simple diary, in which you write down which skills and tactics you employed, why you did so, and what the result was. For example, imagine you have a regular opponent in badminton. You decide that you are going to play in a particular way for one game, to see what happens. Perhaps you will always serve to your opponent's backhand because you have noticed it is a weakness. Or perhaps you will try to engage your opponent in long rallies because you feel your fitness is better and, by tiring your opponent out, you will gain an advantage.

Other ways of keeping a record could include:

■ keeping a video diary

■ obtaining feedback from observers and coaches who watch you play

■ using a simple summary sheet, completed by yourself or a tutor, coach or opponent

■ asking someone to watch your performance and then to discuss it with you.

 Key point

Remember, you need to complete this task for two different sports over a period of time. Use the feedback you receive from others. Change the skills and tactics you use in the light of the results you obtain during matches.

Your two sports must contrast. They cannot be two racket sports, or two events in athletics, for example.

Let's do it!

Many games and sports use special words or terms to signify something. Fill in the table below to define some of these terms.

Term	Sport	Definition
Scrum down		
Double dribble		
Let		
Travelling		
Deuce		
Tumble turn		
Offside		
Service over		
Penalty stroke		
Line-out		

Assessment activity 1: Observational checklist for athletes

To achieve a Pass:

1 In small groups, choose two athletes from any sport that you are familiar with. These athletes might be classmates or players from different teams. With the support of your tutor, draw up an observational checklist that lists:

- the various skills required to perform the sport
- each player's strengths and weaknesses in the range of skills you have identified
- the tactics required by each sport. Look also at the tactics your chosen players use.

2 Discuss how best to record and present your results to the rest of the class. Can you draw any conclusions from your results? (P4)

To achieve a Merit you must achieve the Pass criteria and:

3 Working independently, produce an observation checklist that could be used to review the performance of an individual or a team. (M3)

To achieve a Distinction you must achieve the Pass and Merit criteria and:

4 *Explain* the strengths and weaknesses of an individual or team in one individual and one team sport. Provide specific recommendations relating to improving upon weaknesses. (D2)

6.2 Know the rules, regulations and scoring systems of selected sports

Rules and regulations

All sports have rules and regulations that are written down by the sport's governing body and then administered by referees, umpires or judges. These rules and regulations are needed for a number of reasons.

■ Rules and regulations decide the format of a game – for example, netball players are not allowed to dribble the ball, whereas in basketball, a very similar game, dribbling is allowed.

■ Rules and regulations cover subjects such as the duration of a game, the size of the field of play, the type and nature of equipment that can or must be used, and the number of players and substitutes allowable.

■ Rules and regulations are also vitally important to ensure the safety of players and spectators – for example, an ice hockey goalkeeper must wear certain items of protective clothing.

Section 6.5, Looking at three contrasting sports, gives practical examples of a sports' rules and regulations.

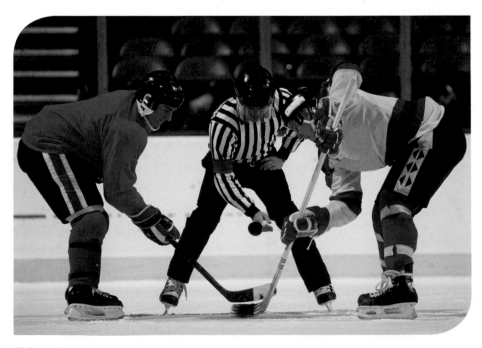

■ Rules for how to begin a game are also set out

Key point

All sports are about overcoming a problem within the confines and restrictions of rules. For example, football is about scoring a goal without touching the ball with your hand, with only ten players in the outfield and without straying offside. Rugby football was invented when William Webb Ellis, who was playing football at the time, picked up the ball and ran with it. At the time, this was not against the rules of football and so a rule was invented to make it illegal. However, others liked the idea of running with the ball in the hand, and so the game of rugby was born.

Scoring systems

All sporting activities have scoring systems. A scoring system refers to all the different ways that points can be scored or lost during a sporting activity. In football, the system is very simple: a goal is scored when the entire ball crosses the goal line, between the posts and crossbar of the goal. Goals can be scored from open play or free kicks, including a penalty. However, in basketball, goals are called baskets and are worth either one, two or three points depending on how they are scored and from where.

Some systems are objective – the winner is determined by who scores the most points, goals or baskets. In other sports the system is subjective – the winner is decided by the opinion of judges.

The rules of the particular game will lay down how and when scores can be made and how a winner is decided. In some sports it is decided by who scores the most (football, basketball, netball). In other sports it is decided by who scores the least (golf, motorcycle trials, show jumping). In other sports, there are set ways in which the game must end. For instance, in darts you must finish on a double to win, while in tennis, the fifth set in a men's game does not go into a tiebreak situation.

For this unit, you need to understand the scoring system used in each of your two chosen sports. Remember, these must be one individual and one team sport.

6.3 Understand the roles and responsibilities of officials in selected sports

This section will look at the various jobs required in any sport to ensure that the rules are observed and safety is maintained.

Roles

There is a wide range of different types of match officials used in sport. Cricket has two umpires on the pitch and a third off-field umpire. Badminton uses an umpire as well as ten line judges and a service judge. Football uses a referee, two assistant referees and a fourth official, while basketball uses a referee, an umpire and a number of table officials. But why are they needed and what do they do?

Match officials undertake a number of different roles when they officiate at a game or match. Roles are those things we expect a person to do. Thus, a football referee is expected to:

- be appropriately dressed
- apply the laws of the game
- communicate with players and other officials
- be responsible for the safety of players and spectators
- be impartial and fair in all their decision making
- keep the match score and details of players cautioned, etc.
- be fit enough to perform the various tasks required
- use a variety of signals to convey what is happening to both players and spectators.

Let us look at the role of a starter at a sprint event in athletics. The starter's roles include calling all the runners to their marks using the correct command 'on your marks'. When all the runners have done so and the starter is happy that all the runners are still, he or she will call the next command, 'set'. Again the starter's role is to make sure all the runners are still and, with the help of another official, that the rules of the start are being met (hands behind the start line, etc.) Finally, the starter will fire the gun to release the sprinters. At this point, the starter might be expected in smaller competitions such as a club meeting to decide if a runner has 'false started' in which case they are called back by the firing of a second gun. The runner who has false started is identified and the process of starting the race is repeated. Can you repeat this for how a sport of your choice is started?

Key points

- A role can be described as a function.
- A responsibility can be defined as an obligation. For example, referees in basketball have a variety of roles, which include enforcing the rules or laws of the game. They also have a responsibility to ensure the safety of all the players and to be impartial and fair in all their judgements.

Responsibilities

In addition to carrying out specified roles, match officials also have jobs we refer to as responsibilities – these are things that match officials are required to do as part of their role. They may be required to make decisions regarding particular matters such as safety, etc. So if we consider the responsibilities of a match official these might include some or all of the following:

- wearing a particular uniform
- checking games equipment such as the ball or goal nets prior to the match starting
- hold, keep up-to-date, and maintain certain qualifications and fitness levels.

During a match or game, the match officials must:

- interpret the laws or rules of the sport in any given situation. Often, players and spectators disagree! Officials must apply the rules in a fair and impartial way to ensure games are fair to both players or teams.
- control players' behaviour while at the same time allowing players to try to win, ensuring that this happens within the rules and in the correct spirit of the game
- ensure the safety of players and spectators. Checking the playing surface and equipment for the game is very important. Thus, before a match, officials will check the surface to be played on, the nets and posts to be used, any obstructions that might endanger players, fire exits, first aid arrangements and so on. The studs on players' boots must be checked to make sure they will not cause undue harm to others. Players' clothing when playing must comply with rules – for instance, no jewellery is allowed unless it is taped over.

In many sports now, match officials have access to a range of technology to help them fulfil their roles and responsibilities. In rugby union and cricket, video reply is available to help make decisions. In rugby it is used to decide if a try has been scored, while in cricket a run out or catch that happened very quickly can be checked to ensure the correct decision is made.

Think about it

Referees of local football leagues need good basic fitness to ensure they are safe to run the 13 kilometres covered in an average match. Lack of preparation and training increase the risk of injury and heart failure.

Finally, match officials have a duty to both players and fans to 'put on a good show'. Officials must balance safety and fairness, for instance, with the need to let a game flow and excite paying spectators. Communication between officials and players/spectators is important and is accomplished through the use of hand signals, a whistle and use of the voice to convey decisions, and so on. If you have access to satellite or digital television, try using the option which allows you to hear what the referee is saying and doing. In rugby union especially, referees are constantly talking to players to stop them from slowing down the game or breaking the rules. This helps to keep the game flowing and provides a much more exciting spectacle for fans.

Communication

Game officials need to communicate with colleagues, players and coaches so that the game is played in the right atmosphere and in the right spirit.

Match officials communicate by:

- using a whistle, e.g. to stop play in rugby or basketball
- talking, e.g. to players and coaches
- using hand signals, e.g. many decisions in basketball are communicated in this way.

In carrying out these tasks the official needs to be confident. He or she needs to be confident when starting the game, when making a decision and in relaying this decision to other people. The official also needs to be confident about using the correct terminology. For example, in badminton the score zero is referred to as love.

Interpreting the rules and making decisions

Referees and umpires need to interpret the rules, and make decisions based on their interpretation. Examples of this kind of decision making in action include:

- a football referee deciding if a player in an offside position was actually interfering with play
- a basketball referee deciding whether a player who was fouled was disadvantaged as a result
- a badminton umpire deciding whether a player's movement during a serve was legal or not.

The more experience a match official has, both as a player and through taking charge of games and matches at a variety of levels, the more informed his or her decision making will be.

Let's do it!

Look in a basketball rules book or watch a football referee to see how hand signals are used.

Key point

- In football the game starts when the referee blows a whistle.
- In badminton the game starts when the umpire calls play.
- In swimming the race is started with a hooter.

Let's do it!

Consider your chosen sports.

- *What decisions do match officials often need to make during a game?*
- *Can you think of any recent decisions that you feel really affected a game?*
- *Why do you think these decisions are taken?*

Assessment activity 2: Observational checklist for officials

To achieve a Pass:

1 Using one team and one individual sport, draw a chart and *describe* the main roles and responsibilities of the officials, for example:

- wearing a specific uniform
- their role during a game or match
- maintaining a stated minimum fitness level
- accepted methods of communication used. (P3)

6.4 Be able to analyse the sports performance of an individual or team

Part of this unit requires you to be able to assess how well other players and teams perform in a particular sport or activity. The following section offers some advice on how this is done.

Section 6.5, Looking at three contrasting sports, provides more practical examples and analysis of three sports – basketball, badminton and swimming.

Performance

As a sports studies student, you need to be able to identify strengths and weaknesses in other players. This might be in how they produce various skills and techniques, as well as the tactics and strategies they employ to be successful. There are a number of criteria you could use, including:

- the starting position for a skill
- the follow-through used
- positioning of the body before, during and after the skill
- the type of footwork used
- positioning on the court/field, etc
- the end result (e.g. did he or she score the goal?)
- the tactics and strategies employed during a game or match.

There are also a number of ways to examine the performance of another player or team. These include:

- observing him or her play, in order to identify strengths and weaknesses
- measuring performance using graphs, charts and tables – these could record, for example, the number of passes made or shots on target
- analysing performance, perhaps by taking a video of a player or team and then discussing it with him or her, the coach, or even the whole team.

Let's do it!

Choose a player at school, and examine his or her performance using the methods described on page 256.

Compare your player to other players, or even to an elite performer. For instance, compare the top goal scorer in your school or college football team with Michael Owen. Look at the way they each perform a specific skill, for example, taking a penalty.

Analysis

Once you have collected information about a player's performance, it is important that it is presented in a clear and easy to understand format. This not only allows you to understand what you have observed, but also helps you make decisions about future action to improve performance.

Tables, charts and graphs

There are various ways in which you could record your observations. You can compare performances by collecting statistics and displaying them graphically.

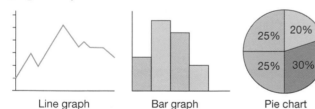

Sport	Per cent
Ballet	10%
Football	50%
Swimming	20%
Cricket	20%

Line graph   Bar graph   Pie chart   Simple table

■ *Examples of graphs, a chart and a table*

For example, you could record:

■ each lap time in a race for two different runners

■ how many shots on goal each player made in a game of football

■ how many tackles each player made in a game of rugby

■ how many assists each player made in a game of basketball.

Your tutor will be able to help you decide which method would be best suited to your chosen sports.

Tables

A table like the one at the top of page 258 allows you to look at a player's or team's performance, make observations, and then address any issues raised in training. This will hopefully help to improve your player's or team's performance.

Skill	Taking a Penalty	
	Michael Owen	**Your star player**
1. Approach to the ball	Head still, concentrating on the ball. Relaxed approach	Head too high. Not concentrating on the ball
2. Body position on contact	Still. Looking at the ball. Left foot beside the ball. Head over the ball	Left foot slightly too far back resulting in body leaning away from the ball. Head moving
3. Leg swing	Long swing of the right leg	Good swing but not as far as Michael Owen
4. Follow-through	Good follow-through	Short follow through
5. Body position	Balanced Relaxed	Stiff Appears nervous and tense
6. Balance	Very good	Good Not leaning to one side or the other
7. End result	Ball struck wide to the keeper's left. Keeper sent the wrong way. Goal scored in bottom right-hand corner	Penalty scored but lacked power and placement. Goal would have been saved if keeper had stood still
8. Strategy	Looked once at the goal and then focused on the ball	Kept looking at the goal before taking the penalty

The following table includes a tally chart, and has been completed for two basketball players.

Skill	Player A	Player B	Comments Player A	Comments Player B
Shots on target for 2 points	12	8	Often off balance	Provides for other players
Shots on target for 3 points	2	0	Lacks a 3-point shot	Rarely in 3-point shooting position
Passes made successfully	55	43	Good range used	Lacks a long javelin pass
Passes misplaced	3	2	Occasionally rushes release of the ball	Sound use of the ball
Assists made for team mates	7	18	Tends to 'go' herself rather than pass	Pivotal player for the team
Interceptions made	6	3	Always threatens ball on defence	Not a strong part of game
Defensive rebounds made	2	20	Lacks height	Tallest player on court. Strong rebounder
Offensive rebounds made	1	24	Lacks height	Tallest player on court. Strong rebounder

Charts and graphs

Charts and graphs are useful for the following reasons.

■ They show a player's performance in an easy-to-read way. A chart showing a batsman's score can also be designed to show where he has scored his runs. This might help an opposing captain devise a way of stopping this player scoring so many runs next time.

■ They can show times or periods when a player disappears from the game. This might be due to tiredness or loss of concentration.

■ They can show tactical flaws in a team's game plan or a player's game strategy, which can then be addressed by the coach. For instance, in basketball, a player may not occupy the correct space when playing a zone defence.

The chart below shows the points scored in a basketball game by one player during each quarter. It also shows how many two and three point shots were scored. Displaying information in this way can help you to look at several aspects of the performance in a very visual way.

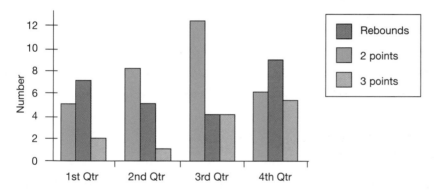

■ *Chart showing points scored by one basketball player during each quarter*

Improvements

When analysing sports performance, what should you look for? Players and teams might improve in a number of ways. Similarly, trainers and coaches might be looking for a particular area of improvement such as fitness or defensive organisation. For instance, a coach might wish to improve an individual player's skill level in a particular area, such as getting free in a basketball game to receive the ball and be able to use his or her good outside shot. Once the reason for the weakness is identified, a programme of activity can be planned, agreed and implemented with testing undertaken to find out what improvement has been achieved. It might be that the player is tactically naïve and needs to be coached through the various systems that the coach wishes to use. The coach must try to ensure the player understands what the strategy is to achieve or the reason for using a particular tactic in a game. What you are trying to improve will determine the method of testing to be used.

Improvements might be focused on the team in terms of the team's cohesion on the court or pitch, their fitness levels or, again, their tactical awareness and proficiency.

But how might these improvements be brought about? Modern technology now plays a vital role in improving both individual players and team performance. Video analysis, computer simulation and monitoring systems such as Prozone used in football allow players and coaches to see exactly what players are (or are not!) doing during a game.

The batteries of fitness tests now allow all aspects of a player's physical and mental fitness to be assessed and monitored. Increasingly, coaches might turn to particular specialists to get extra information and guidance. These include sports nutritionists, sports psychologists and the designers of sports equipment, all of whom have an increasingly important role to play in improving sports performance.

 Let's do it!

1 *Draw up a chart listing all the various sources of help available locally to you that might help you improve your sporting performance. On your chart briefly describe the help available.*
2 *Now repeat this exercise and identify a national source of the same services.*

Assessment activity 3: Rules, regulations and scoring systems

To achieve a Pass:

1 *Describe* the main rules of an individual sport to a small group. Produce a handout that each member of the group can take away. Keep it simple and make it easy to understand. Then do the same for the scoring system used. Choose some simple game situations and explain these to a complete beginner.

2 Look at how the rules or laws are used in each of your chosen sports. Ask yourself the following questions.

- What is the purpose of each rule? (For example, it might be to ensure safety or to keep the game flowing.)
- Which rules or laws are used most in your sport?
- How is the score relayed to players, spectators and other officials?
- Is the system easy to understand for all involved?

3 Draw up a poster which *describes* the basic rules employed in this sport. You should include information on player uniforms and any scoring equipment needed.

Now repeat the three activities above for a team sport. (P2)

To achieve a Merit you must achieve the Pass criteria and:

2 Watch a video of one individual and one team sport with a tutor or classmate, or take a partner to watch them live. *Explain* the scoring system, giving examples where possible. (M2)

6.5 Looking at three contrasting sports

This book is not a coaching manual for any particular sport. Instead, it is designed to guide you through the assessment criteria for each unit. It does this by giving examples of what you might undertake to achieve each criterion and so complete this unit. You will need to conduct further research of your own, especially if your two chosen sports are not included in this chapter.

We are going to look at an example of a team sport – basketball, a racket sport – badminton and an individual sport – swimming.

Each example will offer suggestions as to how you might approach the study of your chosen sports. Remember that your chosen sports must contrast with each other. Do not choose sports that are very similar (for example, tennis and squash). Your level of personal performance is not assessed but it is recommended that you choose sports that you actually enjoy.

Team sports – basketball

Basketball is a fast, athletic team game played between teams of ten players, five of whom are on court at any time. The object of the game is to score points by passing a ball through a hoop suspended ten feet from the floor, while at the same time preventing your opponents from doing the same.

Skills, techniques and tactics

The game requires a number of basic skills.

■ *Basketball skills*

Before you can assess either your own or another player's performance, you need to have a model available that shows you what a particular skill looks like when performed. This section will provide models for selected skills. For other skills, you will need to look at specific basketball coaching manuals to find the information you require.

Passing

The main types of pass used in basketball are the:

- chest pass
- bounce pass
- overhead pass
- javelin pass.

The chest pass can be used as an example of a model. The key points to look for in a chest pass are as follows.

1. The ball should be held in two hands with fingers spread apart.
2. The ball should travel from chest to chest.
3. The arms should be extended and the fingers point to the target after releasing the ball.
4. The player should try to step into the pass.
5. The pass should be flat and fast.

Dribbling

When a player dribbles in basketball he or she should:

1. be able to dribble with both the left and right hand
2. keep his or her fingers spread and the wrist bent to push the ball onto the floor
3. keep his or her knees slightly bent
4. put his or her body between an opponent and the ball for protection
5. keep his or her head up looking for team mates, opponents and so on.

Shooting

Shots in basketball include:

- the jump shot
- the hook shot
- the lay up shot
- the set shot.

We will use the set shot as a model. When performing a set shot:

1. the shooter's eyes should be looking directly at the basket
2. the elbow of his or her shooting arm should be pointing at the target
3. the shooter's feet should be apart so that he or she is balanced
4. the shot should begin with a bending and then straightening of the legs, followed by a straightening of the shooting arm
5. the shooter's hand and fingers should point to the basket after the shot
6. the non-shooting hand should be used to stop the ball going left or right
7. the shooter should aim for the centre of the basket.

■ *Taking a shot*

Rules, regulations and scoring system

Basketball is governed by English Basketball. This is the national governing body, and is responsible for:

- promoting the game
- training coaches and match officials
- developing talent through award schemes and skills awards
- developing initiatives to encourage people to participate in the sport
- choosing representative sides and organising various competitions
- raising finance and generating sponsorship.

The main rules of the game are reproduced on the following pages. These extracts are taken from the England Basketball Level 1 Coaching Manual. They are simplified rules, which would allow you to control a game for young players learning the game.

The scoring system

Points are awarded to your team every time the ball goes through your opponent's basket. Two points are awarded when a basket is scored from inside the three-point line and three points are awarded if the basket is scored from outside this line.

When a player is fouled in the act of shooting then he or she is awarded free throws – either two for a two-point shot or three for a three-point shot. Each successful shot is awarded one point. It is important to note that you can score an 'own basket' by scoring in your own net. If you do this the opposing team will get two points. Points are added together during the game and the team with the most points at the end of time is declared the winner. If the scores are tied then two periods of extra time are played to determine the winning team.

Assessment activity 4: Rules, regulations and scoring systems

To achieve a Pass:

1 *Describe* the key rules and scoring system that would enable some beginners to play a basic game of your two chosen sports. Produce a list in the form of a leaflet or handout that you could give to a new player. (P2)

To achieve a Merit you must achieve the Pass criteria and:

2 *Explain* some of the laws of one team and one individual sport to your partner. Assume they know absolutely nothing about the game. Use practical explanations and demonstrations where possible, by using a court to show how the laws apply. (M2)

Roles and responsibilities of the officials

Two officials control a game of basketball on court: a referee and an umpire. During play, they must work together to control the game. In basketball, events can happen very quickly.

During the match, one official is always in front of the ball while the other official remains behind the ball. When possession of the ball changes, these roles are reversed. Officials should always try to ensure there is a line of sight between them. The official behind the ball (the trailing official) watches the player in possession. The other official watches events off the ball.

Off the court, there are table officials who are responsible for carrying out a number of other duties. These include:

Key point

In basketball each coach is allowed a number of one-minute breaks called 'time outs'. These breaks allow the coach to bring the team together to give fresh instructions on how the game should proceed.

- recording and displaying the score
- recording and displaying fouls committed by individual players or teams
- recording the taking of time outs by team coaches
- checking the game clock is properly monitored, started and stopped, to ensure the game is played for the correct amount of time
- completing the score book, which provides a written record of the game.

Let's do it!

Look at the table below, which identifies the different roles and responsibilities of officials for the three sports in this chapter.

Role/responsibility	Basketball referee	Badminton umpire	Swimming judge
To keep game time	No	N/A	Yes
To record the score	No	Yes	N/A
To call fouls	Yes	Yes	Yes
To discipline players	Yes	Yes	N/A
To maintain a certain fitness level	Yes	No	No
To record player bookings/cautions	No	N/A	N/A
To apply the game rules	Yes	Yes	Yes
To check players' uniforms and dress	Yes	Yes	Yes
To carry a whistle	Yes	No	No
To carry other special equipment	No	Pen, score-book	Stopwatch
To wear a set uniform	Grey shirt, black trousers and shoes	Smart dress generally worn, e.g. shirt and tie for men	White clothing worn

1 *What other criteria could have been used in this table?*
2 *Make a table of your own, contrasting your two chosen sports.*

Case study

Matthew

This is an extract from a diary kept by a basketball player called Matthew. He plays for a team called Bourne Bullets in the Peterborough under-16 basketball league. This extract refers to a game he played against a team from Spalding.

Date Sunday 21 September 2003
Venue Bourne Leisure Centre
Event Match v. Spalding Sonics

In this game, we were confident of getting the season off to a good start. We had played Spalding in the last game of the season and had won convincingly. In this game we wanted to do the same. I play point guard for the team and am also the captain. I need to set a good example to the rest of the squad, and lead by example. In training, I have been lacking a consistent 2 point shot. Our coach has told me that I do not follow through with my shooting hand when making a shot. I want to concentrate on improving this.

In defence we began with a 2-1-2 zone to allow us to see what our opponents had to offer. In attack, we began with a traditional 'horseshoe', playing two deep, two high from the basket with me acting as the play maker. During the game I demonstrated the following skills:
- dribbling with both hands
- lay ups
- free throws - six in this game, of which I scored four - a 66% completion rate
- set and jump shots for two points - 14 points from a possible 28 - a 50% success rate
- set shots for three points - I scored two - a 66% success rate

In addition, I was involved in five assists and stole the ball from the opposition four times.

At the start of the game, the opposition played a 2-1-2 zone. To play against this, we played an offence with a strong side and a weak side. This means we had more players on the strong side than there were defenders. This allowed us to use 'give and go' moves and 'back doors' to get a player into their zone to score. Later, they switched to a 'man for man' defence in order to pressure us and steal the ball. This meant switching our attack and using screens to free a player to score.

As a result, we won the game 58-49.

I think my strengths against my opposite number were:
- stronger dribbling skills on my weaker hand
- a higher percentage of free shots scored
- better rebounding both on offence and defence.

My weaknesses were:
- a poorer set shot from outside the key
- a weaker overhead pass
- I was often drawn out of position on defence when playing a zone defence.

I need to improve my ability to use a change of pace or a fake to create space for my offence. At present, defenders are often not tricked by my fakes and dummies. My stamina began to go after about four minutes of the last quarter. I need to carry out more training during practice to improve this.

Assessment activity 5: Looking at your own performance

1 Using a diary like Matthew's or any other suitable method of keeping a record (video diary, observation sheets, witness statements, etc.), *record*, over a suitable period of time, your participation in one individual sport and one team sport. In your diary you must record information on:

■ the practical skills you have used

■ the different ways, or techniques, you have used when using these various skills

■ the different tactics you have used or tried to use when playing in games or matches.

This will provide evidence for P1 in this unit.

2 Now choose another performer from your class or group or from elsewhere – maybe a local professional or an international player – and assess the skills, techniques and strategies they use when playing.

Remember, you must choose an individual, or team, in one individual and one team sport.

3 Design a form that you will use to assess the performance of the player in the individual sport and the team (or individual in the team) playing your chosen team sport. Think about the skills, techniques and tactics you covered in task 1. Think about how they should be performed. For tactics, think about the role each player should adopt. Remember to include columns where you record strengths and weaknesses.

This will provide evidence for P5 and P6.

Performance of other players

When looking at the performance of other players, it is important that you choose the most appropriate way of carrying this out. As an observer you will need to look for:

■ strengths and weaknesses

■ use of various skills

■ the techniques used to perform these skills

■ the tactics they employ as either an individual or team player.

In addition, you will need to choose a method of displaying your results to your tutor, subject or even your class. This might be a graph, chart, video clip or written observation. You will also need to decide on what you are going to look at – for instance, in basketball it might be points scored or assists given to team mates; in swimming it might be the technique used for breathing; in cricket it might be where a batsman tends to score his or her runs in a match.

Racket sports – badminton

Badminton is an indoor racket sport played either between two players (singles) or four players (doubles). When playing doubles, the pairs can be male, female or mixed. When played at the top level, badminton is a fast and dynamic game and requires a number of different skills.

Skills, techniques and tactics

The game requires a number of basic skills.

■ *Badminton skills*

In addition to the above, players need a variety of physical qualities, including high levels of stamina, agility, speed and mobility to cope with the demands of the game.

Tactics and strategies

The tactics and strategies for a singles game and a doubles game are different.

Singles

In singles you try to make your opponent move every time he or she plays a shot. Use the four corners of the court to make your opponent move as much as possible. If you are serving using a long, high serve, try to play down the centre line. That way, your next shot requires less movement on your part. If you decide to serve short, again aim for the centre line.

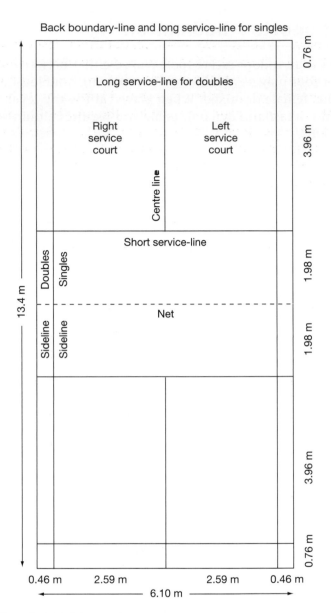

Back boundary-line and long service-line for singles

0.76 m

Long service-line for doubles

| Right service court | Left service court |

Centre line

3.96 m

Short service-line

1.98 m

Doubles · Singles

Net

1.98 m

Sideline · Sideline

3.96 m

0.76 m

13.4 m

0.46 m   2.59 m   2.59 m   0.46 m

6.10 m

■ *The dimensions of a badminton court*

When choosing your tactics, it is important that you consider the following:

- your own strengths and weaknesses
- your opponent's strengths and weaknesses
- previous matches.

There is little to be gained from serving long if your long serve lacks height and distance.

Doubles

In doubles play, the service area is shorter but wider. There is less free space in which to hit the shuttle and so tactics involve moving opponents around to create the free space into which you hit the shuttle. In general, when serving, you should serve short to bring the receiver into the net. If your opponent lifts the shuttle (hits it up), then you and your partner should attack the shuttle (hit it down). You should then adopt positions which put one player in front at the net and the other player behind and in line, covering the rear of the court. This is shown on the diagram below.

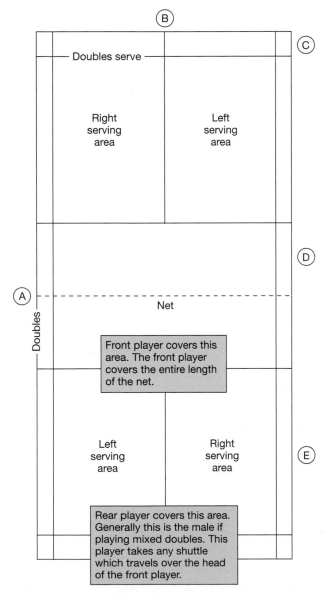

■ *The position of doubles players on a badminton court (front and rear)*

If you are forced to lift the shuttle, then you are defending and should adopt a side by side formation, as shown below.

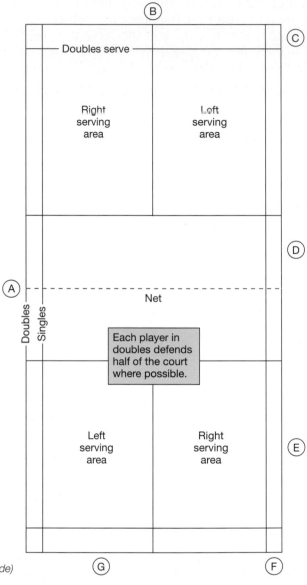

■ *The position of doubles players on a court (side by side)*

Doubles tends to be a faster game because the shuttle is being intercepted more frequently.

Rules, regulations and scoring system

The object of the game is to put the shuttle on to the floor on your opponent's side of the net, or to put the shuttle over the net in such a way that your opponent:

■ cannot reach the shuttle to return it

■ can reach the shuttle but cannot play it back over the net successfully

■ hits the shuttle out of the court when trying to return it.

Serving

A badminton court has service areas which are shown in the diagrams on pages 271 and 272.

The badminton court differs for singles and doubles, as shown in the diagrams. The singles service area is often described as thin and long, while the doubles service area is described as short and fat.

There are a number of rules attached to serving in badminton, such as:

- the server's feet must not touch any of the lines on the court
- on impact, the shuttle must be below the waist of the server
- on impact, the racket head must be below the hand holding the racket
- the server can only serve when their opponent is ready
- no feinting is allowed
- the receiving player cannot move until the serve is made.

A shuttle landing on a line is deemed to be in.

Let's do it!

Visit the World Badminton website at www.heinemann.co.uk/ hotlinks to discover more about the rules of the game.

The scoring system

The reader should be aware of the following.

- The sport's governing body, the International Badminton Federation (IBF), has introduced a series of experimental rule changes to make the game faster and more entertaining.

- Under the old system the first player (or team) to reach 15 points won the set, except in women's singles when the target was 11 points.

- However, both men and women now play up to 21 points. If the score reaches 20–20, the winner is the player or team with a two-point advantage. If the score goes up to 29–29, the winner is the first to reach 30 points.

- In badminton the serve is of huge importance. Points used to be won only on serve. But this has been scrapped under the new changes, so a player or team can win the point without holding serve.

- A team now has only one serve in doubles, rather than two as under the old rules.

Roles and responsibilities of officials

Badminton is controlled by an umpire, whose responsibilities include:

- administering the toss
- keeping and announcing the score
- dealing with lets and rule infringements, and any issues concerned with the laws of the game.

A service judge is placed at the net. His or her role is to watch for infringements of the rules of service.

There are various ways of starting the game, for example, a coin may be tossed. Whatever means is used, the winning team has three options: to choose to serve, to choose to receive (the opposing team serves) or to choose ends.

In badminton, the score zero is referred to as love. When the umpire is ready for the game to begin, he or she calls 'Love all – play'. The umpire always calls the serving player's score first, for instance, 'Five – love'. When one side has finished serving, the umpire calls, 'Service over', followed by the score.

The service judge looks for any infringements of the rules of service (see the rules given under serving on page 273).

In addition to these two officials, there are ten line judges who signal if a shuttle is in or out. The positions of these officials are indicated on the World Badminton website at www.heinemann.co.uk/hotlinks.

Line judges are responsible for deciding if a shuttle is in or out. If the shuttle lands on a line, it is regarded as in.

Performance of other players

You can look at a badminton player's performance in various ways, for example:

- movement around the court

- use of, and effectiveness of, forehand and backhand strokes. Does she or he score a point?

- rallies won on the player's own serve and on his or her opponent's serve.

To help you do this, it is helpful to have a model in your mind of what a particular shot should look like. You can then compare your player's performance against it. Investigate how certain shots should be performed by reading badminton coaching manuals or watching coaching videos.

 Key point

You could use a variety of methods to compare players, for example:

- calculating the percentage of serves that win a player points

- timing the length of rallies

- observing the range of shots used

- identifying the tactics and strategies employed.

Let's do it!

Video a match in one of your chosen sports. Draw up a chart and analyse the performance of one player in the game or match, using some of the methods discussed. Produce some charts, tables or other visual displays which allow you to show some analysis of that player's performance.

From this analysis, make some suggestions to the player as to how they could improve.

Your chart might look like this.

	No. of forehands	No. of backhands	No. of successful smashes	No. of long serves	No. of short serves	Average length of rally when serving	Basic tactics
Player A	52	35	14	20	10	4	Kept opposing player on back line and then used a drop shot/net shot
Player B	64	15	8	15	15	7	Tried to use opposite corners each time to make opponent move as much as possible

Case study

Badminton log book

This is taken from a badminton player's log book. It shows you how you might choose to complete your own.

Date Thursday 8 January 2004
Place school sports hall
Event Match v. Stanground College

During this inter-school match, I was selected to play a singles match over three sets for the school. I had never played my opponent before and so I decided to employ the following tactics:

- serve long to the middle of the court
- engage my opponent in long rallies in an effort to tire my opponent for the second and third sets, since I believe I have a high level of personal fitness.

Match Result I won the match 15-12, 13-15, 15-9

Report

During the first set, I quickly discovered that my opponent had a good smash and net shot. However, his backhand strokes lacked power and distance and his footwork was poor when put under pressure. I decided to change my tactics and varied my serve to make my opponent move as much as possible. This created a number of opportunities to play net shots, as my opponent was unable to control the shuttle sufficiently to keep it low to the net on return. Most of my points came from mistakes made by my opponent.

Match strengths

I returned to the 'T' position well and my serving was reliable and accurate. The distance on my clears was good and my footwork was balanced and sure. My attacking net play was satisfactory but needs to improve in future games. I was stronger on my forehand than my backhand

Match weaknesses

I lacked a strong backhand clear and was unable to cope with shots played onto that side of my game. My short serve was let down by a poor flick serve which hit the net too often. I was unable to keep my opponent moving as much as I wanted. Although this did not cause problems in this game, it may do against other opposition, and needs to be improved.

These comments were written down after talking to my P.E. teacher, who has written a witness statement to go with this diary entry.

Assessment Activity 6: Observational checklist for racket-based games

First:

- Choose whether you are going to use your racket sport for your individual or team sport

- Now decide whether you are going to look at the whole team or just one of the players.

1 Now *identify* the main skills, techniques and tactics that apply to your chosen racket sport (e.g. forehand and backhand shots, serves and volleys, etc). Now identify how they should be performed (grip, position of feet, follow-through, and so on). Draw up a sheet that includes this information and add columns where you can write about what you see. Include spaces for recording strengths and weaknesses. This provides evidence for P4. For M3 do this without help from your teacher!

2 Now set up some practices or drills and ask your player or players to perform these practices. Observe their performance and record what you see on the sheet that you have designed.

3 Repeat this exercise in a game or match to observe the tactics and skills used. Once again, using the sheet you have designed, record your observations.

Tasks 2 and 3 will provide evidence for P5 and P6.

4 Now write up your evaluation. Remember to *describe* what your player or players are good and bad at. This provides evidence for M4.

5 Try to suggest reasons why the strengths and weaknesses you have identified exist. Is it fitness? Poor footwork? Positioning? Lack of communication between players? How might the players you have observed improve the weaknesses in their playing performance? Try to make a number of different suggestions.

This activity will provide evidence for D2.

Individual sports – swimming

Swimming is a water-based activity. Other examples of water-based sports are synchronised swimming, diving (springboard) and water polo. Swimming is controlled by the Amateur Swimming Association (ASA), based in Loughborough.

Skills, techniques and tactics

Swimming is both a team and individual sport. It comprises a variety of disciplines, including the major strokes:

- freestyle (or front crawl)
- backstroke
- breaststroke
- butterfly.

These strokes are swum over a variety of distances. There are also medley relays, where individual swimmers swim each of the four strokes. In addition there are relays of four swimmers, either all swimming freestyle, or each swimming one of the four main strokes. Swimming is not a mixed sport: events are for men or for women.

Skills and techniques

The skills and techniques used in swimming are all designed to allow the swimmer to move through the water as fast as possible and to change direction at the end of each length quickly. At all times, the swimmer is trying to apply as great a force as possible on the water to propel himself or herself forward with the maximum speed. To achieve this, swimmers use specific arm and leg actions designed to allow rapid movement through the water.

The performance of a swimmer can be analysed by breaking the stroke down into:

- the arm action
- the leg action
- the body position
- the breathing sequence
- timing.

Tactics

The techniques used in swimming are less varied than in other sports. Each stroke is governed by a variety of rules, which outline what a swimmer can and cannot do. As a result, the athlete has little opportunity to alter the action used. Similarly, the tactics employed are limited mainly to the pace swum and, in relays, the order the swimmers will swim in. There is no defence and attack to worry about, so there is no concern over defending or attacking formations. Since you swim in your own lane, an important tactic is ensuring that you qualify well from heats to ensure a middle lane draw for swimming finals. This is important, since the middle lanes suffer from less water disturbance during a race.

Another consideration a swimmer must think about is the breathing technique used. If you are in a lane with competitors on both sides then bi-lateral breathing (breathing alternately left and right) is important because it allows you to see where your competitors are. Swimmers may also change when they breathe, for example every stroke, every four strokes, and so on.

Swimming rules and regulations

The basic rules of the sport relate to a number of features, including:

- the start
- turns at the end of each length of the pool

■ the stroke itself.

The rules vary depending on the stroke concerned. The governing body for swimming in this country is the Amateur Swimming Association (ASA) and the international governing body for world swimming is Federation Internationale de Natation (FINA). You can check out both their websites on www.heinemann.co.uk/hotlinks. The rules shown below are set by FINA and apply to competitive swimming from 2003–2005.

THE RACE

SW 10.1 A swimmer swimming over the course alone shall cover the whole distance to qualify.

SW 10.2 A swimmer must finish the race in the same lane in which he or she started.

SW 10.3 In all events, a swimmer when turning shall make physical contact with the end of the pool or course. The turn must be made from the wall, and it is not permitted to take a stride or step from the bottom of the pool.

SW 10.4 Standing on the bottom during freestyle events or during the freestyle portion of medley events shall not disqualify a swimmer, but he or she shall not walk.

SW 10.5 Pulling on the lane rope is not allowed.

SW 10.6 Obstructing another swimmer by swimming across another lane or otherwise interfering shall disqualify the offender. Should the foul be intentional, the referee shall report the matter to the Member promoting the race, and to the Member of the swimmer so offending.

SW 10.7 No swimmer shall be permitted to use or wear any device that may aid his or her speed, buoyancy or endurance during a competition (such as webbed gloves, flippers, fins, etc.). Goggles may be worn.

SW 10.8 Any swimmer not entered in a race, who enters the water in which an event is being conducted before all swimmers therein have completed the race, shall be disqualified from his or her next scheduled race in the meet.

SW 10.9 There shall be four swimmers on each relay team.

SW 10.10 In relay events, the team of a swimmer whose feet lose touch with the starting platform before the preceding team-mate touches the wall shall be disqualified, unless the swimmer in default returns to the original starting point at the wall, but it shall not be necessary to return to the starting platform.

SW 10.11 Any relay team shall be disqualified from a face if a team member, other than the swimmer designated to swim that length, enters the water when the race is being conducted, before all swimmers of all teams have finished the race.

SW 10.12 The members of a relay team and their order of competing must be nominated before the race. Any relay team member may compete in a race only once. The composition of a relay team may be changed between the heats and finals of an event, provided that it is made up from the list of swimmers properly entered by a Member for that event. Failure to swim in the order listed will result in disqualification. Substitutions may be made only in the case of a documented medical emergency.

SW 10.13 Any swimmer having finished his or her race, or his or her distance in a relay event, must leave the pool as soon as possible without obstructing any other swimmer who has not yet finished his or her race. Otherwise the swimmer committing the fault, or his or her relay team, shall be disqualified.

SW 10.14 Should a foul endanger the chance of success of a swimmer, the referee shall have the power to allow him or her to compete in the next heat or, should the foul occur in a final event or in the last heat, he or she may order it to be re-swam.

SW 10.15 No pace-making shall be permitted, nor may any device be used or plan adopted which has that effect.

THE START

SW 4.1 The start in freestyle, breaststroke, butterfly and individual medley races shall be with a dive. On the long whistle (SW 2.1.5) from the referee the swimmers shall step onto the starting platform and remain there. On the starter's command 'take your marks', they shall immediately take up a starting position with at least one foot at the front of the starting platforms. The position of the hands is not relevant. When all swimmers are stationary, the starter shall give the starting signal.

SW 4.2 The start in backstroke and medley relay races shall be from the water. At the referee's first long whistle (SW 2.1.5), the swimmers shall immediately enter the water.

At the referee's second long whistle the swimmers shall return without undue delay to the starting position (SW 6.1). When all swimmers have assumed their starting positions, the starter shall give the command 'take your marks'. When all swimmers are stationary, the starter shall give the starting signal.

SW 4.3   In Olympic Games, World Championships and other FINA events the command 'Take your marks' shall be in English and the start shall be by multiple loudspeakers, mounted one at each starting platform.

SW 4.4   Any swimmer starting before the starting signal has been given shall be disqualified. If the starting signal sounds before the disqualification is declared, the race shall continue and the swimmer or swimmers shall be disqualified upon completion of the race. If the disqualification is declared before the starting signal, the signal shall not be given, but the remaining swimmers shall be called back and start again.

Stroke	Some of the rules
Freestyle	Freestyle means that the swimmer can swim any style in the race. Some part of the swimmer must touch the wall at the end of each length and when they finish the race.
Backstroke	Prior to the starting signal, the swimmers shall line up in the water facing the starting end, with both hands holding the starting grips. The feet, including the toes, shall be under the surface of the water. Standing in or on the gutter on bending the toes over the lip of the gutter is prohibited. Upon the finish of the race the swimmer must touch the wall while on the back. The body may be submerged at the touch.
Breaststroke	All movements of the arms shall be simultaneous and in the same horizontal plane without alternating movement. At each turn and at the finish of the race, the touch shall be made with both hands simultaneously at, above, or below the water level. The head may be submerged after the last arm pull prior to the touch, provided it breaks the surface of the water at some point during the last complete or incomplete cycle preceding the touch.
Butterfly	Both arms shall be brought forward together over the water and brought backward simultaneously throughout the race. All up and down movements of the legs must be simultaneous. The position of the legs or the feet need not be on the same level, but they shall not alternate in relation to each other. A breaststroke kicking movement is not permitted.

■ *Two different swimming styles*

Medley swimming

SW 9.1	In individual medley events, the swimmer covers the four swimming styles in the following order: butterfly, backstroke, breaststroke and freestyle.	
SW 9.2	In medley relay events, swimmers will cover the four swimming styles in the following order: backstroke, breaststroke, butterfly and freestyle.	
SW 9.3	Each section must be finished in accordance with the rule which applies to the style concerned.	

Roles and responsibilities of officials

Swimming competitions take many forms, from club championships to Olympic finals. For open meetings, where swimmers enter under their own name, the ASA state that the following is the minimum list of officials required:

- a referee
- a chief timekeeper for each lane
- a starter
- one timekeeper for each lane
- a check starter
- a male and female competitors' steward
- two placing judges
- a recorder

- two stroke judges
- an announcer
- two turning judges.

Visit the British swimming website, at www.heinemann.co.uk/hotlinks, to find out what each official does.

Performance of other swimmers

The assessment of a swimmer's performance is relatively simple. You can compare his or her swimming action against an accepted model of a good stroke. A swimming stroke is normally broken down into:

- head position
- body position
- leg action
- arm action
- breathing
- timing of stroke.

Recording performance and involvement

If your chosen individual sport is swimming, it is a good idea to ask someone to video you while you swim. You can then replay the video tape and analyse your strengths and weaknesses. Similarly, you can video or observe other swimmers, and assess their performance. It is a good idea to concentrate on one aspect of the stroke at a time, for example, the arm action or leg action. Compare yourself or your subject against a model.

Using statistical information (graphs and charts for example) is sometimes not as easy for individual sports as for team or racket sports. Swimming, for example, is a continuous skill, so the athlete is simply repeating the same action over and over. You might record pace notes for every 25 or 50 metres swum to analyse a performance, or count the number of strokes used to complete each length of the pool. Breathing technique is another area that you could record, for example when and on what side the swimmer breathes.

The type of leg kick used in some strokes can also be analysed. In freestyle, a six beat leg kick is often used (six leg kicks to one left and then right arm pull). In long-distance events like the 1500-metre freestyle, the leg kick is almost non-existent, as swimmers use their arms and shoulders to do almost all the work. In backstroke and breaststroke, you can analyse the distance travelled under water after each turn, and compare these figures.

Let's do it!

1   *The table below provides a general model for an efficient backstroke. Watch someone you know swimming backstroke. In the third column of the table, write your observations of his or her performance. Compare your swimmer's stroke with the model.*

2   *Visit the Amateur Swimming Association website at www.heinemann.co.uk/hotlinks to look at the models for the other major strokes.*

Stroke area	Comments	Observation of performer
Head and body position	Almost horizontal, straight and streamlined Back of head in water Head kept still Shoulders roll in a controlled way Chest clear of water Hips and bottom slightly submerged under the water Eyes looking up and forwards slightly	
Feet and legs	In line with body using an alternate kick Feet near to surface but knees under Toes pointed, knees bending slightly Small splash by feet at the surface	
Hands and arms	As hand enters water, elbow is straight, little finger enters first At deepest point, elbow bends and hand presses round and back towards the thigh Thumb leaves water first and arm travels straight and back to the entry point	
Breathing	Regular and naturally in time with the effort made by the arms	
Timing	Should produce a consistent and continuous stroke	

Case study

Training diary

This training diary entry records the details of a training session.

> **Date** Sunday 11 January 2004
> **Location** Ponds Forge Swimming Centre
> **Session** Under 16 Advanced Training Session for Front Crawl
>
> Today I did the following training:
>
> **Warm up**
> 50m front crawl, 50m backstroke
> 30 seconds rest followed by:
>   25m front crawl - fast
>   25m breaststroke - steady
>   25m butterfly - fast
>   25m backstroke - steady
>
> **Main session**
> 20 x 25m front crawl, followed by 25 m 'catch up'. In catch up drills, the full stroke is swum but only one arm is working at one time. One arm pulls and 'catches up' the other arm, which then pulls.
>
> **Kickboard work**
> 50m kickboard, front crawl.
> 50m arms only front crawl
> 10 seconds rest
> Repeat for a total distance of 800 m
>
> **Fin work**
> 400m front crawl (fast) with fins - concentrate on arm action
>
> **Warm down**
> 300m front crawl (slow) to warm down
> Total distance swum = 2700m
>
> **Comment**
> Felt good throughout the session. Arm action worked well and my coach was happy with the length of my pull. Felt fatigued towards the end of the session but the previous day's weights session was probably to blame. Good advice to keep water on poolside throughout to top up my fluids.

Assessment activity 7: Tactics

When playing either an individual or team sport, players will need to adopt and use appropriate tactics and strategies to try and win the game. When deciding what tactics or strategies to use, a number of factors might need to be taken into account.

1 Observe your two chosen sports – one individual and one team sport – in a competitive situation. Watch how the player in the individual sport, and either the whole team or an individual within the team, play the match. Look for the types of shots played, the speed of the game, swim or run, the team formation used, etc. Observe the following:

■ How effective is the performance observed? Do they win the game or match?

■ Do the tactics/strategies work? Do they win the game because of the tactics used, or despite them?

■ What type of opponent is played – more or less able? Fitter than your subject? Can you identify weaknesses in the opponent that would suggest you should play in a particular way?

2 Why do you think your individual/team uses the tactics observed? Were they the right tactics to use? If so why? If not, why not?

3 Can you suggest how your team or individual could improve their tactical ability? What do they need to try to do better? How could this be achieved?

This exercise will provide evidence for D1.

Summary

In this unit, you have learned the following.

1 Sport requires the performer to make use of a variety of skills and techniques to succeed in particular situations. Skills are learned and require training and practice. There are various types of skills, including individual and team skills.

2 Tactics and strategies are the various ways in which we might play a match or game – they include team formations and individual player positions. It is important to employ a range of tactics and strategies and to be able to change these during a match.

3 You need to be able to assess a player's performance by looking at the skills he or she uses in a game. You can do this using a variety of methods, for example, observation, statistical methods such as graphs, or discussion with the coach or player.

4 You need to be able to assess your own performance. This allows you to identify strengths and weaknesses, plan how to improve your performance and play better and more successfully in the future.

Check what you know!

Look back through this unit to see if you can you answer the following questions.

1 Name four types of skill.

2 Describe and explain one individual skill from a sport of your choice. You should point out the key factors of the skill. Repeat this for a contrasting sport.

3 Describe and explain one team skill from a sport of your choice. Explain the strengths and weaknesses of this team skill. Repeat this for a contrasting sport.

4 Choose a tactic from your chosen sport and explain why it might be employed in a game or match. Explain how an opponent might play against your chosen tactic.

5 Why might you change the tactic employed?

6 Choose three key rules from your chosen sports and explain them to the class.

7 Explain the role of an official from one of your chosen sports.

8 List all the officials required by one of your chosen sports.

9 How might the role of match officials be compared?

10 List five functions of a match official in your chosen sport.

9 Psychology for Sports Performance

Introduction

Success in sport depends on more than being skilful in a particular event or position in a team. We also need to be physically fit for our sport and have the appropriate mental skills if we are to achieve our potential. Most of us are prepared to spend many hours working not only on improving the techniques and skills we need but also ensuring that we are fit enough to maintain our skill level throughout competition. Few of us put the same amount of preparation and training into the mental side of sport, which could be a costly mistake during the challenges of competition.

In this unit we will introduce the concept of sports psychology – that is, using our knowledge of how our mind works to improve our sports performance. You will also consider the impact of personality, aggression and motivation on sports performance. Finally, you will put these ideas into practice by analysing your own mental toughness and by completing a six-week programme aimed at developing attitudes and mental skills connected with your own performance.

▶ Continued from previous page

How you will be assessed

This unit will be assessed by an internal assignment that will be set and marked by the staff at your centre. It may be sampled as well by your centre's External Verifier as part of Edexcel's on-going quality procedures. The assignment is designed to allow you to show your understanding of the unit outcomes. These relate to what you should be able to do after completing this unit.

Your assessment could be in the form of:

- video recorded presentations
- case studies
- role plays
- written assignments.

After completing this unit you should be able to achieve the following learning outcomes.

1 Understand the psychological demands of a selected sport.
2 Understand the impact motivation can have on sports performance.
3 Understand the effects of personality and aggression on sports performance.
4 Be able to assess your own attitudes and mental skills, and plan a programme to enhance your attitudes and mental skills in relation to sports performance.

9.1 Understand the psychological demands of a selected sport

When our physical skills are evenly matched it is usually the sportsperson who has the stronger mental approach who comes out on top. A strong mental approach can be called **mental toughness** – the confidence that you will pull through in any situation.

We often use our mind to work against us by finding different reasons to justify our failings. For example, we convince ourselves that we felt too tired or that the conditions were too difficult. However, most successful sportspeople use their minds positively in order to perform well under any circumstances.

Read the passage on the next page and then work in pairs to see if you can agree answers to the questions which appear at the end of the passage.

When we take part in sport purely for pleasure and the result is of no importance, then our mental approach is almost irrelevant. As soon as the result takes on some importance for us then our mental approach becomes significant. For example, jogging in the forest does not involve the same mental approach as playing in a competitive football match.

■ *Does jogging for pleasure require a strong mental approach?*

The stress and uncertainty of sporting competitions places many psychological demands on the performer. In order to be successful, all performers need mental toughness. Mental toughness in sport means having the confidence that you will pull through in any situation.

Case study

Game, set and match

Ravi was annoyed with himself and his dad. He knew that he was the fittest he had ever been and felt able to win today's regional knockout competition. He also knew that he had wasted time on his computer yesterday evening instead of getting his kit ready for today's match. This had then delayed them leaving home this morning. It was the first time that he had competed at this particular indoor tennis centre and his dad had taken much longer than expected to find it. He was also annoyed with his dad because at one stage during the drive he had commented, 'I hope that you win after I have given up all day for you yet again.' Ravi had responded by saying, 'How do you expect me to play well when I am already stressed by being late for the competition?'

Ravi had changed quickly and completed a much shortened warm-up session with his coach, who had made it clear that he was not happy with him for arriving just in the nick of time. During the warm up Ravi was thinking about Larry Diver, his first opponent in this knockout competition. Although Ravi was ahead 3-2 in matches already played, Larry had won the last two. Ravi was hoping that Larry's serve was not as fast and accurate as it had been the last time that they had met.

He wished he had discussed how best to play Larry with his coach, Bill, but Bill had upset him during their last training session when after a poor shot he had commented, 'I have a five-year-old son who can hit the ball more cleanly that that.'

It was time to play, and during the five-minute warm up before the match started, Ravi noticed that Larry was hitting his ground strokes very sweetly and with a great deal of power. Ravi also started to think about his last training session with his coach when they worked on his backhand drive, which was one of his weaker shots. He hoped that his backhand would hold up against Larry.

Ravi served first and got through to 40–love without difficulty. He then double faulted and as he took position for his next serve he thought 'I did this the last time I played Larry. I can't afford to lose this game.' His first serve hit the base of the net and as he prepared to take his second serve he decided that he did not like the lighting at the centre. He played a weak second serve but fortunately Larry's return was long. Ravi went on to win the first game.

Six games later and with the score at 2-4 and thirty–forty, Ravi was about to take his first serve. 'I can't afford to double fault again. This one must go in or I'll be in real trouble,' he thought. He served: the ball cleared the net but was called long. Ravi could not believe it. He started to argue with the umpire who assured him that the call was correct. Ravi threw his racket on the floor; picked it up and walked very slowly back to the base-line to take his second serve. The umpire warned him about his future behaviour and on this occasion Ravi kept quiet.

Ravi's second serve, although not fast, was accurate and Larry made a scrambled short return to Ravi's backhand court. Ravi decided to play a backhand drive and as he stepped in to play the short he thought, 'I hope that my practice session was worthwhile.'

Now answer these questions.

1 Do you think Ravi is likely to win this match? Be prepared to justify your answer.

2 In pairs, complete the table below which lists the emotions which Ravi felt during different parts of the day. Say whether the emotion is likely to help or hinder his chance of winning the match. The first two are completed for you.

We will revisit this activity later in the unit.

Action or thought	Emotion	Help	Hinder
Dad not knowing the way	Anger at father		✓
Ravi not being prepared in time	Annoyed with himself		✓

We all know that we can improve our sporting skills and fitness through regular training. In the same way, we can improve our mental toughness through training and experience.

Key point

Any mental toughness training programme should include:

- focusing
- confidence
- performance routines
- breathing
- mental rehearsal

- thinking techniques
- thought stopping
- self-talk
- body language.

■ *Sport places strong psychological demands on players*

Psychological demands

Focusing

By focusing we mean concentrating our attention on every detail that will make our performance successful. As performers we have a vast amount of information to consider. Some of this information is external, coming from the environment around us such as the strength of the wind or the noise of the spectators. We also get information about our physical condition, for example whether or not our muscles feel tired or how fast we are breathing. Our internal thoughts and feelings are also important for our performance. They reflect our level of confidence and how relaxed or excited we feel. Successful performers learn to select only the information which will ensure a good performance.

Think about it

Try to recall the last time that you were involved in a sporting event, the result of which was important to you.

- *What were your feelings just before the start of the event?*
- *Were you aware of people watching you – your parents, coach, spectators?*
- *How did your body feel – were you in good shape physically?*
- *Were there any distractions around you?*
- *Did you feel that any of these factors affected your performance?*

■ *It is important to focus attention on all the details that will help us succeed*

Confidence

Confidence is a measure of how likely you feel that you are to succeed. It is not merely hope but rather it reflects your expectations about what you think will actually happen. Success in sport is likely to come to people who retain a confident, positive, optimistic outlook even when things are not going well. This helps them to prevent them 'choking' under the pressure of competition. Positive thoughts can improve confidence, while negative thoughts destroy confidence.

Confidence can be affected by uncertainty and anxiety. However, uncertainty is an important part of all sport. To reduce uncertainty sportspeople must concentrate on what they themselves have under their own control and avoid wasting energy on factors beyond their control. For example, skiers should ensure that they are in top physical condition for the event and do not worry unduly about the likely weather conditions.

Think about it

Try to recall the last time that you were involved in a sporting event, the result of which was important to you.

- *Did you go into the competition expecting to win?*
- *Did you have any anxieties at all?*
- *Did you feel you were in control of the sporting situation?*
- *Did you feel that any of these factors affected your performance?*

Performance routines

In order to be in the best possible frame of mind for competitive sport it is helpful to have a routine in the period leading up to competition. This would include such things as familiarising yourself with the competitive arena, ensuring transport arrangements are in place and that all kit and equipment is checked and ready well before it is needed. We would refer to this as a pre-performance routine.

All sportspeople warm up before training and competition. The activity prepares the body physically for the action to come by stretching muscles and increasing blood flow. It also helps to prevent injury. The development of a regular, systematic warm-up routine also helps sportspeople to focus on the performance ahead of them. This focusing procedure can involve **mental rehearsal** – the recall in detail of a past successful performance. The imagery used can generate confidence and improve our mood. Mental preparation may also involve repeating prepared positive statements to remove any negative thoughts.

Let's do it!

In pairs, explain your own performance routine for a major competition or match using the following headings:

- *Activities the day before including any training or relaxation periods*
- *Any special arrangements for diet and sleep*
- *Transport arrangements on the day of competition*
- *Preparation of kit and equipment*
- *Practice or warm up sessions before competition*
- *Relaxation techniques leading up to the actual competition*
- *Any mental rehearsal or positive self-talk patterns used before the competition.*

■ *Performance routines can help with mental as well as physical preparation*

Breathing

Our breathing can usually be controlled before, during and after both training and competition. Concentrating on breathing deeply and rhythmically allows our body to relax. This in turn helps us to concentrate solely on our performance. This can be very helpful before competition or in some sports, for example tennis, during natural breaks in the performance.

Mental rehearsal

Many sportspeople prepare for sporting activity by mentally rehearsing their actions. In their minds they imagine that they are performing a very successful action. They make their images realistic, clear and successful. For example, golfers imagine how they will swing the club and hit the ball. However, this is not all. They will also try to recall many details about the occasion such as what the weather was like, how short the grass was, how strong the wind was and from which direction the sun was shining. These details will give them some sense of the occasion but the golfers will also try to recall how they felt, their relaxation and their confidence that the shot would be a good one.

Thinking techniques

When taking part in sustained repetitive sporting activity such as running, swimming, cycling and rowing our minds are also active. Sometimes this thinking is helpful to our sporting activity but it can also have a negative effect. Many sportspeople use particular techniques to ensure that their thinking is as helpful as possible to their sporting activity.

- **Association** – When using this technique we concentrate on the feelings we get from our body during the activity. For example, how are muscles are feeling, how fast our heart is beating or how strong our breathing is. We can use this information to help us cope with the intensity of the activity.

- **Dissociation** – When using this technique we actively think of something quite different from what we are doing. This would include listening to music, planning a party, counting all the red cars we see, and so on. We do this in order to distract us from the demands of the activity – for example, how tired we are feeling, or if our muscles are aching and our breathing is difficult.

Thought stopping

We do not want negative or worrying thoughts to distract us when we are performing. For example, having lost a point as a result of a poor shot, the badminton player should not be thinking about this last shot but focusing entirely on receiving the next serve. To maintain our concentration we can use techniques such as saying 'Stop' verbally, snapping our fingers or imagining a red light or stop sign. We can then refocus quickly on positive thoughts and give our full attention to our performance. Above all we need to focus on solutions not problems in order to be successful.

■ *Negative thoughts stop here*

Think about it

Try to recall the last time that you were involved in a sporting event for which the result was important to you.

- *Can you recall how you felt when you made a mistake during the sporting activity?*
- *Did you suffer from negative thoughts at the time?*
- *How did you deal with these negative thoughts?*
- *Did these negative thoughts have any effect on your performance which followed?*

Self-talk

Quietly talking to ourselves before, during and after a competition can be helpful. It has the potential to help us cope with the stress of the competition and any problems with our performance. It should always be positive, focusing attention on the present situation, not the past. It may involve repeating a few positive, powerful words over and over again during competition to maintain our focus on the important points for the performance – for example, 'Power and control' when throwing the javelin.

Think about it

Try to recall the last time that you were involved in a sporting event, the result of which was important to you.

- *Did you find the competition stressful?*
- *Did you use self-talk at any stage in the sporting activity?*
- *Can you remember any key words which you used and which were helpful?*
- *Did this self-talk have any effect on your performance which followed?*

■ *Quietly talking to yourself can be useful*

Should our concentration fail or our performance start to deteriorate, we might find it helpful to use trigger words. These are powerful reminders of the important basics of our performance and might include such words as 'Next point', 'Breathe deeply' or 'Head high'. These words can be written on our sports clothing, our equipment or even on our hands.

Body language

A player whose body language shows confidence and energy is likely to gain an advantage in competition against an opponent whose whole posture and demeanour is not so positive. Above all, positive body language shows that the sportsperson is in control of himself or herself and is ready for the competition. Sportspeople often use routines which allow them to stay focused and confident during competitions. For example, a routine for preparing to serve in tennis, for taking a place kick in rugby or a free shot in basketball.

■ *Look confident and be in control at all times*

Think about it

Try to recall the last time that you were involved in a sporting event, the result of which was important to you. Choose an event in which you played directly against an opponent.

- *Try to remember your first impressions of your opponent. Was he or she looking confident, fit and relaxed?*
- *Did his or her body language suggest that he or she was going to win?*
- *How did you feel? Were you confident, fit and relaxed?*
- *Did the body language of you or your opponent change as the game progressed?*
- *Do you think that body language had any effect on the result of the match?*

Case study

Game, set and match reviewed

Using the knowledge you have gained about the different aspects of mental toughness, look again at Ravi's experience in the game, set and match activity (page 292).

Suggest ways in which Ravi, his dad, or his coach could have improved his chances of winning, either before the tournament or during the match itself. You might find it helpful to use the following table. The table has been started for you.

Activity	Aspect of mental toughness
Ravi checked that all his kit and equipment was ready for the following day, packed it in his bags and had an early night knowing that he was well prepared for next day's competition	Pre-preparation routine

Assessment activity 1: Psychological demands of sport – developing mental toughness

To achieve a Pass:

1 *Describe* the psychological demands, that is, developing mental toughness, for a selected sport. (P1)

To achieve a Merit you must achieve the Pass criteria and:

2 *Explain* the psychological demands, that is, developing mental toughness, for a selected sport. (M1)

9.2 Understand the impact motivation can have on sports performance

We take part in sport for a variety of different reasons. Most of us learn our sporting skills in school as part of a compulsory curriculum. As we get older we can choose to increase our sporting activity if we so wish. Our reasons for playing may change over time as we grow older or develop other interests. For us to continue taking part in sport we need to get something in return. Initially, enjoyment of the activity for its own sake is sufficient, but as we take it more seriously, playing well and winning also become important. If we do not enjoy the activities or are unsuccessful we are unlikely to want to continue. Whether we want to continue in sport or not depends upon the strength of the drive within us. This drive or desire we call **motivation**.

We all vary in our drive to succeed in sport or life in general; that is, we all have different levels of motivation. There are two different types of motivation.

- **Intrinsic (or self) motivation** comes from our own inner drives. Examples include playing for fun and enjoyment, improving fitness and losing weight, the physical pleasure of the activity, performing skilfully and being successful, and the pleasure gained from being with others.
- **Extrinsic motivation** comes from rewards and outside pressures. Examples include winning competitions, being praised for our achievements, to satisfy the expectations of parents, teachers and coaches, and to fulfil our commitment to our team.

Anyone for sport?

An exit survey at a local sports centre revealed the answers on page 302 to the question 'Why do you come to the sports centre?'

Key point

Motivation is the drive within us to keep playing a sport. Different factors affect our motivation, such as our desire to win and personal enjoyment.

Let's do it!

Working in pairs, list the reasons why the people in the survey take part in sport. Can you think of any other reasons. Discuss why you and your partner take part in sport. Share your answers with the rest of the group.

Personal details	Activity	Reasons for participating
Peggy, 26 years old, one 2-year-old daughter.	Aerobics, twice a week	To meet people, to lose weight and keep fit
Darren, 17 years old, student at local college.	Competitive swimming training five times a week with competitions at weekends. Also attends gym three times a week	Has always been an exceptional swimmer from an early age. Enjoys winning trophies more than training. Has always been trained by his mother who is a coach at the club
Aisha, 14 years old, schoolgirl	Centre in netball team. Trains twice a week with a weekend match	Has always enjoyed playing netball and attends with three very good friends. Winning is not very important to her
Henry, 47 years old, competitive rower.	Trains on weights and rowing machine four times a week. Competitions or river work on Sundays	Gains satisfaction from the physical action of rowing and being part of a close-knit team of four. Above all he enjoys performing well
Marika, 21 years old, who wants to join the army.	Five sessions a week including circuits, aerobics and swimming	Failed practical army fitness test. Wants to retake test in three months' time
Wesley, 23 years old, print worker	Trains once a week and plays in local rugby team at weekend	Outstanding player in the team which he captains from scrum half. Now has girlfriend who lives 80 miles away and wants to see him more regularly

Increasing motivation

Most of us are motivated by a mixture of different reasons, some internal, some external. As we get older it is the intrinsic motivation that will keep us taking part in sport when the extrinsic motivators are greatly reduced.

All of us are likely to continue with sport if we enjoy the experience and gain some success. The more skilful we are, the more likely we are to be successful, and this success will increase our motivation. Everyone wants to keep fit and healthy and for many people this is a starting point for physical activity and sport. Sport is usually a social activity involving close interaction with others. We all enjoy the company of others and being with like-minded sportspeople often encourages us to maintain our sporting activity. Therefore, motivation is likely to be improved by making people more skilful, by making them aware of the value of fitness and health and by offering sport in an attractive setting.

We all enjoy achievement in sport, whether it is swimming a width for the first time, gaining a black belt in judo or completing our first marathon. Goal setting can be highly motivating. However, the goals set must be SMART – specific, measurable, achievable, realistic and time-related. Research shows that motivation is closely linked to personal qualities such as personality and mental toughness, the status of people

who give us advice such as parents and coaches and the social situation in which we find ourselves, such as our family and socio-economic status.

Key point

Motivation is our determination to achieve.

There are two types of motivation:

■ intrinsic (or self) motivation
■ extrinsic motivation.

Improving skill and therefore enjoyment

Understanding the value of fitness and health

Motivation may be improved by...

Ensuring sport takes place in an attractive social setting

Setting SMART goals

■ *How to become more motivated*

Assessment activity 2: Motivation

To achieve a Pass:

1 *Describe* the impact of motivation on sports performance, and identify strategies that can be used to maintain and increase motivation. (P2)

To achieve a Merit you must achieve the Pass criteria and:

2 *Explain* the impact of motivation on sports performance and strategies that can be used to maintain and increase motivation. (M2)

To achieve a Distinction you must achieve the Pass and Merit criteria and:

3 *Analyse* strategies used to maintain and increase motivation for sports performance. (D1)

9.3 Understand the effects of personality and aggression on sports performance

The ability to cope with the psychological demands of sport will vary from one sportsperson to another, largely depending on the sportsperson's personality.

Personality

We all think, feel and behave differently from one another. This is as a result of our different personalities. By **personality** we mean the sort of person we are, and it involves such qualities as our character and our temperament. We can also talk about our personality traits, that is, features of our personality: for example, being friendly, being shy and so on. Our traits can influence our behaviour and therefore how we prepare for and perform in sport. Some traits are thought to give us an advantage in particular sports. We should remember, however, that although we may have dominant personality traits our actual behaviour can be affected by both our experience and our environment.

Sports psychologists have suggested many ways of looking at the effect of personality on sport. Three of the most well known theories are as follows.

Extroverts and introverts

Two extreme personalities have been described as extroverts and introverts. Most of us are neither one nor the other exclusively, but somewhere in between. Extroverts are socially outgoing and show great confidence. They are likely to prefer team sports, activities using the whole body and a great deal of activity and uncertainty.

Introverts are less confident and reserved in social situations. They are likely to prefer individual sports, activities with little movement but fine skills and sports with repetitive movements.

Type A and Type B

Type A personalities have qualities such as impatience, intolerance and high levels of stress. Type B personalities have a relaxed, tolerant approach, with lower personal stress. Research has not shown that one particular personality type is preferable to another, although it is likely that Type A would be more likely to succeed in a competitive sporting context.

Hardiness

Hardiness is an important personality trait which has been identified by researchers. It refers to the ability to meet challenges and to cope with difficult times. In sport it would be likely to be linked with mental toughness. People with a high level of hardiness would be likely to have an advantage in the competitive environment of sport. Hardiness involves the ability to make an impact in all sporting situations, to refuse to give up easily, and not to give way to helplessness. At the heart of hardiness is confidence, so that 'when the going gets tough, the tough get going.'

Research suggests that although we differ in our hardiness, the techniques used to improve mental toughness can be used to influence this trait.

 **Key point**

Our personality can influence our likely success in sport. Personality theories include:

■ extrovert and introvert,

■ type A and type B

■ hardiness.

Assessment activity 3: Personality

To achieve a Pass:

1 *Describe* personality and identify how it affects sports performance. (P3)

Aggression

The competitive nature of sport ensures that aggressive behaviour will often be seen. However, some aggression is desirable in sport and some is unacceptable. Aggression usually involves an attempt to harm somebody. In sport we can consider an act to be aggressive if the intention is to harm a person outside the laws of the event, such as punching an opponent in football. This is known as hostile aggression and is totally unacceptable. Another form of aggression occurs when a player uses aggressive behaviour not primarily to hurt the opponent, but as a means to an end. This is known as instrumental aggression and occurs for example when pushing an opponent out of the way in order to receive the ball. Both hostile and instrumental aggression, however, fall outside the accepted rules of most sporting activities and would not be encouraged.

 **Key point**

Aggression is hostile or violent behaviour or actions. It is often unprovoked and caused by frustration or stress.

Aggression or assertiveness

Aggressive behaviour that is within the laws of the game is more properly called assertiveness and not aggression. Assertive behaviour is seen as forceful but acceptable behaviour in sport. It may involve the use of legitimate physical force but does not have the intention to harm or injure anyone. Examples would include strong tackles in hockey, competing for the ball in netball and spiking in volleyball.

■ *Aggressive or assertive behaviour?*

Controlling aggression

Competitive sport brings out strong emotions including frustration and aggression. These emotions need to be channelled into positive action. This in turn is more likely to lead to a successful performance. The following strategies can be used to channel aggression.

- Ensure fitness and skills are sufficient to cope with the competitive demands of the sport in order to minimise frustration.

- Exposure in training to potentially aggressive situations to enable the sportsperson to develop skills to cope in the competitive environment.

- Encourage the sportsperson to focus attention on the next sporting action rather than on what has just happened.

- Develop performance routines which will move the player on from any recent frustration in the sporting activity.

- Develop breathing techniques to use at times of stress to encourage relaxation and to help concentration.

- Encourage thought stopping to remove negative or worrying thoughts which interfere with the sporting performance.

- Encourage self-talk to help cope with the stress of the competition and any problems with the performance.

Key point

Aggression in sport is seen as the attempt to harm others outside the laws of the event. Types of aggression include:

- **hostile aggression** – unacceptable

- **instrumental aggression** – unacceptable

- **aggressive behaviours within the laws of the game (assertiveness)**
  – acceptable.

Assessment activity 4: Aggression

To achieve a Pass:

1 *Describe* aggression and identify strategies that can be adopted to control it. (P4)

To achieve a Merit you must achieve the Pass criteria and:

2 *Explain* strategies that can be adopted to control aggression. (M3)

To achieve a Distinction you must achieve the Pass and Merit criteria and:

3 *Evaluate* the strategies that can be adopted to control aggression. (D2)

9.4 Be able to assess your own attitudes and mental skills, and plan a programme to enhance your attitudes and mental skills in relation to sports performance

Assessment

In order to assess and improve our mental toughness we might find it useful to use a SWOT analysis. By this we mean examining our current strengths and weaknesses in relation to our mental toughness. We can then look at the opportunities available to improve our mental toughness as well as dealing with any threats which might reduce our performance.

 Key point

Using SWOT we can identify the following points in our sporting performance.
- **S** – strengths – positive points.
- **W** – weaknesses – negative points.
- **O** – opportunities – potential to improve.
- **T** – threats – barriers to improvement.

 Let's do it!

Use the case study analysis as a model to carry out a SWOT analysis of your own mental toughness during your most recent competition.

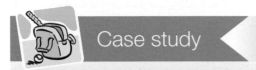

Case study

Game, set and match continued

Look at the following SWOT analysis of Ravi which he and his coach have carried out up to the point in the case study.

	Details
Strengths	Ravi was the fittest he had ever been He felt able to win the competition Ravi had worked on his backhand drive, one of his weaker shots, in training with his coach He started the match well He recovered his composure in the sixth game and produced a good serve at a vital moment
Weaknesses	Ravi was annoyed with himself and his dad Ravi had wasted time on his computer Ravi had not got his kit ready the previous day They were delayed leaving home on the morning of the competition His father was not familiar with the route and did not allow enough time for the journey Ravi was not familiar with this tennis centre His father's comments in the car had put extra pressure on Ravi to which he had responded angrily His lateness in arriving caused a shortened warm up and criticism from his coach He had not worked with his coach to develop strategies in order to deal with his first opponent, Larry Diver He was focusing on the strengths of his opponent's game during the warm up He was not totally confident that his backhand would hold up in the game situation He allowed negative thoughts to flow through his mind after double faulting in the first game and again when he was 2–4 down in games He took his frustration out on the umpire and received a warning for his bad behaviour At the critical moment in the sixth game he allowed negative thoughts to intrude once more
Opportunities	He has the support of his father, which he should show he appreciates. He could improve his pre-preparation by familiarisation with the venue, detailed route planning and timing, early kit and equipment preparation and sufficient rest and sleep He could arrive in plenty of time to be able to relax and go through his pre-arranged warm up with the help and support of his coach Knowing his opponent's strengths prior to the match, he and his coach could have prepared suitable strategies to beat him He could work with his coach in training in order to develop confidence in his own ability Also in his training he could develop the skills of focusing on the strengths of his own game He could use mental rehearsal prior to each serve He could also work on thinking techniques to maintain his concentration during the game In order to avoid negative thoughts he could use thought stopping techniques At critical times in the game he could use self-talk to maintain his focus on the important points of his technique
Threats	His father's support will decline if Ravi does not improve his commitment to the sport and his appreciation of his father His coach's commitment and support will decline if Ravi does not show a more serious approach and improve both his pre-preparation and match preparation Ravi will not fulfil his sporting potential because he does not take the mental training seriously enough Fitness and high level skill are not sufficient at the top level; mental toughness is also a vital ingredient for success

Assessment activity 5: SWOT analysis

To achieve a Pass:

1 Assess your own attitudes and mental skills, *with teacher support*, in a selected sport, identifying areas for improvement. (P5)

To achieve a Merit you must achieve the Pass criteria and:

2 *Independently* assess your own attitudes and mental skills in a selected sport and explain areas for improvement. (M4)

Programme

Once we have assessed our mental toughness using a SWOT analysis we can improve our mental toughness through a six-week training programme. In order for the programme to be successful it is essential to produce a set of goals against which progress can be made. In the mental toughness training programme which we have devised for Ravi we have used the SMART goals as a framework.

Key point

SMART target setting consists of setting targets that are:

S – specific – they say exactly what you mean

M – measurable – you can prove that you have reached them

A – achievable – you can reach them in the next few weeks

R – realistic – they are about action you can take

T – time related – they have deadlines.

Look at the following six-week programme which has been prepared for Ravi based on the SMART goals described above.

Let's do it!

Use this as a model to prepare and carry out a six-week training programme to improve an aspect of your own mental toughness.

Case study

Game, set and match continued

Six-week programme to improve Ravi's mental rehearsal and self-talk techniques:

■ Weeks one to three: teach Ravi to use a mental rehearsal technique

■ Weeks four to six: Ravi to practise mental rehearsal and develop self-talk techniques.

Week one: Sit down with Ravi and ask him to describe in detail one of his most successful serves. Get Ravi to replay it continuously in his mind and ask him to describe what the serve looked like, how he felt about it, the sounds, sights and feelings surrounding the serve. Ravi needs to develop a very clear, vivid picture of this successful serve which he can recall at will. (This process will take 10–15 minutes to complete.) During the rest of the training sessions, from time to time ask Ravi to recall this image of his successful serve, just before he serves in training. Check that he finds this form of mental rehearsal helpful.

Week two: Repeat the process and if necessary refine Ravi's image of his successful serve. Ask Ravi to replay the successful serve in his mind prior to each of his serves in training. Check with him from time to time that he is following this process. Also monitor the number of successful serves compared with unsuccessful serves and give feedback to him as well as asking Ravi for his views.

Week three: Organise a competitive match as part of the training session. Remind Ravi to use the mental rehearsal of the serve before serving. Monitor the results of Ravi's serving. Discuss with Ravi any improvements in the consistency of his serves and how successful the use of mental imagery has been.

Week four: Reminder to Ravi to continue mental rehearsal before each serve during practice. Prior to the start of the training session, ask Ravi to concentrate on his own performance and to be positive at all times. Suggest that he might find it helpful to make a few quiet comments to himself at the end of each rally. Remind him that the comments must be positive and forward looking. At the end of the session

ask Ravi to tell you the words or comments he used as self-talk. Explain that Ravi should try to recall all the unspoken comments and not just those which he may have spoken out loud. Ask Ravi to think about his comments and make a short list of the ones which he thinks were the most effective.

Week Five: Organise a competitive match as part of the training session. Remind Ravi to continue mental rehearsal of the serve. Also remind him to use the comments he has prepared at the end of each rally. Insist that he remains positive at all times and looks for the highlights in his performance. Ask him to look for improvements in his play rather than merely the results of each rally.

Ravi should not dwell on his mistakes. After the match, ask him to write down his mistakes on the left-hand side of a sheet of paper. Then, on the right, he should write down what he needs to do better next time. Ask him to tear the sheet in half, throw away the left-hand side and set about achieving those things listed on the right in training and competition.

Week Six: Organise a competitive match as part of the training session. Remind Ravi to continue the mental rehearsal of the serve and to use the self-talk practised previously.

During the match observe very carefully Ravi's response to winning and losing points. After the game, ask Ravi to describe the self-talk he used and whether he thought it was worthwhile. Review particular parts of the game where Ravi was especially successful or unsuccessful and ask him to describe what he was feeling at the time.

Following up this six-week programme, Ravi should now be able to use a mental image of his serve and also use self-talk effectively in the match situation. Hopefully this will result in improved performance. He and his coach can now look at other aspects of mental toughness in order to further improve his performance.

Recording

It is important that you keep a record of your SWOT analysis and any other evidence you used to assess your current mental toughness. Evidence which could be collected prior to the six-week programme could include:

- video of you taking part in a competitive sporting situation.
- comments from your coach, friends or parents about your mental strengths as well as areas which could be developed. These comments could be written down or recorded on video or audio.

■ *Recording information*

During the six-week programme you will need to keep a diary or log-book in which you should keep a record of your progress.

Diaries and log-books

One of the easiest ways in which to record and assess a performance is by keeping a diary or a log book. This should focus on all elements of the training session or event – even the weather!

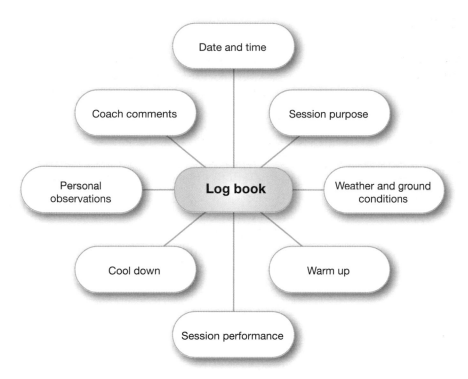

■ *Log book*

Case study

As part of Ravi's training programme he has kept a diary of his preparation.

Date: 20th August   **Day and time:** Thursday evening 7–9 pm.

Mental training detail: Bill (my coach) got me to think about my most successful serve and asked me to picture it in my head. He then got me to describe it in detail to him, not just the serve but also everything else that I could picture – the sounds, smells, thoughts in my mind, etc.

As we continued the training session, Bill kept asking me to picture this successful serve in my mind just before I was about to serve. At the end of the session Bill asked me if I thought that imagining a successful serve was helpful. I said I did not think it made a lot of difference, but Bill said that with practice it should make a difference.

My thoughts on the training session: I quite enjoyed trying to get a clear picture of one of my successful serves and describing it to Bill. I gave him a lot of detail which I thought he would not want to hear but to my surprise he asked me if I could give any more detail. I found it quite helpful to picture it just before I was about to serve, but once we started proper training again, I forgot to do it consistently. Bill reminded me about once every ten minutes. I don't know if I will be able to remember to do it in the heat of competition.

Now complete these activities.

1 Create your own diary for a day of your own training schedule.

2 Discuss your activities with other members of your group and compare how each of you differs in your preparation.

Let's do it!

Use the case study as a model to prepare and carry out a six-week training programme to improve an aspect of your own mental toughness.

Video and audio

Visually recording a performance provides the opportunity for you to review specific actions and movements and analyse these in your overall programme. Keeping a visual log will also enable you to assess improvements and determine areas of weakness. These materials can also be shown to others for comment.

Audio recordings can be used by trainers and coaches to take notes as the sportsperson is in action, providing a real-time account that can be analysed and discussed as part of an ongoing assessment.

Evaluation

You have already carried out a SWOT analysis of your own attitudes and mental skills and also created a six-week training programme in order to develop your mental toughness. You set targets for your six-week programme using SMART goals.

To carry out an evaluation of your six-week programme it is necessary to compare your progress against the goals which you set yourself. The evidence you use for your evaluation will depend upon your sport, the way that you recorded your progress over the six-week programme and the type of targets or goals you set yourself.

When Ravi evaluated his mental toughness training programme he gained feedback from the following:

- statistics from before, during and after the programme showing the percentage of successful first serves and double faults

- video footage of his serves in competitive matches before, during and after the training – looking for evidence of improvements in body language, mental preparation before serves, and the way emotions are displayed during matches

- his own personal thoughts about the training programme

- feedback from his coach, his parents and his colleagues

- reviewing his diary to note progress during the training programme.

Based on this evaluation Ravi and his coach have decided to reinforce the mental image practice on a regular basis. To improve his ability to create a really clear mental image, his coach was filming his serves during matches on a regular basis in order to be able to play some perfect ones back to Ravi at the start of training sessions. They have also agreed to further develop Ravi's self-talk, both when on the court and between games.

You should carry out a similar process of evaluation for your training programme, identifying the successful aspects as well as those needing improvement. You should then suggest how the programme can be modified to bring about these improvements.

Assessment activity 6: SMART analysis

To achieve a Pass:

1 Plan, and carry out, a six-week training programme, *with teacher support*, to improve attitudes and mental skills in a selected sport. (P6)

2 Evaluate the training programme, identifying areas for improvement. (P7)

To achieve a Merit you must achieve the Pass criteria and:

3 *Independently* plan a six-week training programme, to improve attitudes and mental skills in a selected sport. (M5)

4 *Evaluate* the training programme, *explaining* areas for improvement, and making suggestions in relation to how improvements could be achieved. (M6)

To achieve a Distinction you must achieve the Pass and Merit criteria and:

5 *Evaluate* the training programme, *justifying* suggestions relating to improvement, including specific activities relating to improvements in own attitudes and mental skills in a selected sport. (D3)

Summary

In this unit you have considered the psychological demands of sport. You need mental toughness to be able to cope with these demands; this means you will have the confidence to pull through in any situation. You looked at focusing, confidence, performance routines, breathing, mental rehearsal, thinking techniques, thought stopping, self-talk and body language.

You then went on to consider the effects of personality, motivation and aggression on sporting performance. Finally you used the SWOT analysis and the SMART guidelines in order to plan a six week programme designed to improve your own mental skills in relation to your sports performance.

Check what you know!

Look back through this unit and see if you can answer the following questions.

1 Explain what is meant by mental toughness.

2 List five different aspects of mental toughness which a training programme should include.

3 Chose one of these aspects of mental toughness and suggest how it could be developed to improve your own performance.

4 Give three examples of self-talk for a sport of your own choice.

5 Explain why confidence is so important in sport.

6 Give an example of the performance routine you use in your sport.

7 Explain the difference between intrinsic and extrinsic motivation.

8 Give three ways in which school leavers could be motivated to continue taking part in sport once they leave school.

9 Describe the difference between an introvert and an extrovert. Suggest types of sport which would be most suitable for each type of personality.

10 Explain the difference between assertiveness and aggression.

11 Suggest three ways in which an aggressive sportsperson might be encouraged to keep within the rules or laws or his or her sport.

12 What does SWOT stand for?

13 Explain how the SMART guidelines can help you achieve goals in sport.

12 Lifestyle and Sports Performance

Introduction

There is no doubt that leading the correct lifestyle is a contributing factor towards success and an improvement in sports performance for any athlete. It is important that all athletes adopt a professional approach to their training, taking into account things that could be harmful to their career, for example drugs, excess alcohol or how they spend their free leisure time.

Elite athletes will usually have to deal with lots of media attention – this could be giving interviews on TV or radio or being photographed daily by the paparazzi. Therefore it is important to represent the sport that they play, the team or country that they play for and ensure nothing untoward happens which could bring the sport and their personal reputation into disrepute.

Success in sport is not only about training hard and achieving great physical fitness. It is also about interaction with the coach and other athletes, effective communication, listening and responding to feedback as well as setting and working towards achieving those goals.

This unit will provide you with information about an appropriate lifestyle for an elite athlete or for those competing at a high level. To pass this unit successfully it will help if you play sport competitively or train outside of your school or college.

How you will be assessed

This unit will be assessed by an internal assignment that will be set and marked by the staff at your centre. It may be sampled as well by your centre's External Verifier as part of Edexcel's on-going quality procedures. The assignment is designed to allow you to show your understanding of the unit outcomes. These relate to what you should be able to do after completing this unit.

Your assessment could be in the form of:

- video recorded presentations
- case studies
- role plays
- written assignments.

You are required to keep a paper based or electronic diary showing realistic planning and prioritisation of work commitments – for example, study, sports training, competition, any employment and also your leisure time.

After completing this unit you should be able to achieve the following learning outcomes.

1 Be able to plan and manage your work commitments and leisure time.

2 Understand appropriate behaviour for an elite athlete.

3 Understand the factors that influence the effective planning of a career.

4 Be able to communicate effectively with the media and significant others.

12.1 Be able to plan and manage your work commitments and leisure time

Work commitments

To be successful in sport it is important that an athlete is able to plan and manage many aspects of their life that impact on each other such as their work commitments, training and leisure time. They do this in order to prioritise and use their time efficiently so that their goals and aspirations can be achieved. There is no doubt that planning can be time-consuming. However, it will make it easier for an athlete to compete, reduce any fears or concerns and allow the athlete to see what to do in order to make it to the top by planning work, study and leisure time around the main priority of training and competition. Insufficient training due to other commitments will be detrimental to the career of an athlete. So it is imperative that effective planning and prioritising is carried out as soon as possible.

Training and competition

Training is essential for progression in sport. Enough time must be dedicated in order to allow for achievement of set goals or objectives. A training plan must be devised and, where possible, adhered to. A training plan can be devised for a week, month or year depending upon current level of training, season, fitness or preparation for competition.

Stages of training

Any planning will have to take into consideration the four different stages of training.

1   Pre-season preparation phase.
2   Early season preparation phase.
3   Competition phase.
4   Recovery phase.

Stage 1: Pre-season preparation phase: In the preparation phase an athlete must start to develop their physical and cardio-respiratory fitness dependent upon their sporting activity. This is the time when an athlete has just returned from the rest and recovery phase. It is also a time to develop techniques that are specific to the sport and to start goal setting.

Stage 2: Early season preparation phase: Training becomes more specific in this phase ready for competition; both training and intensity start to increase. The athlete may start to enter a few competitions for training purposes but is obviously still preparing and focusing for the big events.

Stage 3: Competition phase: This is the main competition period, where an athlete is looking to produce a high level performance to the best of their ability in key or major competitions and events. The athlete will aim to peak at certain times in relation to important competitions or events.

Stage 4: Recovery phase: The period involves a period of complete rest and recovery. Light activities such as swimming or gentle exercise may be undertaken here to allow the body to recover from all of the stresses placed upon it through the preparation and competitive phases.

Employment and flexibility

An athlete will have to balance work commitments or other employment with training and competition. The stages described above give an indication as to how much work is involved in training for competitions. Planning for the year would be an advantage; an athlete could take his training plan to his workplace manager and discuss a working pattern around training commitments. Some employers will be very supportive and may offer a degree of flexibility and allow an athlete to work when they can. Other employers may not be so willing or may not find it a practical situation on which they could operate their business.

The athlete may also have to offer a little flexibility if it is necessary.

Studying

If an athlete is studying at school, college or university then they will receive a timetable of all their classes for the academic year. It is harder in these circumstances to plan training around study because of the fact that a lot of important classes or modules are part of a main qualification aim and if this is missed it could be detrimental to overall success.

However, there may be some exceptions if the athlete is studying for a sports diploma or degree where the entry criteria requires them to be a training or competitive athlete. The athlete might go to a university that supports sport and so will be able to study politics, for example, but over four years instead of three. In these instances the educational establishment is usually flexible and will want the best possible outcome for the athlete's sporting career. The athlete will also have to be flexible and ensure that they catch up any missed work and attend regular development sessions.

Within a school environment, any training will have to be worked out around the timetable, after school, during lunchtimes and at weekends as it is not advisable to miss school.

Informing others

It is important to forge good relations with employers, peers, coaches and so on. If you are going to be late for a track meeting, or late for work because you are held up in training, a telephone call may be the answer. It is good practice, courteous and polite to inform others. Ensure that you have a mobile phone with all of the necessary telephone numbers stored in the memory.

Leisure time

Leisure time can be defined as time away from work or training, relaxing or doing leisurely activities such as gardening, swimming, visiting art galleries, walking, spending time with family and friends and so on. We need to keep our bodies fit and healthy and this includes letting the body rest.

Social life

A social life can be defined as having and enjoying contact with other people. Everyone needs a social life. People enjoy meeting up with friends, developing new friendships, taking part in leisure activities together, going to bars, to a nightclub, going to restaurants to eat, as well as, for example, going to the cinema or bowling. These are classed as social activities. Maintaining a social life will allow you to forget about the stresses of work, and allows an individual to take time out and have fun. However, it is important that an athlete doesn't let his or her social life impact on his or her training or sporting career.

Inappropriate activities

Inappropriate activities include:

- drinking too much alcohol
- smoking
- taking drugs.

Alcohol

It is important that an aspiring athlete doesn't spend their leisure time drinking copious amounts of alcohol.

Alcohol can affect the performance of an athlete. It is dangerous to play sport or train when alcohol is in your system. This could be dangerous not only to yourself but to other participants. Alcohol can:

- slow down reaction time
- affect balance and coordination
- cause severe dehydration
- affect the way in which you think
- slow down recovery time.

Think about it

Think of sports which are dependent upon a quick reaction time, good balance or coordination. Discuss what might happen to a sportsperson's performance if they have consumed alcohol.

Key point

Alcohol is a diuretic, which means it can make us urinate more than usual.

Smoking

The red blood cells in our body carry oxygen to all of the cells and organs in our body.

Smoking:

- produces carbon monoxide
- can reduce lung function
- can affect the ability to breathe efficiently
- can increase the risk of cancer
- can significantly reduce fitness levels and increase blood pressure.

Key points

- Normal carbon dioxide levels in the blood are about 1% for non-smokers and 10% for smokers.
- Performance is affected when carbon monoxide levels in the blood reach 3% and maximal aerobic power decreases at 4.3%.

From *The Fitness Leader's Handbook*, 1998: B Franks and E Howley.

■ *Smoking does not help sports performance*

Drugs

Some drugs are substances which we use when feeling ill, such as aspirin and paracetomol, or when we are suffering from an injury. These drugs are controlled – they may only be prescribed by a qualified doctor or dispensed by a chemist – and are taken for our benefit, for example, to help relieve pain or reduce swelling.

Other drugs, which people take for recreational use, are usually stimulants and produce adverse or exaggerated reactions in an individual.

Amphetamines: These are addictive drugs, which stimulate the central nervous system. They reduce pain and mask the feelings of fatigue and tiredness, making it possible for an athlete to overtrain or overexert themselves. They can alter a person's mood causing anxiety, apprehension and aggression. They also make the heart beat irregularly, a lot faster and also have an effect in increasing blood pressure and body temperature which is dangerous and can lead to heart failure.

Caffeine: This substance is found in coffee and other soft drinks which people drink every day because the stimulant or the effect is mild.

However it does, like amphetamines, increase the heart rate and blood pressure. Caffeine in very high doses has been used by athletes in the past to make them more alert and reduce tiredness. It produces nervousness and insomnia.

Ecstasy or 'E': This is a recreational drug, which some people have reacted badly to, and some people have died from its effects in the past. This drug makes an individual become 'high' and they may lose all sense of reality.

LSD: This is another dangerous drug which causes an individual to lose the ability to think clearly, it will cloud their judgement and alter their perceptions.

Appropriate leisure activities

Appropriate leisure activities for an aspiring athlete should include rest and recovery – especially if they are balancing work with training or study. It is important to rest the mind as well as the body. Activities such as golf or going to the cinema with friends are less strenuous and will allow the athlete to relax.

Let's do it!

Do some research to find out about the drugs listed below.

- Cocaine
- Heroin
- Marijuana/cannabis.

1 Why do people take them?
2 How do they affect people?
3 How do they affect a sportsperson's performance?

Let's do it!

1 Make a list of the activities that you do in your own leisure time. Do you consider them to be appropriate or inappropriate for you as a young sports person?
2 Complete the table below with a list of inappropriate and appropriate activities that an athlete should/ shouldn't do in their leisure time.

Appropriate activities	Inappropriate activities

Living away from home

Some people might go away to study or may go to another city or country to further their career in sport. Living away from home can be both exciting and frightening. It is exciting because everything's new, a new place to explore, new friends to meet and you are also required to be independent. It is frightening because you are leaving what you are used to – friends, and family and so on – and you may have feelings that you will not be able to cope initially. However, in your leisure time you need to plan and be able to make time to go back home for a visit.

Pressures

When trying to plan and mange your work commitments and leisure time it is not easy juggling activities and work and trying to please lots of different people, such as friends who may want you to go out with them socially, teachers who may require you to study or work harder, coaching staff who may want you to train for longer periods of time, or family who may want to see you.

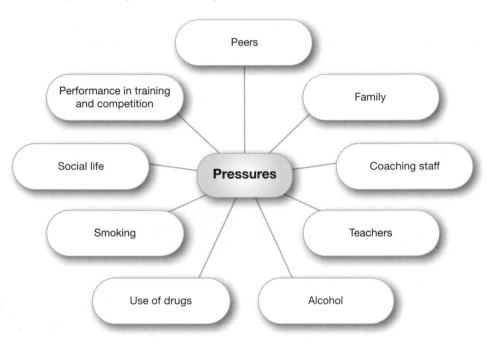

■ *Pressures on sports people*

All of the above factors would put any individual under pressure as well as the conflict between the needs of the sport and the performer's other responsibilities.

Peers, alcohol consumption and drugs

Throughout life you may have to deal with problems or make some difficult decisions on your own. However, sometimes other people or your peers may get involved and try and pressure you one way or another.

Peers are very influential people. Peers are usually our friends and in a similar age group to us. They can make us feel awkward, pressurised and embarrassed if, for example, they are drinking or smoking and we refuse to join in. Lots of young people start drinking and smoking because of peer pressure, not wanting to feel the 'odd one out' and doing it just to 'fit in'.

It is the same with using drugs. Some friends or peers may coerce you into trying drugs, saying it won't hurt you and is just for fun – this is an example of **negative peer pressure** – and other good friends may steer you away – this is an example of **positive peer pressure**.

Another example of positive peer pressure occurs if your friends are involved in the same sport as you. They can be very influential in ensuring that you are keeping to training schedules, offering encouragement and support.

Performance-enhancing drugs

You may be pressurised into taking anabolic steroids or other performance-enhancing drugs, which are banned and are illegal in sports competitions. They are injected or taken orally by those who feel that they need to improve their physique or who have a strong desire to succeed at any cost. Some athletes take them if they feel that their competitors are better or stronger than them, and feel it will improve their chances of winning. Others seem to have the certainty that they will not get caught... which certainly isn't true.

 Let's do it!

1 *Look at the table below on the effects of steroids.*
2 *Look at the column of what steroids can do for you and then read about the negative effects and the psychological factors. Would you still consider taking steroids to enhance your performance?*
3 *Discuss the arguments for and against the use of steroids.*

What steroids do	Negative effects of steroids on men	Negative effects of steroids on women	Negative mental effects of steroids
Increase muscle mass	Increase growth and thickening of pubic hair	Increase growth and thickening of pubic hair	Increase desire to win
Break down protein more quickly	Deepen the voice	Deepen the voice	Increase aggressiveness
Increase blood haemoglobin, which carries more oxygen around the body	Increase blood pressure	Increase blood pressure	Change behaviour and mood
Increase the amount of calcium in bones	Increase facial hair	Cause an irreversible increase in facial and body hair	Reduce feelings of pain
	Cause spots or acne	Cause spots or acne	
	Cause baldness	Cause irregular periods of menstrual cycle	
	Cause men to develop larger breasts	Cause liver and kidney damage	
	Cause liver and kidney damage	Can lead to an early death	
	Can lead to an early death		
	Increase the risk of prostate cancer		

Effects of steroids

Key point

Remember drugs are dangerous substances, can be harmful to the body and can even kill.

Let's do it!

There have been some high-profile cases in recent years of athletes taking performance-enhancing drugs. Discuss the outcomes of some of these cases that you know about within your group and attempt the following tasks.

1 *Using newspapers, magazines or the Internet, can you find any articles about athletes who have taken drugs or stimulants to enhance their performance?*

2 *With the information you have gathered, produce a poster warning young athletes of the dangers of drugs in sport.*

Family pressure

Your family may put added pressure on you. If you are away from home they may demand or want to see you at every opportunity. On the other hand they may be expecting you to do extremely well in your sporting career as well as in your educational achievements and this can put a lot of stress on you trying to live up to other people's expectations.

Pressure from teachers

Additional pressures can come from teachers who may feel that your studying or work is suffering due to your sporting commitment. Therefore it is important to discuss these issues with your tutor to see how they can help you.

Level of performance in training and competition

If you and your coach feel that you are not performing to the best of your ability then this could put additional pressure and stresses on you to perform better or to win. Your level of performance in training and competitions can be affected by all of the pressures that we have discussed including the use of drugs and alcohol consumption.

Other factors that can affect performance

In addition to the factors you have considered in this section, there are a number of other factors that can affect the performance of a sportsperson. These are based on the nature of the sport itself.

The sports we play can be divided into two categories.

1 **Individual sports** – with one person playing another.
2 **Team sports** – where two teams compete against each other. For example, volleyball is played between two teams with six players on

the court at any one time. Rugby Union has teams of 15 players. A badminton doubles team consists of two players and this pair may be of the same gender or a mixed team.

Many factors affecting sports from these different categories are the same. In many events, both individual and team, the competitors are required to produce set routines or to perform combinations of set moves upon which they are judged. Ice skating, where competitors must complete set skills in the routines they perform, is an example of this. However, there are also a variety of different factors that come into play, depending on whether the sport is played as an individual or as a team.

If you play an individual sport, the following factors may affect your performance.

- **Personal fitness level and performance** – you have to be fitter than your opponent to have a chance of success. In a boxing match, the boxer with greater strength or stamina, or faster reflexes, is likely to prevail, all else being equal.

- **Motivation to succeed** – you need to be motivated to succeed because there are no team mates or peers to 'keep you going' when things get tough.

- **Tactics employed** – for example, a swimmer must decide at what pace he or she will swim each length of a race. If the pace is too fast the swimmer may run out of energy too early but if it is too slow, there may be too much distance to catch up.

If you play as part of a team, different factors come into play.

- **Teamwork** – as a team, all members must work together to promote the success of the team and the individuals within it. Jonny Wilkinson's now famous winning drop goal in the 2003 Rugby World Cup is a good example. He was able to perform only because the rest of the team had all played their parts in taking the ball up the field to get him sufficiently in range. A single error by any of the other 14 players, a missed pass or an infringement of the rules might have meant the chance was lost.

- **The strengths and weaknesses of individual players** – in any team game, each side will have strengths and weaknesses within their players on the field. These may be physical, skills-based or to do with tactics. The way in which a team plays to its strengths, compensates for its weaknesses and exploits the weaknesses of its opponents may have a major effect on the result of the game. For example, in basketball, teams will try to match up their best player with the opponent's weakest player to gain an advantage.

- **Substitutions** – these are allowed by many (although not all) team games. This means that players who are having a poor game, who have sustained an injury, or who are fatigued, can be replaced. This, of course, is not possible in individual sports.

■ **Stopping play** – in many team games, the coach is able to stop play to give teams advice on how to play. Basketball and volleyball both allow coaches to call time out for this purpose.

Dealing with pressures

Pressures are a normal part of life. Studying, working and trying to follow a sporting career brings a whole batch of new pressures. What really matters is not how much pressure you have but how you deal with it.

There are many different ways in which to deal with pressures that may be affecting your daily life.

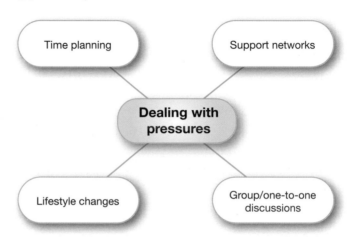

■ *Dealing with pressures*

Support networks

Support networks are usually groups of people who are in the same situation or facing unique challenges. These networks are intended to provide people with encouragement, advice and most importantly a feeling that they are not alone.

Discussions

Group or one-to-one discussions will allow the pressured individual to discuss their concerns and feelings with others and a suitable outcome may be achieved.

Lifestyle changes

Lifestyle changes will alleviate some pressures, changing the amount of time spent working or socialising will help to reduce feelings of anxiety and stress. Lifestyle changes could also include a change in diet, efficient budgeting and financial planning.

There are advisors who will work with you and your coach, who specialise in and offer support to athletes wanting to pursue their career. They help you effectively plan your career and training while still having time for work or social activities with family and friends.

Key point

Diet can be regarded as everything that a person eats and drinks. It is an important contributory factor in sports performance. Diet has become increasingly more important over the past few years, as our knowledge of nutrition has increased. Now, most international sports performers have a nutritionist, whose role is to give advice about what to eat and drink.

Time planning

Time planning your training and competition schedules around work commitments and study is vital to success and will help to deal with some of the pressures that you may be facing. Without a plan, your training and competitive programme will lack focus and direction. Keeping a record of your progress is also important. It means you can monitor which aspects are going well and which are not, and so identify what further training is required for you to achieve your ultimate goal.

Other methods of dealing with pressure include:

- reading
- light exercise
- visiting the cinema
- asking for help
- taking a break.

Let's do it!

In pairs, discuss other lifestyle factors that could alleviate pressures of work, study, training, competition and trying to maintain a social life.

Let's do it!

Working in pairs, think about and discuss the answers to the following questions.

- *Is all pressure bad or can some be good?*
- *Name any good pressures that you can think of.*
- *Name any bad pressures that you can think of.*
- *Have you felt or are you feeling any pressures?*
- *What makes you feel pressurised?*
- *How do you know when pressure is getting too much?*

Planning aids

A good way to plan is to write things down, either on paper, in a diary, or by keeping an electronic diary. A diary will help you keep track of what you are doing on a daily basis as in the example below.

16th January 2006		
8 am	Training	Don Valley arena
10 am	College – PE	Remember tracksuit
11 am		
12 am	Lunch	
1 pm	College sports science	Homework due in
2 pm		
3 pm	Training Willoughby sports centre	Meet group at 3.15 Plyometric training
4 pm	Time out	
5 pm	Time out	
6 pm	Work – 9pm	

A personal assistant, manger or coach can also help you to manage your time effectively. They can help you to plan your training around study and work commitments and they can also remind you of training events and ensure that you make other appointments, matches or competitions.

Assessment activity 1: Diary

You can only achieve a Pass or Merit for this assessment activity

To achieve a Pass:

1 You are required to keep a diary or log of your work commitments and leisure time for one month. Your diary can either be in an electronic or paper format, but must show how you manage the following.

- All work commitments.
- Training.
- Competition.
- Study.
- Any employment.
- Leisure time.

These commitments need to be prioritised where appropriate. (P1)

To achieve a Merit you must achieve the Pass criteria and:

2 Explain the way your work commitments and leisure activities have been planned. (M1)

Assessment activity 2: Poster

Devise a poster or leaflet which is aimed at a young athlete to inform them of the pressures that they could be faced with and ways in which to reduce these pressures. Use pictures to enhance the presentation of your material. Your poster/leaflet must include the material required for a Pass and Merit grade.

To achieve a Pass:

1 *Describe* three different pressures on elite athletes and identify strategies that can be used to deal with these pressures. (P2)

To achieve a Merit you must achieve the Pass criteria and:

2 *Explain* three different pressures on elite athletes and describe suitable strategies that can be used to deal with these pressures. (M2)

12.2 Understand appropriate behaviour for an elite athlete

Tiger Woods (golf), Thierry Henry (football), David Beckham (football), Amir Khan (boxing), and Andy Murray (tennis) are all elite athletes in their own right... but what is it that makes them elite?

An elite athlete is someone who excels in his or her sport and who is at the top of his or her game. They will be dedicated, committed and constantly striving to achieve new goals. Elite athletes may represent their team and country in competitions – for example, World Cup events or the Olympics and Commonwealth Games – so it is important that they behave in an appropriate manner and avoid doing anything that might harm their reputation and the reputation of their team, or anything negative that might capture media attention.

Let's do it!

1 Make a list of five sportspeople who you think are elite athletes.
2 What is their sport?
3 Discuss the factors or characteristics which you think make them an elite athlete.

Behaviour

Adherence to rules

All sports have different rules and governing bodies depending on the level of play. The governing bodies set the rules that have to be adhered to by the participants; umpires and referees oversee this process throughout play.

Rules and regulations of sports are set for particular reasons.

- They safeguard and maintain the health and safety of the participants, for example, by making personal protective equipment to reduce the risk of injury compulsory.

- They encourage fair play.

- They specify the duration and format of play, such as the number of players.

An elite athlete must adhere to rules at all times. These may be rules set by the governing body or rules given by the coach. Failure to abide by rules can result in accidents, foul play or may result in someone being seriously injured.

Respect for peers and others

There will be other athletes in the same athletic club or football team striving to achieve their goals, and during competitions, meets or matches there will be other competing athletes. Therefore, it is important to create a harmonious situation and display sportsmanship. For example, games may start and finish with players shaking hands to demonstrate a good sporting spirit.

Key point

Sportsmanship can be defined as competing or training with others in a way which takes into account the rules and the intended spirit of the sport.

■ *It is important to respect your peers*

Let's do it!

1 *Think about a time when you were playing sport and you didn't agree with a call from a referee. How did you feel and how did you act?*

2 *Have you witnessed athletes or sportspeople arguing with referees or other officials on television? Discuss what happened.*

Respect for the coach

The coach is a person who an elite athlete will work closely with. The coach will help the athlete set realistic goals and will be there to help and suggest ways in which to achieve the goals. A coach will have a vast amount of knowledge and experience in their sporting area and about different methods of training and will try to get the best out of the athlete. The athlete at times may not agree with a suggestion or feedback from the coach, but it is important to deal with this in an appropriate manner, by talking and coming to an agreement, or trying new ideas.

Respect for officials

The role of the official will be to control play, enforce the rules of sport and communicate with players or other officials. For example, a linesman may have to signal to an umpire, or a referee may have to issue a player with a warning or a yellow or red card. They have to use judgement, make decisions and may suffer verbal abuse from players. The officials are there to ensure that the participants apply or follow the rules and to ensure safety and fair play at all times.

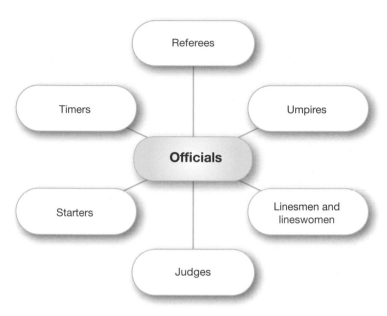

■ *Different officials*

Respect for spectators

Spectators are people who usually pay to watch sporting events such as football and rugby matches or athletic meets. Sometimes they travel great distances, and even overseas, to watch and support their favourite team or sportsperson perform. Elite athletes should therefore remember that they do have supporters, acknowledge them where possible and have respect for them.

■ *Always remember your fans!*

Acting as a role model

David Beckham inspires many young footballers who aspire to play football like him and who want to live the dream like him. They see him as a role model, someone to look up to. It is therefore crucial for any elite athlete to remember this, that young children or young adults are very impressionable and may act in a way in which their idol or role model behaves. The press or media will be there to report any misbehaviour from famous or elite athletes.

Role models are very influential and can easily influence those who look up to them; they should therefore encourage youngsters to do well at school or college and should encourage participation in sport.

Appropriate clothing

Appropriate clothing is an essential for sport. A particular sport may have rules on what a participant or competitor must wear. These may include personnel protective equipment (see Unit 2, page 84) such as gum shields for boxers, shin guards for footballers or a protective hat for show jumping.

As well as protective clothing athletes must dress in accordance with the rules and regulations of their sport. For example, footballers are required to wear their strips and track athletes may be required to wear spikes.

Let's do it!

Complete the table below.

Sport	Appropriate clothing	Personal protective equipment
Football	Football strip Football boots	Shin pads
Netball		
Hockey		
Ice hockey		
Rugby		
Boxing		
Show jumping		
Karate		

Conduct and manners

The attitude, behaviour and conduct of an elite athlete will be under scrutiny by the press, other media and by other people. It is the athlete's responsibility to conduct himself or herself in an appropriate manner, be it during training, at social functions or gatherings or during competitions. Imagine if during a social event a top athlete drank heavily and began to swear or verbally abuse the press or other peers. This would be reported by the media and create a bad reputation for the athlete. It is therefore imperative that they conduct themselves in a professional manner and avoid doing anything which could harm their career or give their sport or team a bad name.

Elite athletes will find themselves in many different situations during their sporting career. They will train at different venues, they may enter competitions in the UK, in Europe or overseas. They will find themselves being invited to social functions, for example, charity events to support or create awareness of a good cause such as breast or prostate cancer. Elite athletes could be invited to attend openings of sporting facilities or to give talks in schools, colleges or universities. It is therefore important that they learn how to behave or conduct themselves in these different situations.

Situations

During training and competitions

Training and competition are fundamental to any sport. It is therefore important that an athlete turn up on time to organised training sessions, in the appropriate clothing and in the right frame of mind ready to start working and striving for improvement in his or her performance.

Elite athletes have the ability to perform their sport to a high level. Successful athletes need to be physically and mentally strong and this will be developed through regular training and competition. Appropriate behaviour and conduct is therefore necessary in order to succeed. This could include listening to the coach, asking questions and responding positively to feedback or criticism during training.

During competitions appropriate behaviour would include displaying sportsmanship and adhering to the rules and regulations of the sport.

At home

When at home away from the spotlight it is amazing how there is still a great media interest in an elite athlete. David Beckham and Wayne Rooney sell newspapers and magazines – it is not just their performance on the field but their lifestyle off the pitch that attracts media attention.

At social functions

Elite athletes, because of their high profile, will be invited to many different social functions throughout their career. These could range from small functions to raise awareness or money for a charitable cause to larger-scale events such as the 'Brits', Sports Person of the year or other televised award shows. Whatever the size or venue of the social function, the elite athlete must remember that they have been invited for a specific reason and should not do anything to embarrass the organisers or themselves. Television cameras may be recording the event, so it is important that they act as though they are on camera all the time as they may not be aware when they are being filmed and when they are not. There is often a lot of alcohol at social functions but the elite athlete must limit their alcohol consumption and avoid getting drunk.

Let's do it!

Use newspapers, magazines and the Internet to see if there are any reports of elite athletes misbehaving or conducting themselves in an inappropriate manner. You may be able to recall seeing a report on the TV or in magazines, which you can use.

- *Discuss the incident with your group.*
- *What was the outcome?*
- *Did the incident bring the athlete and sport into disrepute?*

Assessment activity 3: Appropriate behaviour

We have seen that it is important for athletes to conduct themselves and behave in an appropriate manner.

To achieve a Pass:

1 *Describe* appropriate behaviour for elite athletes in three of the different situations given below.

- A cameraman is taking photographs of an elite athlete when she is out with her partner and children. The photographer is getting very close and is taking lots of photos.

- An elite athlete has been invited to a school to give a talk to pupils aged 12+ on participation in sport.

- During training the elite athlete and his coach have an argument about specific training procedures. The elite athlete reacts by storming out of the training session.

- During a social function, the athlete drinks too much alcohol and starts to sing at the top of his voice. He says horrible things to all of his team mates and tells the coach what he really thinks of him. (P3)

To achieve a Merit you must achieve the Pass criteria and:

2 *Explain* appropriate behaviour for elite athletes in the three situations you have chosen. (M3)

To achieve a Distinction you must achieve the Pass and Merit criteria and:

3 *Evaluate* the effects and consequences of the behaviour of elite athletes. (D1)

12.3 Understand the factors that influence the effective planning of a career

Goals

When planning a career we usually think about setting goals that we want, to achieve things that we want to do in the short term and in the long term. For example, in the short term an athlete may want to develop his or her cardio-respiratory fitness in order to be able to run a marathon in the long term.

Examples of goals

Short-term goal: To improve cardio-respiratory fitness within three months

Medium-term goal: To develop cardio-vascular fitness further and be able to run 15 miles without becoming too fatigued

Long-term goal: To complete the marathon

SMART goals

Goals should be SMART.

- **Specific** – Goals should be specific and should clearly define and emphasise what you are going to do, why you are going to do it and how you are going to do it.

- **Measurable** – You must be able to gauge success and effectiveness.

- **Achievable** – There is no point in setting goals which are way out of your reach or outside your scope of training. Although it may make you work or train harder it can also quickly demotivate and leave you feeling deflated if you do not meet the goals set.

- **Realistic** – Goals should be challenging but realistic and should be set and agreed by both coach and sports performer.

- **Timed** – A specific time frame should be set in which to achieve the realistic goal, in order to motivate and enthuse the sports performer. Setting a time frame will also help with psychological preparation. For example, the performer will know that he will have three months to achieve a specific goal, so will ensure adequate and effective training is carried out.

Goals set at different periods may run together. For instance, a 100 metre sprinter aiming to make the team for the Olympics may set the following goals:

- Short term – this year: win county title; improve personal best to 10.16 seconds.

- Medium term – within two years: win AAA title; improve personal best to 10.00 seconds.

- Long term – within four years: qualify for British Olympic Squad; achieve Olympic qualifying standard.

Identifying strengths and weaknesses

When you plan your goals, you will need to decide upon targets to be achieved along the way. These targets may be physical, to improve basic strength, for instance. They could involve setting actual times or distances to be achieved within a certain timescale. They could involve competitions or events to be used as a training exercise or performance guides.

- You will need to analyse your performance and identify your own strengths and weaknesses.

- Each training session should be planned, so that you know in advance the duration of each session, its content, the type of training you will undertake, and so on.

- You need to think about mental preparation in addition to your physical training. How will you try to improve it? When will this take place?

- When you examine your diet, analyse strengths and weaknesses. For instance, do you eat too many fatty foods? Are your meals eaten too close to training and competition?

Once you have all this information, you can begin to design and plan your training and your career.

Athletic career

World-class performance programme

To be a world-class or elite athlete involves making many sacrifices. Only those dedicated, extremely talented and committed enough will be able to earn money and make a successful career out of their sport. They will face many struggles on their way up to the top, working to earn enough money to live on and fitting in a comprehensive training schedule designed to achieve specific goals, in order to pursue their sporting career.

Because of the pressures that elite athletes face, and to enable athletes to compete in world-class competitions, a programme was created by UK Sport and Sport England to help athletes reach and perform to the highest levels – the World-Class Performance Programme (WCPP).

Each sport will have its own World-Class Performance Programme, all of which have the same aims and objectives – supporting and further developing the skills and careers of talented athletes in their training and maximising their competitive potential. All athletes will be nurtured and inspired to win medals and be the best that they can be.

As an elite athlete your coach or sporting governing body or world-class training programme will have certain expectations of you. As an elite athlete you will also have certain expectations of them.

Current expectations as an elite athlete

Funding

Funding for elite athletes usually comes from lottery funding, sponsorship or prize money. If this is the case this may alleviate the pressures of work, thereby giving them adequate time to plan and sufficient time to undertake any training, travelling or competition requirements.

Some athletes receive a personal award from the World-Class Performance Programme. This award is to help with living costs and buying equipment.

Medical back-up

Injury can have a disastrous effect on performance levels. Many athletes have suffered injuries at some time in their career because of their training schedules and constant use of their muscles. This usually means that training and competition has to stop until the injury heals. This can take many weeks or even months. The effects of sports injuries are taken very seriously today. Top performers or elite athletes can be expected to have access to doctors, physiotherapists and sports massage therapists to ensure that:

- injuries are avoided, as far as possible, through correct training and exercise
- when injury occurs, it is treated promptly using the best facilities and expertise, to ensure the athlete can return to competition as quickly as possible.

While teams will be able to employ a vast array of staff at a match or tournament, individual players will not. Tournaments in sports like tennis and athletics provide doctors and physiotherapists for the athletes and players competing. The table on page 340 shows the different roles in medical back-up.

Medical Staff	Role
Physiotherapist	Treats injuries using massage, electrotherapy and exercise instead of drugs
Sports massage therapist	Performs pre-, inter- and post-event massage Prepares the muscles for activity and after activity Treatment here is designed to reduce the likelihood or reoccurrence of injuries Advises on exercise working closely with the physiotherapist, coach, doctor and athlete
Injury consultant	Diagnoses an injury so that the correct treatment can then be administered, using exercise or drugs

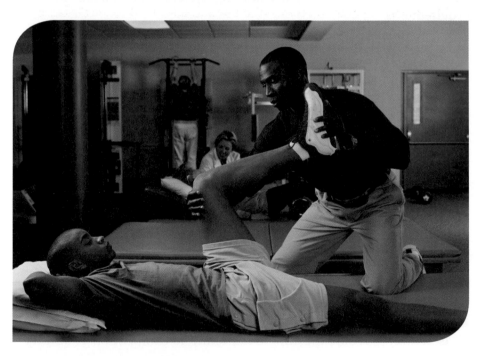

■ *It is important to have medical back-up*

At the lower levels of sports performance, access to medical assistance is more difficult. Local GPs are able to offer some non-specific treatment and local sports centres may offer access to a physiotherapist, but treatment can be expensive. This cost may prevent a player from receiving the treatment required. Some local semi-professional teams may have a club trainer or physiotherapist. Local colleges may also offer sports therapy classes, and so might be able to provide the treatment needed.

Biomechanical/performance analysis

Elite athletes can expect feedback on performance. This enables them to adapt their training if necessary for greater improvements and will also give them the opportunity to discuss any problems that they may have. Biomechanical analysis is an ideal way to assess training and developmental needs and involves a team of experts who all work together in the best interest of the athlete to help improve and increase performance. Let us use the example of a runner.

- Biomechanical analysis would at first involve a discussion with the runner, physiotherapist and coach about injuries, treatments and training methods/ schedules.

- Secondly the runner would be observed in action on a track where his or her techniques/running style and body position may be observed and/or video recorded in order to assess the runner's form.

- The runner may then be asked to use a treadmill which is linked up to a computer and can detect the length of the runner's stride (stride pattern) and the amount of pressure going through the heels or feet as the foot strikes the ground. This is an excellent method of helping an athlete to improve their technique/performance and reduce the risk of injury occurring.

Let's do it!

- *Do some research on training or biomechanical analysis.*
- *What are the different ways in which it is carried out?*
- *What are the benefits to an athlete of biomechanical or performance analysis?*

Access to facilities and training

Training and competition are fundamental to any sport and require:

- **facilities** – such as pitches, courts, and athletic tracks
- **services** – such as doctors and physiotherapists.

As you progress in a sport, you will encounter better facilities and support to help you fulfil your sporting potential. There are many centres of excellence which are run by the English Institute of Sport. This organisation provides many services and facilities to elite athletes. Visit it at www.heinemann.co.uk/hotlinks to find out more about your area and a particular sport.

Practical coaching expertise

An athlete can be expected to be provided with a high performance coach with knowledge and expertise in the field, who can help with all the training and planning needs of the athlete.

A competition programme

An elite athlete will be provided with a competition programme which will allow certain goals to be tested and the athlete's competition status can be monitored and reviewed.

Let's do it!

- *Can you think of other expectations an athlete or coach may have?*
- *What would you expect from a governing body or World-Class Performance Programme?*
- *What do you think they might expect from you?*
- *Discuss in small groups then share your ideas with the rest of your class.*

Elite athletes are expected to:

- aim to win medals in a safe manner
- prioritise their training over social/work commitments where possible
- be dedicated and show a high level of commitment to their sport
- behave in an appropriate manner and maintain a high level of professional etiquette at all times both in training and away from training
- follow their training programme, liaise or communicate with the coach at all times
- attend all training sessions, medicals, competitions or meetings
- not undertake any work, such as hard manual labour, which could jeopardise their career as an elite athlete
- manage their time effectively
- deal with the media or press in an appropriate manner
- accept responsibility for their performances and management of their daily lives.

Key review dates

There will be many key review dates in the career of an elite athlete. These dates will include the following.

- Review of short-term goals or targets.
- Review of medium-term goals.
- Review of long-term goals.
- Funding.
- Annual calendar of events or competition.

Review of goals or targets set

These are key dates that need to be reviewed at stages throughout training and competition, and will let the athlete and coach know how the athlete is improving, if they are or are not reaching goals and will allow for new goals to be set if necessary.

Funding

The funding and support of an athlete is usually reviewed annually.

Annual calendar for elite athletes

This calendar will have dates and information about meets or competitions. Together, a coach and athlete will review the list and decide on entries and aims for the year.

Change of coach or club

Reasons for change of coach include the following.

- Arguments about politics, funding or competitions.
- Athlete not performing or achieving desired goals.
- Specialist coach required e.g. for strength and conditioning.
- Personality clash.
- Desire for different training methods.

There are different types of coaches and elite athletes may need to change to a coach who has specific expertise in an area in which they need to develop. For example, if they need to improve strength, they may change to a strength and conditioning coach.

Throughout their athletic career they may have to change coach for other reasons, including moving to those who have a greater knowledge or experience in their sport or those who apply different training principles or methods.

They may change their coach if they are not performing well or getting the results that they want. A coach and athlete may argue about politics or may not agree on goals or competition.

They may change to a coach who uses different methods of coaching or who has had a number of successes in their sport.

Athletes may also change the club that they represent. This could be to make advances or if they feel that it would be beneficial to their career as an elite athlete.

Contingencies for illness, accidents and injury

A contingency plan is a back-up plan. Imagine if you were an elite athlete who relied on prize money to earn a living – what would happen if you fell ill or you were severely injured during training or competition? This could be the end of your athletic career – what would you do?

You should always have a back-up plan. In life there are no certainties, we do not know what the future holds or when we will be ill or injured. So it is imperative that an elite athlete has something to fall back on. Many athletes may turn to coaching children or young adults in their sport. Many athletes try to study while holding down a career in athletics. However, at times this can prove difficult because of heavy training commitments.

Effective contingency planning for injuries or illness is advisable for all athletes, this is a plan that should be formulated in advance just in case something happens to jeopardise their athletic career.

Case study

Contingency planning

Joanna is an elite athlete who is training to compete in the Olympics. During a long training session, Joanna stumbles over the hurdles and breaks her leg in two places and sustains a severe wrenching and tearing of the ligaments in her ankle. Her leg is plastered at the hospital and she is given the devastating news that she will be out of action for at least six to eight months. After that she will have to go through a rehabilitation programme, which could last a further two to three months.

Joanna hasn't any contingency plans in place because she thought it would never happen to her and relies on the prize money offered at competitions to earn a living.

Now pretend that the accident never happened. Prepare a contingency plan for Joanna.

1 Think of possible scenarios that could happened to Joanna as an elite athlete and hurdler.

2 Suggest some feasible contingency actions.

3 Tabulate your information using the example below – work in pairs, discuss your ideas and complete the table.

	Worst case scenarios	**Contingency plan**	**Action required**
1	Relies heavily on prize money to earn a living	Sports coaching Sports education	Identify what she is good at, and what qualifications, knowledge and experience she has. Seek advice or employment Further training
2	Out of action for nearly a year	Physiotherapy Sports massage therapy	
3			
4			

■ Contingency plan for Joanna

Second career

Many elite athletes may have the opportunity to develop or take on a second career while still training in their sport. This is mostly for financial reasons, to help pay for travel to and from events especially if these are not paid for by the athletics association or World-Class Performance Programmes.

Lots of athletes today are involved in a second career, especially those who are not yet earning enough money from their sport to live on. They may also have to take on a second career because of the possibility of the unknown (as discussed in contingency planning).

At the other end of the scale there are elite athletes such as Thierry Henry and David Beckham who are earning extra money while still competing. David Beckham continues to model and promotes many products, sporting merchandise, footwear, sunglasses and hair products. Thierry Henry promotes and features in Renault advertisements.

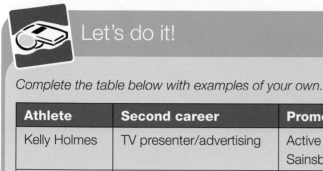

Let's do it!

Complete the table below with examples of your own.

Athlete	Second career	Promotes/endorses
Kelly Holmes	TV presenter/advertising	Active Children – Sainsbury's
Thierry Henry	Model Advertising	Renault Clio

Coaching

Elite athletes may choose to work in sport coaching. They may assist a coach or help others to develop the skills and athletic performance in their chosen sport. In this situation the youngsters who they are coaching would see them as a role model because of their experiences and achievements.

Coaches work with teams, individuals, amateurs or professional sportspeople to help develop their skills and ability within the sport that they participate in. They help towards achieving the full potential of each individual they work with.

A coach may have a specific speciality, such as a strength and conditioning coach or a speed and agility coach. Other coaches work in fitness and exercise including aerobics and weight training (sometimes these are referred to as instructors).

Qualifications

To coach elite athletes you are required to have:

- a qualification in sports coaching
- a degree in sports science specialising in elite athletes
- at least three years experience working within your sport
- extensive knowledge and experience of different methods of coaching and training
- the ability to assess individual needs.

■ *Coaches work with sportspeople to help them develop their skills and abilities*

To coach children under the age of 16 or to assist a coach in doing so you are required to have:

- a qualification in sports coaching
- at least a BTEC National Diploma in Sports (specialising in sports coaching)
- a certificate in Child Protection
- experience within your sporting field
- knowledge of different methods of training and assessing the individual needs of children
- undertaken a CRB (Criminal Records Bureau) check before working with children in sport.

Further study is required to specialise in sports injuries or sports medicine.

Teacher

Teachers in school who work in sport are known as PE teachers or sports teachers. Their roles and responsibilities include working with children of all ages to develop their skills and abilities with physical activities and sport. A teacher's role also involves planning and preparing lessons, marking work, writing reports and interacting with parents.

Sports teachers can also be involved in setting up and running after-school clubs in netball, football, rugby and so on and also organising events and matches with other schools.

Teachers in colleges are known as lecturers and can teach sports studies or a practical sports-based course.

To become a teacher in school, study is required to obtain a BEd (Bachelor Of Education) degree or PGCE (Post-Graduate Certificate in Education) at university. To become a lecturer you will need a degree in your subject area or a sports-related discipline and also a PGCE or Certificate in Education (CertEd).

Second career in the media

Careers in the media can include:

- sports journalism
- television presenting
- match or event reporting
- commentating.

Working in the media is a popular career choice and to be successful it is important that you know as much as possible about the industry. Writing about their sport would hopefully come easily to an athlete. This type of work involves travelling around the UK and to many other countries where sports events are held. It involves meeting top sportsmen and women.

Sports journalism is difficult to get into. However, those who are talented, have experience or those lucky enough to have the right connections may make it into this field.

Radio and television

Working in these two fields as sports reporters or television presenters is competitive as positions that arise usually go to those people who have prior experience of working in the same or a similar capacity.

Television and radio companies sometimes run training programmes. If you are interested in these then you will need to contact the relevant company for more information.

Let's do it!

Can you think of any other skills required to work in a media position?

Assessment activity 4: Career goals

You are an elite athlete in a sport of your choice. You are aware that your career will not last forever due to pressures and the impact of training on your body.

To achieve a Pass:

1 You must *describe* realistic goals in a personal career plan and discuss a second career choice. (P4)

To achieve a Merit you must achieve the Pass criteria and:

2 *Explain* your goals and your second career choice. (M4)

To achieve a Distinction you must achieve the Pass and Merit criteria and:

3 *Justify* your goals and your second career choice. (D2)

Sports development

The role of a sports development officer is to try to promote sport, and develop interest in sport and/or physical activity. They try to improve access and opportunities for all.

Sports development officers work for:

- city or county councils
- youth organisations or trusts
- sports councils
- national governing bodies.

The work of a sports development officer involves:

- developing and promoting term-time sports activities
- promoting events
- developing partnerships within the community
- monitoring activities and making necessary adjustments.

■ *Where sports development officers work*

Qualifications

A sports-related degree or HND (including an element of sports development) is normally required. Experience of working in sports development is always advantageous but not always necessary, as organisations will give you training.

Physiotherapist

To be a physiotherapist an athlete would have to have the necessary qualifications to gain entry into university to study for a three- or four-year degree, where subjects such as anatomy, physiology, injury management, musculoskeletal sciences or electrotherapy would be studied.

Anyone wishing to study physiotherapy should possess three or four A-levels, preferably in human biology, chemistry, PE or physics. This will vary according to the entry requirements for different universities. Upon qualification a BSc (Bachelor of Science) in Physiotherapy will be awarded.

Physiotherapists treat people of all ages with various conditions, from heart and respiratory problems to sports injury rehabilitation. However, further study is required to specialise in sports injuries or sports medicine.

Skills required to be a physiotherapist

- Patience.
- Effective communication skills.
- Ability to motivate.
- Sensitivity.
- Good listening and responding skills.
- Ability to use own initiative.
- Ability to work within a multi-disciplinary team.
- Ability to work in different situations/ environments.
- Patience, sensitivity and tact when dealing with injured players.
- Ability to apply theoretical knowledge into a practical context.

Let's do it!

Can you think of any other skills required for a physiotherapist?

Where physiotherapists work

- Football and rugby clubs.
- Private clinics.
- Athletics clubs.
- Hospitals.

Sports science support

This role would involve trying to help develop and enhance the performance of an athlete through methods such as biomechanical analysis, fitness testing and generally looking at physiological and psychological areas of an athlete's performance.

Sports science support might involve working alongside other sports scientists, coaches and athletes, so it would be essential to possess the right skills to help succeed in the role.

To work in sports science support the following skills and qualities are needed:

- knowledge of sports science
- an in-depth knowledge of sports performance
- ability to communicate with others including athletes, coaches, doctors and physiotherapists
- sensitivity
- patience
- ability to motivate and enthuse
- ability to apply theoretical knowledge into a practical context.

Let's do it!

Can you think of any other skills required to work in sports science support?

Financial management

Sport is big business! Apart from the various personal factors that affect how well you play a sport, there are a number of other external factors that also need to be considered and one of the most important is money.

Sport costs money. Money is needed for equipment, for travel, for competing, even for basics like food and a home. In the initial stages of their development, most sports performers will be 'funded' by their parents. Later on, they might have a part-time job that provides the money needed to play a sport. At the lower levels of sport, money may be available in the form of grants. The better an athlete becomes and the higher the level at which they play, the more expensive sport becomes. At the very top, sports performers are training and competing full time – they live and breathe sport! Their income comes from sponsorship, prize money and being paid to appear at events.

Sponsorship

Sponsorship is a very important source of income. Each sponsor pays a large sum of money to be associated with an elite athlete's success.

All Premiership football teams have kit sponsors. Many players also have individual sponsorship deals to wear a particular make of boot, or to endorse a particular product. At a more local level, a local business or individual might sponsor a team or a particular sports performer.

Appearance money

Top players and teams may also receive appearance money, for simply turning up. If players who are not the very best were unable to earn a living from the game, they would not be able to play. This would mean that big tournaments would not be able to take place. There would not be enough players to allow the various rounds to take place and make the tournament what it is. This is particularly important for sports such as tennis and snooker, where tournaments require a large number of players to allow the tournament to take place.

A number of players make a living just by playing in a variety of tournaments. Appearance money is very important to sport and its future. Other examples include the contracts that are given to players to play for their country. The England Test Match Cricket squad are all on England contracts, which pay them a lucrative sum of money for playing for England. Obviously, the better the player, the better the reward from the contract.

Prize money

Prize money is paid to the winner, and often the runner up, of a tournament or event. In horse racing in the UK £94.1 million was paid in prize money in 2003.

If there was no prize money in horseracing:

- there would be no incentive to be the owner of a racehorse
- there would then be no need for stables and trainers, or grooms and jockeys
- your high street bookmaker would struggle to stay in business.

Financial responsibility

It is important for any athlete who is in the position to earn money and who is earning money from their sport to take some form of financial advice. This could be from the Inland Revenue, an independent financial adviser, a coach or from another athlete who has had similar experiences.

If self-employed then you must register with the Inland Revenue. It is your responsibility to ensure that you pay national insurance contributions and tax. Each year you will have a reminder from the Inland Revenue and will have to complete a form declaring profits or money earned, on which you will be taxed. Failure to take the necessary advice and actions could leave you with hefty fines from the Inland Revenue.

It is important that you keep records of any money you have coming in (income) and money you are paying out (expenditure).

Income

Income can be defined as any money that you have coming into your household. This includes income from:

- employment
- awards
- prize money
- a playing contract
- sponsorship
- appearance money/endorsements
- publishing
- tax credits
- any benefits
- a lottery award.

Expenditure

Expenditure refers to the money you are paying out – for example, on travelling to and from competitions, household bills or food.

There are two types of expenditure that a sports person should be concerned with.

- **Revenue Expenditure** – These refer to items that are purchased for sport and have a relatively short life span, such as trainers, sports clothing or tennis racquets.
- **Capital Expenditure** – Refers to items which are purchased for your sport but have a shelf life of a year or more. An example would be fitness training equipment.

Keeping track of your monthly income and expenditure is important.

Taxation

If you are a professional athlete, earning a living from your sporting career, earning money from competitions or from endorsements or prize money then you will be liable for taxation.

Even if you received a lottery award, because you seek to earn or make a living from competitions this award would become taxable too.

An elite athlete who is classed as self-employed will be liable to three different types of tax.

- National Insurance.
- Income tax.
- VAT – Valued Added Tax.

National Insurance

When we work we pay National Insurance contributions. The more you earn the more you pay. Paying these contributions will enable you to qualify for certain benefits when you need them. These are:

- State pension.
- Widow's pension (for women).
- Maternity allowance.

Tax

Everyone who earns money is liable for income tax, be it money from employment or money as a sports person; this is the main tax that is deducted from any wages or earnings. VAT is a tax on non-essential goods and services. However, what is seen as a luxury for some may be an essential to others. For example, sports clothing and footwear are needed by most sportspeople and thus theoretically should be tax exempt for them. Vat is currently 17.5%.

Case study

Jacob has been training and competing in competitions as an athlete for the past two years on a full-time basis. Each year he needs to raise in the region of £8000 to cover his personal sporting expenses.

He was invited on to his local news show to discuss sporting and financial issues facing elite athletes and subsequently because of his appearance was sent a donation of £4000. His family and friends rallied around and managed to raise another £2000. Jacob was then awarded £2000 from the lottery award. He became worried that he would have to pay tax and therefore spoke to the Inland Revenue about his situation. He was told that because he wasn't seeking to earn or make a professional profit from his sport, he was not regarded as a professional and therefore was not taxed on his lottery award.

Working in small groups answer the following question. You may need to do a little research or ask your tutor for help.

Jacob started to win competitions, receive sponsorship deals, promote sports on television and so on. His lottery award was increased from £2000 to £5000.

1 Explain what would happen and why with regards to taxation.

Savings

The difficulty of saving is that until you become established it is hard to justify not spending all your income trying to further your career. Once you are established your earnings need to be managed in a way that covers the post-career phase.

Investments

Investments are linked to savings in that when an athlete becomes successful they must manage their income for the long term, to benefit from a relatively short career.

Insurance

Having insurance means that you have thought about life's uncertainties. There are many different types of insurance that would benefit an athlete. These include:

- **personal accident insurance** – provides cover if the athlete is injured
- **life assurance** – pays a lump sum to a beneficiary if the athlete should die
- **medical cover** – will cover physiotherapy and other necessary medical services which an elite athlete might need to access frequently, especially if they have been injured.

Insurance taken out by the club or association would include:

- **public liability insurance** – this insurance protects athletes and other members of the organisation should a claim arise from negligence by the club or organisation which resulted in injury or death
- **professional indemnity insurance** – this insurance is taken out by clubs to cover coaches/trainers and anyone who works closely with the athlete giving professional advice. An athlete could make a claim against a coach or trainer for giving wrongful advice or instructions during training or competition, which resulted in an injury.

Key point

Insurance is normally arranged through an insurance or financial broker.

Pension

A pension is a type of savings scheme for your retirement which you pay in to. If employed, your employer may make a contribution towards your pension and as well as money being deducted from your wages each month.

Some people choose to pay into a private pension scheme.

Legal and contractual requirements

In relation to financial management, the athlete will have legal and contractual obligations that he or she will have to fulfil in order to maintain funding and sponsorship deals. These obligations may include:

- working a number of hours in a set period to promote the funding body, its products and services
- attendance at special promotional events to represent the company
- personal use of the company's products/services where appropriate

- allowing the use of the athlete's name to endorse the products/services
- commitment to photographic, advertising and merchandising rights
- legal restrictions to limit the range of other sponsorship opportunities for similar brands of products/services.

Case study

Audley

Audley is a 19-year-old, junior international 100-metre sprinter and has been training with various coaches, including a technical sprinting coach and a strength and conditioning coach. During training the strength and conditioning coach was motivating and coaching Audley to lift weights, using the leg press, leg extension and leg curl. The coach recommended and encouraged Audley to lift larger weights and advised him that this would help to increase his strength endurance. In attempting to lift weights well in excess of previous sessions, Audley sustained quite a severe hamstring injury, which resulted in a three-month lay-off from training and competition.

Audley sought legal advice from his sports governing body (AAA) and he was successful in making a claim against the coach through the Professional Indemnity Insurance Scheme. The grounds for his claim were that the coach gave incorrect advice, gave inappropriate

instructions and failed to take into consideration the athlete's personal limitations and previous training records.

As a result Audley was able to make a claim in relation to:

- physiotherapy and other medical costs
- loss of earnings/ potential earnings
- rehabilitation and travelling expenses
- out of pocket expenses
- legal expenses.

Now answer these questions.

1 After you have read the case study, discuss in small groups whether you think it was just that Audley made a claim against his coach.

2 Share your views/opinions with the whole group.

Assessment activity 5: Financial issues

Your tutor should act as an elite athlete and you as a financial advisor who specialises in financial issues for elite athletes.

To achieve a Pass:

1 *Describe* three financial issues that an elite athlete has to consider. Note that the elite athlete must ask appropriate questions and the financial adviser must give good advice. (P5)

12.4 Be able to communicate effectively with the media and significant others

Communication

Pursuing a career in sport, be it as an elite athlete, a coach or even working in sports retail, will require you to communicate and work with others. Effective communication is crucial and it must be remembered that it is a two-way process, which involves speaking and listening, responding and understanding.

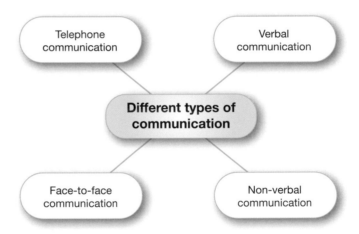

Telephone communication

Verbal communication

Different types of communication

Face-to-face communication

Non-verbal communication

■ *Different types of communication*

Verbal communication

Verbal communication is characterised by speaking. When we speak we change our tone to denote expression. We may vary the pace or speed and the volume of our spoken words. Verbal communication is used in face-to-face and telephone communication.

During verbal conversation it is important to speak clearly and address your audience, be it your coach or a group of athletes. Make yourself understood!

Verbal communication, as mentioned previously, is a two-way communication process. While you are speaking, others will be **actively listening** to what you are saying, understanding and possibly responding. While they are responding you will be actively listening, trying to understand and responding to what has been said.

Responses may be in the form of asking the appropriate key questions:

- how
- when
- why
- what
- where
- can I
- do you?

Responses could also be in the form of performing an action or task which the coach or others have asked you to do, or a response could be a simple gesture (non-verbal communication).

Responses in verbal communication include:

- questioning
- performing a task
- gesture or signal
- expressions.

Effective verbal communication involves:

- listening
- responding
- questioning
- understanding
- controlling and varying tone of voice
- varying pace
- the avoidance of slang
- addressing your audience.

Non-verbal communication

Non-verbal communication involves sending signals or making gestures and includes the use of facial expressions and body language when communicating with others. For example, a coach may make a signal or gesture to his athlete from the sidelines which they will interpret and understand. An example of where non-verbal communication is important could be at a large sports stadium where verbal communication would be ineffective due to the noise of the crowd and other players.

Written communication

Communication through letters, reports, emails, press releases, training and guidance notes are just some examples of the different types of written communication. It is important, however, for the sender to decide on the best method of communication in order to get the message across to the audience or recipients.

Written communication must be clear, logical and uncomplicated, therefore it is important that you ensure spelling, wording, punctuation and grammar are correct.

Writing style

Your writing style may vary depending on who you are writing to. For example, if you are writing a letter or sending an email to a friend you may choose a less formal style. If you are writing to a prospective employer your writing style must be formal, as the employer will be looking to see how well you communicate on paper. They will make a judgement about you from your written communication and this could make the difference in you being invited for interview or not! The table below sets out some forms of written communication.

Formal written communication	Informal written communication
Reports	Emails to friends
Letters applying for jobs	Notes taken in a lecture
Assignments	Memos to friends
Training and guidance notes	
Workplace emails/memos	
Minutes of meetings	
Proposals	

Issues to consider in formal written communication include:

- being clear and concise
- making your message clear and aiming it at the right audience
- having a good structure
- avoiding 'text' language, e.g. gr8, b4, wot
- avoiding incorrect spellings
- avoiding the use of slang words.

Think about it

When might you use written communication as an athlete or sportsperson?

Communicating accurately and clearly

Communicating accurately and clearly means ensuring that in your spoken or written communication you are getting the right message across to another person or group of people.

Communication can be distorted if the recipient doesn't understand what you are saying. Therefore, we must speak clearly and at a pace that allows others to understand us. When we write, it must be written accurately, neatly and it must be clear to others what we are trying to say.

 Good posture helps you communicate clearly

Let's do it!

Chinese whispers

- *Think of a message to pass on – for example, 'Coach says we have to meet the morning of the 11th at Paradise Pacific Park stadium, and we must bring our entry cards, kit and equipment.'*

- *Quickly whisper this into the ear of the person sitting next to you and so on until the whole group has heard the message.*

- *The last group member should repeat the message aloud that was given to them.*

- *Is the message the same as the original?*

- *Now repeat the activity again speaking at an appropriate pace and clearly.*

- *Did you notice any differences? Discuss.*

Discussion

Throughout your sporting career you will have many discussions with different people which may include discussions with coaching staff, managers, advisors and other athletes. A discussion is a meeting between two or more people where the following can be undertaken.

- Decisions can be made.

- Information can be shared.

- Views and opinions can be expressed.

- Ideas can be developed.

In discussions it is important to listen to what others have to say and respond appropriately. A discussion gives you the opportunity to voice your opinions on the subject matter in hand. There could, for example, be a discussion between coach and athlete about a new training regime which you may or may not agree with.

Key points to remember when taking part in a discussion are:

- pronunciation – pronounce words correctly
- avoid speech mannerisms – for example, saying 'right' or 'Ok' after each word or sentence can distract the listener
- actively listen
- express your views and opinions
- don't be aggressive or lose your temper
- don't be personal by, for example, badmouthing others.

Key points from written material

If you have a piece of written material it is useful to be able to identify and extract the key points, as this will help you to understand what the written piece is about.

Working with other people

Think about it

What do we mean by **effective** *working relationship?*

Working relationships

Throughout your career you will work with many different people, which may include coaching staff, managers, advisers and other athletes. It is important to create an effective working relationship, maintain it and develop it further.

Your relationship with your coach will be different from that with a teacher, and your relationship with a manger or adviser will be different than with other athletes.

If working relationships are effective then you will probably find that you work or perform better. If working relationships are poor, this may hinder your performance, as you will work less well with others.

Effective working relationships include:

- communication
- team work/good team leadership (this could be a coach or a manager)
- discussions/keeping people informed
- avoiding or being able to deal with conflict
- valuing the team
- listening/responding

- motivation
- compromise
- support.

Effective working relationship with coaches

A coach and an athlete must have an effective working relationship. They will have to work together to create training programmes to maximise career and competition potential. The athlete should have respect for the coach because of his or her experience, knowledge and ability to get results. The coach should have respect for the athlete because of his or her commitment to training and desire to achieve.

Effective working relationships with managers

Case study

Manchester United played a match in the fifth round of the FA Cup and lost 2–0 to Arsenal. It is alleged that the manager, Sir Alex Ferguson, was angry and stormed into the dressing room and kicked a shoe. The shoe struck David Beckham above his left eye, which needed several stitches.

This action showed a weakness in his management techniques and a poor working relationship, the result of which:

- showed the manager instantly lost control of the situation by losing his temper

- could have demotivated the team

- resulted in an injured player, which could have weakened the team

- gained much negative publicity and threatened the reputation of the manager.

Discuss the above case study within your group and answer the following questions.

1 Do you think the above actions affected the relationship between David Beckham and Sir Alex Ferguson. Justify your answer.

2 If a coach and athlete didn't respect or trust each other then this would certainly affect the athlete's performance because it would create a poor working relationship. Discuss how this could happen. Can you think of any examples in your personal sporting career or that of an elite athlete?

Effective working relationships with advisers

A relationship with an adviser must be professional for it to be effective. An adviser will be knowledgeable in their area of expertise, be it financial, sports injuries or nutrition related. The adviser would have to build a good rapport or relationship with the athlete in order to gain his or her trust.

Effective working relationships with other athletes

Imagine if a football, rugby or netball team had poor working relationships, if players didn't get on with each other on and off the field – how do you think this would affect their performance or the dynamics of the team?

It is important in any team situation to foster good working relationships in order to be able to work together. If a team can't work together it is unlikely that they will be effective. Everyone has to know what motivates everyone else.

Reviewing and improving relationships

Effective communication is the key to reviewing and improving working relationships. This can be achieved by:

- keeping individuals and/or the team fully informed
- monitoring and reviewing working relationships.

These key elements will help to build on existing arrangements and will allow athletes, coaches, managers and advisers to establish and develop long-term effective working relationships.

Recognising the causes of poor working relationships

Recognising the causes of poor working relationships will allow you to review and improve your techniques. Effective working relationships provide the basis for effective performance and success in sport. Some causes of poor working relationships include conflict or disagreements, lack of communication or poor decision making.

When thinking about reviewing and improving techniques the following must be looked at or evaluated.

- **The success of an individual or team** – if a sportsperson or a team is not succeeding, then we need to know why. Is it because they don't understand what is being asked, is it because they don't agree with their coach or is it because of poor communication?

- **Discussions** – is the discussion a two-way process or is it just the coach and the manager involved in the discussion and the athletes listening? A discussion should be a forum to allow everyone to share their points of view.

- **Review any previous targets set** – if the coach has previously set a team or an individual five targets and these targets have not been met, this could mean that communication may not have been effective.

Media

Being an elite athlete doesn't only involve training and performance, it also involves working with the media to some degree.

An elite athlete will be open to many media opportunities, especially if they have been successful or achieved certain goals. They will be encouraged to behave and conduct themselves in an appropriate manner and also keep themselves in the public eye, which could help to enhance their finances by getting more endorsement contracts or sponsorship.

The media includes:

- TV
- radio
- press
- print media.

Interviews with the media can help to:

- get more coverage for the athlete or sport
- promote the sport
- promote the country
- promote the team or individual as professional athletes
- create more opportunities for individuals or teams.

TV

Television is probably the most powerful medium that there is today. It is important to create the right image for TV, not only through the way you appear but also through how you act and how you put your point across. In a television studio it is important to act like you are on camera all the time because the camera may pan to you when you least expect it, maybe for the audience to see your expression or how you have reacted to what someone has said. Don't forget that body language speaks a million words!

Radio

Radio is a huge medium with many different stations and millions of listeners. A radio interview may last between 3 and 15 minutes and is usually much milder and less intimidating than a TV interview.

With radio, you could be invited into the studio or a reporter could meet you at a different venue and record an interview from there. Radio also allows you the advantage of being able to use script sheets or prompts, as there are no cameras present.

Your pre-interview checklist will be similar whether for TV or radio.

- Find out how, when and where you will be interviewed.
- What is the interview about?
- Will you be live or will it be pre-recorded?
- What is the purpose of the interview and how will it be used (news, sports bulletin, etc)?

Press

The press comprises reporters who represent different magazines, newspapers or television channels. They are usually found at events and they try to get an immediate interview. In this case, if you decide to give the interview you will have to think quickly, communicate effectively and get your point across.

Press conferences are pre-arranged meetings where there will be lots of reporters and cameramen representing various magazines or newspapers. A press conference is like an interview – however, the press get the opportunity to quickly fire questions at you which can be very nerve-racking. Sometimes you will have to be quick on your feet. You don't have to answer all of the questions, or the awkward ones; you just have to prepare an answer for dealing with them in case they crop up.

For example, you may be asked about your thoughts on a fellow athlete who has been banned for taking performance-enhancing drugs. In this case you could say, 'At the moment I am just concentrating on areas of my performance.' This should silence them, and then move on to the next question.

Print media – local, national and international

Print media refers to newspapers or magazines. You may be interviewed for a magazine or publication, or you may be asked to contribute to or write an article.

Again, it is important to find out the purpose and what exactly they are after. Whatever you write or say may be edited, so it is important to ask to see and check the edited version before it is printed.

Planning

It is important to plan ahead and work out what you want to say, what message you want to get across and what you want to achieve before the interview.

Don't think that you can get away without planning – you would probably embarrass yourself, and this would affect public opinion of you and could result in sponsorship being withdrawn or loss of endorsement contracts.

Planning considerations include:

- Who is your audience?
- Why are you doing the interview?
- What do you want to achieve?

Let's do it!

Look through sports, health and fitness magazines, or newspapers, for interviews given by sports people.

- *Can you easily identify the key points of the interview?*
- *Did the interviewee get their point across well?*
- *Discuss your findings with your group.*

Key point

Be positive! Remember, anything you say could be reported in a newspaper.

Purpose

You need to be clear on the objectives and purpose of the interview. Are you there to discuss a new record, or a medal/ competition, which you won?

Anticipating likely questions

Consider the types of questions you may be asked and think about good answers to those questions before you are interviewed. The worst scenarios are being caught off-guard, not being able to answer a question properly or not having a good positive answer.

 Let's do it!

Imagine the following situation.

You scored the winning goal in a recent football or netball match for England and at the moment you are hot property! You have only been playing for the team for one year. However, in that time you have gone from strength to strength and all of your performances for the team have been outstanding. There is now a lot of media interest in you.

BBC Radio Five has invited you to an interview, which will be heard by over five million listeners.

Think about and list the questions that the presenter/interviewer may ask you and complete the table below with notes on possible answers.

Possible questions you may be asked	Notes to include on prompt or script sheets if necessary
Why do you think there is a lot of media interest in you now?	
What do you feel you bring to the sport?	Enthusiasm Fresh talent A love of the game
Children may see you as a role model. What do you have to say to them?	

For example, in athletics, after a win, an athlete might be interviewed live for television, straight away, even before they have got their breath back. The interviewers may ask the athlete to take them through their race and ask them how they were feeling at different stages. In this case an athlete might say something like, 'As soon as I heard the gun I knew what I had to do, I came out of the blocks hard and fast and was conscious that the favourite was a little ahead of me, I straightened up and my adrenalin was flowing, I pumped hard and could see the finish line, I looked either side of me and I knew I had it as I dipped my chest over the finish line.'

Never speak badly or ridicule your opponents if they have performed better than you, no matter what the reason. This will make the general public, coach and other competitors see you in a negative light, which could affect any future opportunities.

Scripts and prompt sheets

These are notes that you might make to help you with your TV or radio interview. They may be used as a safety net to help you out if you get stuck and are used to jog your memory.

If using scripts and prompts for a television interview:

- keep them on the table or out of sight of the camera
- don't write long sentences – keep notes short, use single words to prompt you
- ensure that they are clear and legible
- only look at them when you know the camera is off you.

Rehearsals

Rehearsals are important to allow the person being interviewed to acclimatise to new, and possibly unfamiliar, surroundings, and most importantly to prepare them with some questions that may be asked to make sure that they can handle themselves.

TV or radio interviewers might fire questions at the athlete and may ask the unexpected, so planning and rehearsals are essential.

Appearance and presentation

Appearance is important for television. The way in which you dress or carry yourself will create a first and lasting impression with the audience.

Tips for how to dress for TV include the following.

- Dress smartly although not necessarily in a suit.
- Dress to look confident, as you would for a job interview.
- Avoid heavy make-up or lots of jewellery.

- Avoid colours such as bright whites, yellows or browns, or a heavy mix of colours.
- Avoid large stripes or checks.
- Tidy or brush your hair.
- Ensure your make-up isn't smudged.
- Ensure your tie is straight.

It's always important to check your appearance before your TV interview. However, athletes are often interviewed after an event and they will break these rules.

Sources of help and advice

If you need help or advice about how to handle the media, there are many different organisations and individuals experienced in media relations, and they will be able to offer advice and assistance.

- Athletic Association
- UK Sport
- Sport England
- sports agents
- team mates who've been through it before
- coach
- manager.

Delivery

When giving an interview, people use a combination of speech (verbal communication) and gestures and facial expressions (non-verbal communication) to get their message across. The effective use of speech involves voice projection, pronunciation of words and speaking clearly, as well as a combination of pitch, pace, clarity and intonation.

Pace

The pace needs to be just right in order for the audience to be able to understand. If you speak too quickly, there is a good chance that people will not understand you. On the other hand if you speak very, very slowly, your audience will switch off from what you are saying.

Intonation

Ensure that you pronounce the words correctly and you do not speak in a monotonous, single tone. You need to be able to emphasise words where necessary, and to be successful in your interview, your voice must rise and fall naturally.

Let's do it!

Intonation practice activity

You will need a tape recorder or Dictaphone for this activity.

1   *Working in pairs, one of you act as the interviewer, one as the interviewee. The interviewee should say the following passage in a monotonous tone. The interviewer should record it.*

Athletics has always been in my life. Both of my parents were sprinters, so this I think is where I got my ability. I started training when I was eight and joined various clubs throughout my life and learnt so much not only about training, but also about nutrition and injury management. My greatest achievement to date has been winning gold in the Commonwealth Games. I aim to do the same at the Olympics in 2012 and to beat my personal best.

2   *Listen to the recording. How did it sound?*

3   *Now both of you decide where the interviewee's voice needs to rise and fall and where to place emphasis on the words to make the interview sound more interesting. Repeat the activity.*

4   *Discuss the activity and what might happen to the audience if the interviewee spoke in a monotonous voice.*

Clarity

Speak clearly so that your audience can understand you. Try to sound lively and enthusiastic about your subject matter.

Body language

In your interview you must be aware of your body language. Use light hand gestures where necessary but don't exaggerate. Maintain eye contact with the interviewer. Don't slump in your chair or cross your arms. Be aware of the expression on your face at all times.

Let's do it!

Body language activity

1   *Working in small groups, half of the group come up with different facial expressions, gestures and so on to communicate a simple message, and perform them. You are not allowed to speak.*

2   *The other half of group should guess what they are trying to say. Discuss your answers and then swap roles.*

Confidence

An interview can be like a sporting performance – you need to radiate confidence. Confidence comes when you know your subject matter inside out. Rehearsals and pre-empting questions will also contribute towards gaining more confidence.

Use of equipment

Microphones may be used during an interview. There are many different types of microphones, and the press could use the small ones that attach to your clothes, or the larger ones associated with singing. Speak clearly, don't put your mouth on the microphone and, most importantly, don't shout. It's important to be able to practise speaking into a microphone before any interview.

Assessment activity 6: Media interview

For this assessment you are required to plan for and take part in a media interview. Equipment required:

■ video recorder

■ microphone.

Note to tutor
Arrange this assessment so that all students have the opportunity to be interviewed.
Choose two of the case studies below. One must be from the television interview section: *Do not choose two from the same group*.

TV interviews

1 You play football for a local team and you have just been talent spotted by a scout for Arsenal Youth Academy with the intention of playing for the first team within a year. The press have been tipped about a big story and about what a talented player you are. You are now receiving lots of media attention; therefore a television interview has been arranged so that the public and the sporting world can get to know all about you.

2 Your accomplishments in hockey have been outstanding for your local club. Unbeknown to you, an England talent scout is watching your game and decides that she wants you to try out for the England team. During the trials you play exceptionally well and have won a place in the squad.

Within three months you play in your first match for England and score eight out of the ten goals scored. The press are going wild about your achievements and forceful play. An interview has been arranged for BBC Newsnight.

Assessment activity 6: Media interview continued

Radio interviews

3 You have been invited to appear on a BBC Radio 1 sporting feature. You are a 1500-metre runner and your role model is Kelly Holmes. You have won a variety of medals but have been in the news recently for winning gold in the Commonwealth Games. It has been picked up that your family life hasn't been wonderful – your father is in prison and you were in trouble with the police several times when you were younger. You have been invited to talk about your achievements but the interviewer asks you a few personal questions.

Press conference

4 You are representing England and have just won the 60-metre indoor sprint event in 6.19 seconds, which is a new world record. A press conference has been organised for two hours later, as the press want the story. One of the questions that the press asks is if you have taken performance-enhancing drugs. Don't forget the cameras are on you at all times.

Tasks

Your tutor will put you in groups.

Television interview – this will be video recorded.

Interviewer

Your role will be to prepare and ask questions based on the scenarios. Please note there can be more than one interviewer – your tutor will decide on the format.

Interviewee

Your role will be to anticipate the questions and prepare appropriate answers. Make use of script sheets or prompt notes to help you, but remember to keep these out of the view of the cameras.

Radio interview – this will be tape-recorded.

Interviewer

Your role will be to prepare and ask questions based on the scenarios. Please note there can be more than one interviewer – your tutor will decide on the format.

Interviewee

Your role will be to anticipate the questions and prepare appropriate answers. Ensure that you think about the clarity of your voice and eliminate speech mannerisms such as 'er', 'um' or 'you know what I mean'.

Press conference – this will be video recorded.

Interviewer

A group of students needs to represent the press from different newspapers, TV programmes or magazines. You role will be to fire questions quickly at the interviewee. Prepare these questions beforehand but do not let the interviewee know what you are going to ask.

Assessment activity 6: Media interview continued

Interviewee

Your role will be to anticipate the questions and prepare appropriate answers. Make use of script sheets or prompt notes to help you, but remember to keep these out of the view of the cameras.

To achieve a Pass:

1 Plan for and be the subject of a media interview, *describing* you own strengths and areas for improvement. (P7)

To achieve a Merit you must achieve the Pass criteria and:

2 *Explain* your strengths and areas for improvement when participating in a media interview. (M6)

To achieve a Distinction you must achieve the Pass and Merit criteria and:

3 *Present recommendations* on how to improve your media interview skills. (D3)

Note to students

■ Start your interview in the correct way, introduce your guest and say why they are there.

■ End in the appropriate manner by thanking your guest.

■ Treat it as though you were really on the TV or radio.

Summary

In this unit you have studied a variety of issues relating to lifestyle and performance, and how certain factors such as pressures, drugs, alcohol and an inability to balance leisure time with training or work commitments can affect the performance of an athlete.

We have also looked at the issues surrounding elite athletes, inappropriate behavioural issues, how to deal with media interviews and financial management.

As a sports performer or elite athlete it is important that second career choices are investigated, as a back-up or part of a contingency plan, should a severe injury be sustained which sadly puts paid to your athletics career.

Check what you know!

Look back through this unit to see if you can you answer the following questions.

1 What is the importance for an athlete of planning work commitments and leisure time?

2 Describe and briefly discuss three pressures that an elite athlete may be faced with.

3 Give three examples of how an elite athlete might reduce or eliminate those pressures described in question two.

4 Give examples of a second career choice for an athlete, describing skills and qualifications required.

5 Devise a personal career plan for an athlete and describe realistic goals.

6 List three financial issues that an elite athlete may be faced with.

7 Describe how an elite athlete should behave at a press conference, at a social function and at a sports event.

8 What skills are necessary for effective communication?

9 What skills are required to work effectively with others?

10 What are the important points to consider when giving a television or radio interview?

11 How could you improve your own media interview skills?

Index